Ad Litteram

Issues in Systematic Theology

Paul D. Molnar
General Editor

Vol. 5

PETER LANG
New York • Washington, D.C./Baltimore • Boston
Bern • Frankfurt am Main • Berlin • Vienna • Paris

K. E. Greene-McCreight

Ad Litteram

How Augustine, Calvin, and Barth Read the "Plain Sense" of Genesis 1–3

PETER LANG
New York • Washington, D.C./Baltimore • Boston
Bern • Frankfurt am Main • Berlin • Vienna • Paris

BT
695
.G717
1999

Library of Congress Cataloging-in-Publication Data

Greene-McCreight, Kathryn.
Ad litteram: how Augustine, Calvin, and Barth read the "plain sense"
of Genesis 1–3 / K. E. Greene-McCreight.
p. cm. — (Issues in systematic theology; v. 5)
Includes bibliographical references and index.
1. Creation—History of doctrines. 2. Bible. O.T. Genesis I–III—Criticism,
interpretation, etc. 3. Augustine, Saint, Bishop of Hippo—Contributions
in doctrine of creation. 4. Calvin, Jean, 1509–1564—Contributions in
doctrine of creation. 5. Barth, Karl, 1886–1968—Contributions
in doctrine of creation. I. Title. II. Series.
BT695.D717   222'.1106'09—dc21   97-39226
ISBN 0-8204-3992-4
ISSN 1081-9479

Die Deutsche Bibliothek-CIP-Einheitsaufnahme

Greene-McCreight, Kathryn:
Ad litteram: how Augustine, Calvin, and Barth read the "plain sense" of
Genesis 1–3 / K. E. Greene-McCreight. –New York; Washington, D.C./Baltimore;
Boston; Bern; Frankfurt am Main; Berlin; Vienna; Paris: Lang.
(Issues in systematic theology; Vol. 5)
ISBN 0-8204-3992-4

Cover design by James F. Brisson.

The paper in this book meets the guidelines for permanence and durability
of the Committee on Production Guidelines for Book Longevity
of the Council of Library Resources.

© 1999 Peter Lang Publishing, Inc., New York

Printed in the United States of America.

Contents

Preface

This book attempts to deal with a central question involving the doctrine of scripture. During the course of my graduate studies, it become increasingly clear to me that the fundamental theological problem which Christian theology faces today, indeed which Christian theology has continually faced throughout the ages, centers around the practice of privileging the "plain sense" of scripture, particularly when reading the Old Testament as scripture of the Church. The purpose of this book, then, is to trace a trajectory of the understandings of the notion of the "plain sense" of scripture. The hope is that we might then come to some understanding at least of what is involved in reading the Bible as scripture. The trajectory I chose is one which feeds Reformed Protestant Christianity: Augustine, John Calvin, and Karl Barth.

After sketching the theological and hermeneutical nature and function of the privileging of the plain sense in the catholic Christian tradition, the first chapter of this book then examines key issues and themes, problems and possibilities which are inherent in Christian understandings of the plain sense of scripture. The bulk of the study is then devoted to close readings of the biblical interpretation of Augustine, Calvin and Barth on Genesis 1–3 in which particular attention is paid to their underlying assumptions about what constitutes a "plain" reading for each of them. The key texts analyzed are Augustine's *De Genesi ad Litteram, libri XII*, Calvin's *Commentary on the First Book of Moses*, and Barth's *Church Dogmatics* 3.1.

The categories for the analysis in the second through fourth chapters are drawn in large measure from the issues raised in the first chapter. This includes, but is not limited to, a consideration of the following: 1) how the interpreters understand the task of reading the verbal sense of a specific passage of scripture; 2) how and to what extent they investigate the narrative structure, authorial intention, and historical referentiality of the biblical text; 3) how their readings are informed and shaped by the practice of intrabiblical prooftexting; and 4) to what extent each interpreter's assumptions about the sacred quality of the text impact his reading of the plain sense. It should be pointed out that this book is not a study of these three theologians in themselves, but rather an investigation into the doctrine of scripture, using these theologians as test-probes.

The results of this investigation urge a reformulation of the notion of the plain sense within the theological trajectory represented by the figures studied here. That is, reading according to the plain sense in this trajectory involves negotiating between the constraints of verbal sense and Ruled reading. Basic to the reading of the "plain sense", then, is respecting the verbal and textual data of the text as well as privileging the claims about God and Jesus Christ which cohere with the Rule of faith. Thus the "plain sense" allows for the possibility for scripture to be "self-interpreting": the central narrative of Jesus is taken from scripture (both in the New Testament and its patterning in the Old Testament) and is reapplied to scripture to render a variety of possible plain sense readings.

My thanks, of course, are due to many who helped me to complete this project. For the patience and long-suffering of my teachers, Brevard Childs, Hans Frei, Rowan Greer, Richard Hays, Leander Keck, David Kelsey, George Lindbeck, Abraham Malherbe, Christopher Seitz, and Kathryn Tanner, I am especially thankful. Also, to Yale University I am grateful for its financial support of my work in the form of a Franke Fellowship in Humanities and a Yale University Dissertation Fellowship. I am also indebted to the Pew Evangelical Scholars Trust for their generous grant during the academic year of 1996-97, a portion of which I allocated for revisions of my dissertation which fed into this book. I also owe thanks to Paul Molnar for his encouragement and thoughtful advice on the manuscript. To my parents, Robert and Joyce Greene, who were my first theological teachers, I am grateful for nurturing in me a love for the Word. On a practical level, without Alexandra Farley who helped care for our children, who were both born during the course of my graduate studies, I simply could not have completed my doctoral work. I owe deepest thanks to my husband, Matthew McCreight, who has believed in my abilities even when I could not and encouraged me at every turn. It is to him and to our children, Noah and Grace, that I dedicate this book.

Permissions to reprint portions of the sources I used are granted by the following: *The Bible and the Narrative Tradition*, by Frank McConnell. Copyright © 1986 by Oxford University Press, Inc. "Theology and the Plain Sense" by Kathryn Tanner, *Scriptural Authority and Narrative Interpretation*, edited by Garrett Green, copyright © 1987 Fortress Press. Used by permission of Augsburg Fortress. *Church Dogmatics* by Karl Barth and *Calvin's Old Testament Commentaries* by T. H. L. Parker, used by permission of T. & T. Clark Ltd., Publishers. All rights reserved. Rowan Williams, "The Literal Sense of Scripture," *Modern Theology* (1991) 7, used by permission of Blackwell Publishers. All rights reserved. Raphael Loewe, "The 'Plain Meaning' of Scripture in Early Jewish Exegesis," Papers of the Institute of Jewish Studies, London, edited by J. G. Weiss, used by permission of Magnes Press. All rights reserved. Of course, of inestimable help in this project is the two volume translation of Augustine's *De Genesi ad litteram* in *St. Augustine* (ACW Vol. 41 and 42) translated and annotated by John Hammond Taylor, S. J. © 1982 by Rev. Johannes Quasten and Rev. Walter J. Burghardt, S. J. and Thomas Comerford Lawler, used by permission of Paulist Press. One study which I have been unable to locate but which might have been of help is the unpublished dissertation by R. N. Hebb, "Augustine's *Sensus ad litteram*," (1986) cited by Starnes.[1]

Christmas, 1997

Notes

1. Colin Starnes, "Augustinian Biblical Exegesis and the Origins of Modern Science," in *Collectanea Augustiniana: Augustine, "Second Founder of the Faith"*, eds. Joseph C. Schaubelt and Frederick Van Fleteren (New York: Peter Lang, 1990), 352.

Abbreviations

CD	Church Dogmatics
CHB	Cambridge History of the Bible
CO	Ioannis Calvini Opera Quae Supersunt Omnia
CR	Corpus Reformatorum
CSEL	Corpus Scriptorum Ecclesiasticorum Latinorum
CTJ	Calvin Theological Journal
DcD	De civitate Dei
DDC	De Doctrina Christiana
DGncMan	De Genesi contra Manichaeos
DGnLImp	De Genesi ad Litteram Imperfectus Liber
DGnL	De Genesi ad Litteram
ETL	Ephemerides Theologicae Louvaniensis
HTR	Harvard Theological Review
Interp	Interpretation
JAAR	Journal of the American Academy of Religion
JBL	Journal of Biblical Literature
JSOT	Journal for the Study of the Old Testament
JTS	Journal of Theological Studies
KD	Kirchliche Dogmatik
NPNF	Nicene and Post-Nicene Fathers of the Christian Church
REAug	Revue des Etudes Augustiniennes
RTP	Revue de Théologie et Philosophie
SJT	Scottish Journal of Theology
WTJ	Westminster Theological Journal

Chapter One:
"Plain Sense" in Christian Interpretation of Scripture

My God, my God, Thou art a direct God, may I not say a
literall God, a God that wouldest bee understood literally,
and according to the plaine sense of all that thou saiest?
But thou art also (Lord I intend it to thy glory, and let no
prophane misinterpreter abuse it to thy diminution) thou art
a figurative, a metaphoricall God too: A God in whose
words there is such a height of figures, such voyages, such
peregrinations to fetch remote and precious metaphors,
such extensions, such spreadings, such Curtaines of
Allegories, such third Heavens of Hyperboles, so
harmonious eloqutions, so retired and so reserved expressions, so commanding perswasions, so perswading commandments, such sinewes even in thy milke, and such
things in thy words, as all prophane Authors, seeme of the
seed of the Serpent, that creepes, thou art the Dove, that
flies.   O, what words but thine, can expresse the
inexpressible texture, and composition of thy Word...

John Donne,
Devotions Upon Emergent Occasions, Expostulation 19

The Nature of the Problem

While John Donne may have a rare ability to push theological reflection into
the realm of eloquence, the questions which he raises in the above quote about
the relationship between the subject matter of theology and the language of
scripture are by no means unique.   The question of the "plaine sense" of

scripture has from the very beginnings of Christianity generated profound theological reflection because of the intimate relationship indicated in the above quote between the subject matter of Christian theology and the interpretation of Holy Scripture. Christians historically have claimed, after all, that in the Bible they hear the Divine Voice and perceive the Divine Will in such a way that it is plain and not hidden. While the phrase "the perspicuity of scripture" usually recalls Reformation debates, the notion that Scripture is in some sense clear and understandable in its witness to Jesus and to the life of the Triune God certainly has longstanding precedence.

But what does it mean to read Scripture according to its plain sense? Is the plain sense to be understood as the sense the author intended? The historical sense? The way the words go?[1] How then can Jews and Christians read some of the same texts of Scripture and arrive at very different conclusions as to the plain sense? These questions are rooted in the very content of the earliest Christian claims about Jesus and his relationship to Israel's God.

The Retention of the Old Testament

For the earliest Christian communities, during the period of the passing on of the traditions later collected in the New Testament, the interpretation of scripture *ipso facto* focussed on the texts of what we now call the Old Testament.[2] That the Christian community did not abandon the Old Testament, but continued to understand it as the central textual vehicle of the divine voice and will, is one of the most significant factors in the shaping of specifically Christian understandings of what it means to read scripture according to its plain sense.[3] The Christian community's refusal to discard what was to become the Old Testament, namely, the Bible of the Synagogue, was by no means immediately settled. The problem is apparent in the early church, for example, in *The Epistle of Barnabas* and in the Marcionite and Manichean heresies, and in the contemporary church in some elements of Lutheran theology. With this retention of the scriptures of Israel comes the problem of how to interpret them: how does the new community of Messianic Jews (soon to become an almost entirely Gentile phenomenon) read the Scriptures such that they validate their claims about the identity of Jesus of Nazareth as God's chosen and anointed Messiah? There are in the earliest stages of Christianity at least two broadly understood communities which read the Holy Scriptures of Israel: one reads them in part as foretelling the mission and election of Jesus as Paschal Lamb offered for the sins of the world, while the other denies the applicability of the scriptures to the story of Jesus and vice versa.

In the nascent Christian tradition, there developed therefore a preoccupation with what we will call the "plain sense" of scripture.[4] Various theologians throughout the history of interpretation have used different terms to refer to this preoccupation, e.g., "literal sense", "simple sense", and "historical sense." While these terms each have slightly different nuances, they all tend to overlap insofar as they point to a strategy to cope with the interrelated problems of the relation of the two testaments and the privileging of this Christological interpretive key to the whole of scripture. For the purposes of the present study, the term "plain sense" will serve as a place holder to mark the presence of possible strategies to cope with these problems. This place holder will be "filled in" with considerations from the three theologians to be examined. The term used at any one time in my exposition will be the term used by the theologian being examined. When I am speaking generally without reference to a specific theologian, I will use the term "plain sense."

The plain sense of scripture in Christian reading thus hinges hermeneutically on the problem of the relation of the two testaments, and theologically on the problem of the relation of the covenant with Abraham and the New Covenant made in the death and resurrection of Jesus. The problem of privileging the plain sense of scripture is apparent in the earliest writer in the New Testament, the apostle Paul. Paul agonizes over theological and ethical issues related to the plain sense most notably in Romans 9–11 and Galatians 2–5, and the related hermeneutical issues crop up continuously throughout his writings. In his first letter to the Corinthians, regarding the story of the rock which miraculously gushed forth water in the desert for the thirsting People of God, Paul claims that "The rock was Christ" (1 Corinthians 10:1–5; Exodus 16–17). Paul apparently is not saying that the rock is "Christ-like", nor that it symbolically represents Christ, nor does he indicate that his claim is a midrashic elaboration on the Exodus story, but that the rock in some respect *was* Christ. This should tip off even the casual reader as to the potential complexities of Christian plain sense interpretation.[5]

Paul's interpretation is, he seems to argue, what the text "really says," or at least what it really says when one is equipped with the Christological interpretive key which opens to full view otherwise veiled significations. He is re-reading the Old Testament here according to a new "logic" governed by the understanding of God's decisive act in Jesus' life, death and resurrection.[6] While those Jews who do not agree with Paul would regard his Christological interpretive key as a "new" or even dangerous innovation, Paul himself does not see this to be the case at all. According to Paul, from the standpoint of the cross and resurrection alone can one finally understand what the law, prophets, and writings have been saying all along. Therefore, understanding the rock as

Christ does not entail reading into the story an element foreign to it at all, but is a justifiably plain sense reading in the "last days" inaugurated by Jesus.[7] Thus "plain sense" necessarily becomes reformulated with the inauguration of the eschaton.

Christological Interpretation

The very acceptance of Christological interpretation then poses in turn the problem of how to protect the unsurpassability of this "new" hermeneutical key. How can a Christological reading of the Old Testament assure its own authority and prohibit newer readings from trumping the finality of the revelation in Christ? An ancient example of this trumping would be Montanism; a contemporary example would be Mormonism. How can Paul, for example, make the claims he does about the Old Testament without running the risk of some other teacher offering an interpretation which contradicts his own, based on another subsequent hermeneutical key?

In a seminal article on this subject, Hans Frei points out that the identification of the literal sense, understood as literal ascription to Jesus of the gospel narratives about him, as normative results in two problems: retaining while reinterpreting the Old Testament, and affirming the unsurpassability of the new hermeneutical key.[8] While it may be an insoluble "chicken or egg" question, it might be just as easily said that these two problems, inherent in the Christian community's very understanding of who Jesus was, result in this new "ruled reading" of the plain sense in ascription to Jesus. That is, the plain sense is hammered out as a tool to cope with these two problems which themselves are integral to the Church's understanding and confession of Jesus. Of course, it is fashionable to contest the very claim that there is a pre-kerygmatic "identity" of Jesus as Messiah of Israel, an "objective" given prior to and apart from the church's interpretation of him. However, this claim has been traditionally part and parcel of the church's faith, and as such does not hang on the verdict of socio-historical validation or denial. In examining the problem of the plain sense, one must at least acknowledge that this assumption was (and is in most of the Christian community) intrinsically bound to the understanding of what it means to claim the Messiahship of Jesus.

These hermeneutical problems of retaining the Old Testament while asserting the unsurpassability of Christ as depicted in the New Testament were and continue to be thorny issues for Christian interpretation of the Bible. It can be argued that the "plain sense" reading is that which functions to take account of the data of the biblical text, whether narrative, legal, poetic or kerygmatic, while maintaining an equilibrium between these countervailing forces. In other words, the reading which comes to be normative and convincing is that which functions to negotiate between the primacy of the Christological hermeneutical key and the enduring hermeneutical validity of the "prophecy" of the Old Testament. This is the understanding of the function of the plain sense with which I will be working in the course of my examination of the exegesis of Augustine, Calvin and Barth.

Plain Sense and Ruled Reading

The conceptual relation between plain sense thus understood and the *regula fidei* now begins to emerge.[9] While neither the dating and origin of the Rule of Faith, nor the precise pinpointing of its contents, will be a concern for the present study, one can easily point to places where the Rule of Faith is nevertheless identifiable. We can find early kernels of the Rule of faith which expand on New Testament statements about Jesus and his relation to the Father in Ignatius and Polycarp.[10] References to and longer summaries of the Rule of Faith can also be found in Irenaeus and Tertullian.[11] Tertullian outlines the Rule of Faith in *Concerning the Veiling of Virgins* as follows:

> The rule of faith, indeed, is altogether one, alone immovable and irreformable; the rule, to wit, of believing in one only God omnipotent, Creator of the universe, and His Son Jesus Christ, born of the Virgin Mary, crucified under Pontius Pilate, raised again the third day from the dead, received in the heavens, sitting now at the right (hand) of the Father, destined to come to judge the quick and dead through resurrection of the flesh as well (as of the spirit). The law of faith being constant, the other succeeding points of discipline and conversation admit the novelty of correction...[12]

And again, in *The Prescription Against Heretics*, Tertullian summarizes the Rule of faith as

> that which prescribes the belief that there is one only God, and that He is none other than the Creator of the World, who produced all things out of nothing through His own Word, first of all sent forth; that this Word is called His Son, and, under the name of God, was seen in diverse manners by the patriarchs,

heard at all times in the prophets, at last brought down by the
Spirit and Power of the Father into the Virgin Mary, was made
flesh in her womb, and being born of her, went forth as Jesus
Christ; thenceforth He preached the new law and the new
promise of the kingdom of heaven, worked miracles; having
been crucified, He rose again the third day; having ascended
into the heavens, He sat at the right hand of the Father; sent
instead of Himself the Power of the Holy Ghost to lead such as
believe; will come with glory to take the saints to the enjoyment of everlasting life and of the heavenly promises, and to
condemn the wicked to everlasting fire, after the resurrection
of both these classes shall have happened, together with the
restoration of their flesh.[13]

Soon after identifying the outline of the Rule, Tertullian points out not only
that the faith which saves has been deposited in this rule (14), but that use of
the Rule is evidence of those who truly possess the Scriptures. He makes it
clear in chapter 15 that the Christian should not even deign to argue or discuss
the meaning of the Scriptures with those who do not honor the Rule of faith.
In addition, he claims at the end of chapter 13 that this rule was taught by
Christ himself.

For our purposes it is important to note how the Rule functions: it holds
together theologically God the Creator and Jesus Christ, and hermeneutically
the Old and New Testaments. William Countryman has suggested understanding the *regula fidei* as an oral tradition communicated in performance in the
social location of catechesis, "betraying signs of an anti-heretical origin in its
emphatic coupling of Jesus with the Creator."[14] As such, the Rule of Faith is
a basic "take" on the subject matter and plot of the Christian story which
"couples" the confession of Jesus the Redeemer with the confession of God the
Creator. It is generally understood to have been drawn from scripture, and in
biblical interpretation it is reapplied to scripture. It functions to circumscribe a
set of potential interpretations: within the catholic tradition, a reading can
generally be argued to be justifiable, convincing, authoritative and thus "plain
sense" insofar as it abides by the Rule of Faith which disallows either the
hermeneutical separation or conflation of the two testaments. The Rule of
Faith is in this sense also an outer limit which places constraints on what can
be argued as a convincingly "plain sense" reading.

While the plain sense of scripture thus considered functioned as an
umbrella strategy for maintaining both the unity yet distinctiveness of the Old
and New Covenants, there is a subset of related concepts which are important

to understanding the practice of reading according to the plain sense in the Christian tradition. Most of these fall under the larger topic of authority and authoritativeness. Here, we must consider not only the authority of the text of scripture itself but also the authority extended from it to the religious leader and/or community in teaching and religious formation of its members. The plain sense is appealed to as the authoritative sense, and leaders or teachers diverging from that may find themselves losing their extended authority. Likewise, the plain sense of the text functions to control that extended authority: the authority granted the text can guide, correct and undercut the authority of the religious leadership and/or community. This, of course, was one of the important aspects of the plain sense of scripture which played such a crucial role in the Protestant Reformation. Closely related to these issues is the reader's or reading community's self-location within the biblical narrative. In other words, in order to read the plain sense of a given biblical text correctly in order to access this authoritativeness, one must be able to judge the relationship between the narrative moment of that text and the present moment of the reader or reading community. Reading the plain sense of the sacrifice of Isaac, therefore, will probably involve different strategies and emphases than will reading the plain sense of David's encounter with Bathsheeba, or Psalm 22, or Matthew 5-7, or Galatians 2. This, of course, is in turn a correlate of the unsurpassability of Christological interpretation, which comes full circle back to the notion of authority and authoritativeness. Connected to the notion of authority and authoritativeness is the extent to which plain sense readings lead to some sense of closure or definition of meaning and the extent to which they open up a range of possible meanings from which the interpreter has a degree of liberty to chose.

Authority for Religious Teaching and Practice

One of the most important recent considerations of this aspect of the plain sense of scripture has been that of Raphael Loewe, whose focus is not on Christian plain sense but on plain sense or *peshat* in the Talmudic period. He gives an initial definition of *peshat* as the "plain, straightforward or simple exegesis which corresponds to the totality of the meaning(s) intended by the writer."[15] In other words, he begins with a definition of plain sense as the original writer's intention, and moves from there to examine how this accords with Talmudic exegetical practice. Setting this initial definition up against the evidence of the word *peshat* in exegetical use, he points out the inadequacies of the "ideal" or abstract definition. He notes that the fundamental meaning of *peshat* in Biblical Hebrew is "to strip (a garment), to flatten, to extend or stretch out," and adjectivally the concept is used to convey such meanings as "flat, straight, simple, uncompounded, innocent, unlearned."[16] After examining rabbinic use, Loewe offers the following revised understanding of the term *peshat*:

> ...the essential notion conveyed by the root at this semantic stage is *authority*...the meaning is but a natural semantic development of the meaning *extend*—viz. the extension of an opinion, received by a teacher or elaborated by himself, over a wider body which (by acknowledgment thereof) *broadens* the currency of the authority of the source whence it emanates...The identification of *authority* as the central notion in this use of the root will explain how it comes about that the noun *peshat*...is used in talmudic and midrashic sources to describe exegesis that is by no means always literal.[17]

Here Loewe points to the implicit "slippage" between the terms "literal sense" and "plain sense" or *peshat*. What we might usually think of as literal (author's intention, the way the words go, etc.) is not always a defining feature of rabbinical *peshat* interpretations. In other words, understanding *peshat* as "simple" exegesis will require reexamination.

Up to the end of the Talmudic period, according to Loewe, *peshat* is to be understood as authoritative teaching rather than simple, plain, straightforward interpretation.[18]   This points to the dual aspect of the notion "authoritative": it indicates a give-and-take, so to speak, between teacher and community.   In other words, while a teaching can be propounded by an authority, it must be recognized by a community as authoritative before its authority becomes meaningful.   Loewe thus rejects a positive notion of *peshat* up to the end of the Talmudic period and says that the real distinction between *peshat* and *derash* in this period seems to be that

> *derash* is exegesis naturally, or even experimentally propounded without secondary considerations; if it is popularly received, and transmitted into the body of conventional or 'orthodox' opinion, it crystallizes into *peshat*.[19]

After in effect erasing the usual distinction between *peshat* and *derash*, Loewe suggests that a more helpful way to draw the distinction between these types of exegesis of this period is to use the terms "static" and "dynamic" exegesis.

While he notes that this is a distinction which the rabbis themselves would not have formulated, he believes that this is the most useful for heuristic purposes. "Dynamic exegesis" is concerned "constantly to enlarge the significance of a given text by relating it to new ideas, conditions, or associations in the mind of the exegete himself", while "static exegesis", the broad category into which the term *peshat* falls, indicates a "concentration on the text that would eschew such accretions."[20] Loewe notes that a more sophisticated distinction does not seem to appear until the Gaonic period, partly as a result of the challenge posed by Karaism which rejected the Oral Torah of rabbinic Judaism.

Extended Authority: Social Function of Plain Sense

Thus we see that the relationship between text and community, whether present community or gathered tradition of the community, is a key issue in Jewish reading of the plain sense of scripture. The extent to which this is true also for the Christian tradition of plain sense reading will be important to consider. This question has been raised by Kathryn Tanner, who takes as a partial basis for her discussion Loewe's article. She has sought to examine how the plain sense of scripture within the Christian tradition can function to shape the community. While Loewe indicates that in early Jewish exegesis "the scales are weighed in favor of conservatism,"[21] Tanner points out that in the Christian tradition of plain sense reading the opposite can be the case. In her view, the plain sense, rather than pushing towards conformity, promotes a tradition which is "self-critical, pluralistic, and viable across a wide range of geographical differences and historical changes of circumstance."[22] Adapting David Kelsey's discussion of the location of scripture's authority in its communal function, Tanner suggests understanding the plain sense of scripture not as a property of the text but as a

> function of its communal use: it is the obvious or direct sense
> of the text according to a *usus loquendi* established by the
> community in question...The plain sense is a consensus read-
> ing, interpretation having distilled into conventional opinion
> when a certain approach to the text has come to be a com-
> munity's unselfconscious habit...the traditional sense of a
> text.[23]

The casual reader might wonder at this point whether Tanner is suggesting that the plain sense consists of whatever the community might say any given text "means," but this is not her point. Rather, taking up Loewe's sketch of *peshat*, she says that plain sense in the Christian tradition is the "'familiar, the traditional, and hence authoritative meaning' of a text within a community whose conventions for the reading of it have therefore already become relatively sedimented."[24]

Tanner then considers an array of possible relationships between the privileging of plain sense reading and other interpretive practices which would impact the relationship between text and interpretive community. One of these possibilities, which could be represented by Orthodox Judaism,[25] might make appeals to an oral tradition understood to be parallel to the text but having intersected at their origin. Tanner says that here the critical force of the plain sense for community practice can be undercut by the oral tradition. This way of considering this possibility opens some interesting avenues into understanding ways of understanding plain sense reading in the Christian tradition.

For example, we might test this possibility by considering the following. The Pentateuch command reads, "You shall not boil a kid in its mother's milk" (Ex 23:19b; Dt 14:21b), and the Oral Torah understands this to extend to the prohibition of mixing any meat and any milk in the same meal. Here, an appeal to an oral tradition understood to be parallel to the text increases and expands the *verbal* sense, but does it undercut the plain sense? If the "plain sense" is defined as the authoritative sense, and the community understands the authoritative sense of the Pentateuch passage to prohibit the mixing of meat and milk in the same meal, the Oral tradition does *not* undercut the critical force of the plain sense over communal practice. Rather, the Oral Torah is simply part of that which *establishes* the plain sense. The matter to be debated, then, would be the status of the Oral Torah itself. An analogous debate took place, of course, in the Protestant Reformation over the authority of Church tradition.

Another possible intersection of plain sense and other interpretive practices which Tanner considers is the privileging of applied senses over plain sense. This again affords us a new angle on understandings of the plain sense, for this would be a logical impossibility if one has established the definition of plain sense as the authoritative sense as does Tanner.[26] In this case, the interpretive practice itself would achieve a quasi-scriptural status such that the plain sense would in effect lose its critical purchase over communal practice. One thinks here of much of medieval Christian exegesis, such as in that of Jean Petit's reading of 2 Cor 3:6, "The letter kills but the Spirit gives life." Petit appealed in an interesting if convoluted way to 2 Cor 3:6 in order to justify the 1407 murder of the Duke of Orléans.[27] The critical force of the commandment "Thou shallt not kill," needless to say, was blunted by his exegesis.

In another possible intersection, the priority of plain sense reading converges with the practice of privileging a canon of scriptural texts and classifying the plain sense of these as "narrative."[28] Basing her argument on the work of Hans Frei, Tanner understands plain sense reading in the Christian tradition to fall under this category of narrative. This convergence, according to Tanner, prevents the privileging of plain sense reading from promoting "a rigid uniformity in community life." The canonical limitation of scriptural texts combined with the focus of the plain sense around the central Christian narrative of Jesus Christ will promote exegetical creativity, not limit it. Thus, instead of pointing toward closure and definition, plain sense readings, when identified in narrative terms, can lead to an opening or multiplying of interpretive options.

Tanner's essay has pointed out some very important aspects of, and raised some intriguing questions about, the problem of the plain sense. She has outlined the social function of a convergence of certain possible Christian interpretive practices to show that a community's privileging the "sensus literalis" does not necessarily entail rigid communal practice, politics, and theology. She has implicitly pointed to some key similarities and distinctions between (orthodox) Christian and (Orthodox) Jewish interpretive practices. For Jewish interpretation, reliance on Oral Torah in effect diminishes the interpretive authority of the biblical text itself and emphasizes the authority of the rabbi interpreting the law. It becomes not the Biblical text but the Talmud which is the focus of Jewish learning in matters of *halakah*. For the Christian community, however, the interpretation of the plain sense as being anchored in the narratives of Jesus' life and death and resurrection-appearances renders the problem of the plain sense of an entirely different order. The "fixity" of Christian scripture and its interpretive key in the narratives about Jesus allows an elasticity in interpretation and communal practice, while the "elasticity" of Orthodox Jewish scripture (Bible and Talmud) and its understanding of contemporary rabbinic interpretation fosters a fixity and uniformity in communal practice. Of course, this may be an example of correlation without necessity, and this may point to no more than the classical distinction between Law and Gospel. In either case, the possible understandings of the plain sense Tanner offers, "...'the sense the author intended,' 'the verbal or grammatical sense,' 'the sense that God intends,' 'the sense a text has when included in the canon,' 'the sense Church authorities designate'" will be important in the examination of our theologians' understandings and identification of plain sense in the latter chapters of this book.[29]

Readers' Narrative Self-locating

Since the plain sense is related to the question of religious authority, how readers understand their own relationship to the time and place of the text at hand may also prove an important element in plain sense reading in the Christian tradition. This self-situating vis-à-vis the plotline of scripture entails finding one's place within the "time" of the narrative. For the Christian tradition of plain sense reading, this is tied intrinsically to eschatology and therefore to the resurrection of Jesus, the decisive eschatological event in the biblical narrative which marks the turning of the ages and the New Creation. It is thus the key interpretive position of the narratives regarding Jesus, particularly the passion and resurrection-appearance stories, which gives the distinctive shape to plain and applied readings within the Christian tradition.

The relationship between literal and non-literal senses of scripture has been restated along these lines by Rowan Williams as the tension between diachronic and synchronic styles of reading.[30] He compares diachronic reading to the performance of a drama or piece of music, and the synchronic reading with the way one views a painting. Diachronic reading thus takes seriously for the interpretive act the text's sequence in time and therefore its "intentionality" or internal direction. The synchronic reading views the text as a field of linguistic signs referring backwards and forwards with little regard to uni-directional sequence or pattern of transformation. The Christian tradition of giving primacy to the literal sense thus can be seen as this "dramatic reading," suggests Williams. This dramatic reading understands the diachronic element to be central in Christian interpretation of scripture such that "the time of the text is recognizably continuous with my time."[31] Employing Nicholas Lash's notion of "performance" of the scriptures, Williams suggests that the use of the lectionary moving through the festal cycle is a mediator of the literal sense insofar as it necessitates a diachronic reading where the time of the text becomes our time and vice versa.[32] The congregation during Holy Week takes on the roles of the city that hails Jesus' triumphal entry on Palm Sunday, receives his ministry in the Last Supper on Maundy Thursday, watches with him in Gethsemane and then deserts him on Good Friday. Williams notes the similarity between the enactments here and that of the Passover ritual, in which each Jew understands him or herself as being redeemed from Egypt as though with Moses. Thus, according to Williams, analogy is fundamental to literal reading, for "diachronic reading assumes a continuity between the time(s) of the text and what we recognize as movement and production in our own lives."[33]

Literal reading also takes seriously the reality of discord, says Williams, both that between the testaments, within each testament, and within our communities' different understandings of what it means to be a faithful Christian. The limit to this discord Williams argues is the story of the cross and resurrection, the "unifying narrative moment" both of scripture and of the Church. It is a unifying narrative moment which, however, will not settle for easy resolutions to the discord, for this unity is "learned or produced only in *this* kind of history, the history of counter-claims and debate." For this reason the literal sense might be best reconceived as an "eschatological sense":

> To read diachronically the history that we call a history of *salvation* is to 'read' our own time in the believing community (and so too the time of our world) as capable of being integrated into such a history, in a future we cannot but call God's because we have no secure human way of planning it or thematising it. In other words, so far from the literal or historical sense being a resource of problem-solving clarity, as it might appear to be for the fundamentalist, an area of simple truthfulness over against the dangerously sophisticated pluralism of a disobedient Church, it may rather encourage us to take historical responsibility for arguing and exploring how the gospel is going to be heard in our day...It suggests that what matters is not our ability to finish our business or to secure consensus, as if Christ would be 'audible' only in this mode, but our readiness to decide, to take sides, as adult persons, and to live with the consequence and cost of that within the disciplines we share with other Christians of openness to the judgment of the Easter mystery.[34]

This points to the salient features of the revised understanding of the "literal sense" which Williams offers. It is not to be understood as a resource for problem-solving, for narrowing options and determining a unitary course of action. Like Tanner, Williams sees plain sense reading to be an opportunity for broadening rather than seeking closure in interpretation. While Tanner sees this mainly in terms of its social function, Williams notes the connection with this and a specifically Christian understanding of eschatology. For Williams, the act of reading the "literal sense" itself is caught within the eschatological tension of the Gospel. It is this eschatological tension which threatens to undercut even the community which offers a literal interpretation, much different from the fundamentalist's self-assured correctness argued on the basis of literal interpretation. As will become apparent in this book, while our three theologians would indeed agree with and honor what Williams is calling the "eschatological" dimension of the literal sense, they also did understand the notion of literal sense as a tool for grounding truth claims as do the fundamentalists Williams mentions. While neither Williams nor Tanner makes this explicit, here we see the area where their suggestions meet: the notion of literal reading can be just as easily the foundation on which we stand as it can be the stumbling stone which trips us up, undercutting our own claims and teaching authority.

Plain Sense and Textual Reference: Gospel Narratives about Jesus

We have seen thus far that the importance for the plain sense within the Christian tradition of the stories about Jesus cannot be underestimated. They form, obviously, the *sine qua non* distinguishing factor between Jewish and Christian plain sense reading, and different uses of the Jesus narratives will mark the different approaches within the range of competing plain sense readings within the Christian tradition.

Different uses of the Jesus narratives have been shown to mark the distinction between traditional understandings of the plain sense and that of phenomenological hermeneutics. Hans Frei points this out in "The 'Literal Reading' of Biblical Narrative in the Christian Tradition," where he identifies the traditional understanding of the plain sense as the "literal ascription to Jesus of the Gospel narratives." In other words, traditional plain sense readings assumed that the narratives about Jesus were in fact about Jesus and not about some other referent, whether an ideal or material reality. This Frei contrasts with the assumptions about the literal sense which underlie phenomenological hermeneutics. According to Frei, phenomenological hermeneutics implicitly understands that the Gospel narratives do *not* primarily describe and bear the identity of Jesus Christ, a character within the stories. Rather, phenomenological hermeneutics, represented in particular by the interpretation of Paul Ricoeur and David Tracy, reads the narratives about Jesus as describing universal problems and patterns of human existence and understanding under the "cover" of the character of Jesus. Practitioners of phenomenological hermeneutics tend therefore to view Jesus as

> the verbal expressor of a certain preconceptual consciousness which he then, in a logically derivative or secondary sense, exhibits in action. For example, *that* Jesus was crucified is not

a decisive part of his personal story, only that he was so consistent with his 'mode of being in the world' as to take the risk willingly...The personal world in the hermeneutical scheme is one in which the status of happenings is that of carnal shadows of the true 'secondary' world of 'meanings' 'understood' in 'disclosure.'[35]

Thus phenomenological hermeneutics focuses on a set of attitudes or 'consciousness' rather than on the character Jesus within the story who actuates this set of attitudes. Insofar as this is the case, this approach is more akin to traditional allegorical reading than it is to literal reading, for it views the gospel narratives as veiling beneath or behind the story itself a deeper meaning. Frei quotes an excellent example of this understanding of the interpretation of the Gospels from Ricoeur:

> The ultimate referent of the parables, proverbs, and eschatological sayings is not the Kingdom of God, but human reality in its wholeness. Religious language discloses the religious dimension of common human experience.[36]

One of the advantages of phenomenological hermeneutical theory, when applied to the New Testament, is its compatibility with concepts traditionally important for Christian reading of scripture. Frei identifies some of these as the concepts of revelation, uniqueness, and the claim to normatively valid interpretation. But, says Frei, while phenomenological theory upholds the claim to the unsurpassability of the christological interpretive key (what Frei calls "the New Testament narratives' ascriptive reference to Jesus"), it also wants to deny that this unsurpassability "involves the invidious distinction between insiders and outsiders to the truth".[37] However, these claims are mutually contradictory. This "uneasy alliance of hermeneutical aims" results in the theory's breaking down under the burden:

> Whatever may be the case in its other regional exemplifications, when it is applied to the New Testament narrative texts, the result is that the tradition of literal reading is not only stretched into a revised shape, it breaks down instead.[38]

He indicates in this article that he might want to look for a notion "similar to (though not necessarily isomorphic with it)"[39] Ricoeur's "second naïveté." In other words, he would like to uphold the tradition of literal reading without the pitfalls of confusing the meaning of the narratives about Jesus with their supposed reference, resulting either in "meaning as ostensive reference" or "meaning as ideal reference."[40] This alternative "naïveté" which Frei advocates insists on the logical distinction of "meaning" from "truth" within the interpretive task.[41] He calls this approach "less ambitious" and "less high-powered" than phenomenological hermeneutics, for it will necessarily treat the text more concretely as narrative, noting literary features, rather than dealing in abstract philosophical and generalizing terms.[42]

While this examination of phenomenological hermeneutics is highly instructive, for the purposes of the present study one of the most interesting contributions which Frei makes here is the implicit emphasis places on the Rule of Faith. If one were to look for Frei's own understanding of the interpretive impact of the Rule of Faith, one could point to the following passage:

> First, Christian reading of Christian Scriptures must not deny the literal ascription to Jesus, and not to any other person, event, time or idea, of those occurrences, teachings, personal qualities and religious attributes associated with him in the stories in which he plays a part, as well as in the other New Testament writings in which his name is invoked... Second, no Christian reading may deny either the unity of Old and New Testaments or the congruence (which is not by any means the same as literal identity) of that unity with the ascriptive literalism of the Gospel narratives. Third, any readings not in principle in contradiction with these two rules are permissible, and two of the obvious candidates would be the various sorts of historical-critical and literary readings.[43]

These rules, Frei seems to want to say, have been part of the rules of the "grammar" of Christian biblical interpretation. He says that such rules are the "*minimal* agreement about reading the Scriptures." While he does not use the term "Rule of Faith," nor does he say that he is reformulating it or considering its interpretive use, this seems a fair conclusion to draw. The Rule of Faith would cohere, after all, with the set of rules referred to in the following statement:

> The (largely but not wholly) informal set of rules under which it [Scripture] has customarily been read in the community, in the midst of much disagreement about its contents, has been fairly flexible and usually not too constrictive.[44]

This is exactly how the Rule of Faith functioned in interpretation, for it was allowed to place outer-limits or constraints within which great flexibility and a rich range of interpretive options existed.

Borrowing from the work of his colleague, George Lindbeck, Frei wants to understand Christianity as a "cultural linguistic system" whose theology will be "'intratextual'...the 'normative explication of the meaning a religion has for its adherents'...for 'meaning is constituted by the uses of a specific language rather than being distinguishable from it.'"[45] The specific language of the Christian tradition follows its own rules, and has its own logic. It should not be relied upon to provide ideological coherence for Western culture, says Frei, but should seek to regain its "autonomous vocation as a religion." He says that in this enterprise, the literal sense "may be counted on to play a significant part in such a less pretentious enterprise. It will stretch and not break."[46] While Frei did not make this explicit conclusion himself here, it does seem that one could argue on this basis that the Rule of Faith may play a major role in this elastic, non-brittle understanding of the literal sense of scripture.[47]

Plain Sense and Plain Silence

So far we have been considering understandings of plain sense of the textual, of what is written. This is because for the Christian tradition, plain sense reading was engaged in for the specific purpose of discerning the divine voice and will through the vehicle of scripture. But the conviction that reading the biblical text engaged the reader in an encounter with the Living God meant that every word was of the utmost significance, and it also meant that what was *not* written was also significant. Most modern considerations of "literality," however, tend either to disregard or to deny this as being an important element in interpreting the plain sense of scripture. For example, James Barr makes the following uncategorical statement:

> Literality may suggest: these words supply all that is needed, and one must not go beyond what they actually say. But what of the *silences* of the Bible?... Literality should properly require that, just as nothing that is there in words should be ignored, so nothing that is not there in words should be allowed.[48]

Barr's consideration of the literal sense fluctuates between a focus on how the term is understood among fundamentalists, among the Christian community more broadly understood, and among speakers of English at large.   He sketches a number of salient features of the notion of literality as he sees it: physicality, historicity, authority, textual segmentation, lexical meaning, intentionality.   Unlike Williams and Tanner, Barr seems to understand "literality" as functioning primarily to close off and define interpretation rather than open up a range of interpretive possibilities.   However, we will need to consider carefully how this compares with the practice of biblical interpretation in the Christian tradition, or at the very least within our chosen trajectory.   That is, even when plain sense interpretation is understood as a device to define and bring closure to problematic issues, as indeed has been one of its major functions in Christian biblical interpretation, we will need to ask whether or not the silences in the text are to be excluded as an object of inquiry.   Do different understandings of plain sense which we find in our trajectory allow the narrative spaces and silences of the Biblical text the power to bear the divine voice as the written words of the text are understood to do? If so, to what extent and how is this so?

We have uncovered some important issues with regard to the plain sense of scripture in the Christian tradition.   The notion of authority is of great significance for understanding what plays into reading the plain sense of scripture.   Within the Christian tradition, the reason one reads scripture in the first place is that it bears the voice of the Author and Authority of heaven and earth.   Understanding the text is therefore an existentially crucial task, for it involves answering or being accountable to one's creator, the Lord of the Church.   Not only is the text authoritative in this regard, it also authorizes the religious teachers, leaders, and the entire religious community.   Getting the "sense" of the text at hand is important in adjudicating matters of practice and matters of belief.   Thus the interplay between community and text is also therefore important in considering the notion of plain sense, for plain sense readings tend to allow the Scriptures leverage over against the community and its leaders.   This itself enables the nurturing of a community which is in its practice and doctrine able to adapt to change over time and in spite of cultural and geographic differences.   This is evident even within the first generation of Christianity, which went from an isolated Jewish Palestinian sect to a Gentile urban phenomenon spanning almost the entire known world.   This points also to another key aspect of plain sense reading: its relationship to apologetics, and presumably also therefore to polemics.

We have also seen that in addition to the textual, the non-textual may be also an important consideration in plain sense reading: our preliminary investigation has suggested that implicit communal norms such as embodied in the Rule of Faith may play a role in plain sense reading, as may also "reading between the lines" of the text itself. Likewise, the matter of textual reference and historicity may or may not be important to the theologians we will consider. Consideration of these issues will therefore prove helpful as we frame the questions to be posed of the theologians in the remainder of this study.

The Present Study: Augustine, Calvin and Barth Read Genesis 1-3

We will take up the question of the plain sense of scripture as a systematic problem, examining as test probes into the question writings from three theologians from the history of the Christian tradition. As our brief consideration above has shown, there has been some formal examination of our subject, but little material examination of samples of exegesis from different periods of Christian biblical interpretation as to the varying implicit assumptions about what goes into plain sense reading.[49] This study will assume that the understanding of the very notion of "plain sense" itself may vary over time and from reader to reader; that is, we are not arguing for an understanding of the plain sense as a property within the text itself.[50] With the theologians whom I will be examining, I will be assuming in the course of this study that words are used to "mean," albeit differently by different authors in different settings. Our use of the term "verbal sense" to refer to a theologian's understanding of the "meaning" of the words of the biblical text, while not "essentializing" meaning as a category, does assume a certain degree of givenness to verbal meaning, even if that givenness is mainly in use. This will require, therefore, a certain blending of the systematic and historical tasks. While attention will be paid to historical and contextual factors shaping the theology and reading of each of our theologians, the primary orientation of this study will be systematic.

Since this will not be a purely descriptive exercise in the history of interpretation, the reader will be disappointed who expects a review of what each theologian says about Genesis 1-3. For example, some of the better known comments which Augustine offers in his *Confessions* and *City of God* will scarcely be mentioned here. The goal before us is to examine not so much *what* these three figures say as *why* they say it and *how* they come to the interpretations they offer. This will require making explicit what remains implicit in their own work. Another *caveat lector*: the present study will not attempt to lay out the literal sense of Genesis 1-3. In other words, we will not presume to tell the reader "what the Bible really says" in its opening chapters. The study is of a second order, on *understandings* of the plain sense of scripture in Christian interpretation.

The first three chapters of Genesis will focus our investigation. One might argue that it would have been interesting to examine New Testament texts, especially in light of phenomenological hermeneutics' preference for Gospel parables and Frei's followers' preference for Gospel narratives. However, Old Testament interpretation is one of the key issues with regard to the plain sense. It might be most fruitful therefore to explore interpretations of an Old Testament text. The first chapters of Genesis tell the story of "Creation and Fall," the pivotal episodes that launch the Biblical story (as Christians have read it) in the direction of the Redemption wrought at the cave in Bethlehem, on the cross on Calvary, in the empty tomb at Golgotha. The opening chapters of Genesis have therefore received much attention because of the construals of their doctrinal "content." They have also been at the heart of the debate over the plain sense of scripture from the early church to the Fundamentalist/Modernist controversy.

It is in Augustine's work on Genesis that the problem of the literal sense comes to the fore for him. Certainly Augustine was not the first Christian theologian to have approached the opening chapters of the Bible with questions of interpretation, whether allegorical or literal, but in his own life and work this issue takes on a certain urgency.[51] Augustine becomes converted from a Manichee "hearer" to the Christian faith in part by listening to the allegorical sermons of Ambrose. Yet he regards his own attempts to win the Manichees to an "orthodox" reading of Genesis as a failure, for they were too allegorical. He tries instead to offer literal interpretation. We will examine Augustine's mature work, *De Genesi ad litteram*, by holding his comments up against the backdrop of this tension between the fruitfulness of allegorical interpretation and the necessity of literal interpretation. Next, we will examine Calvin's commentary on Genesis against the backdrop of the tension between the Humanist influences which impel him to a renewed "literal" reading, and the constraints of Ruled reading which he inherits from his Augustinian background.[52] Next we will examine Barth's reading of the opening chapters of Genesis in his *Church Dogmatics* 3.1 as he handles the interplay between dogmatic theology and exegetical investigation.

One might object that we are comparing apples and oranges here; in a certain respect we are. While Augustine is clearly precritical, Calvin is at the cusp of the critical era, and some would call Barth "post-critical."[53] Again, while Augustine and Calvin are writing what they call "commentaries," Barth's exegesis is embedded in his grand theological opus which is organized doctrinally. These observations, while valid, should not deter us from our project. Firstly, the historical contexts of each theologian will be taken into consideration. Secondly, Barth's exegesis, it can easily be argued, is no more or less shaped by his theological commitments than is that of Augustine and Calvin. Indeed, Barth's exegesis, even within the doctrinal framework of the *Church Dogmatics*, is arguably more "exegetical" than that of either Augustine or Calvin as regards attention to philological and literary matters. Thirdly, the exercise is a small one, limited in scope to one example of exegesis from each reader, and any conclusions drawn will therefore be necessarily limited. Finally, these three theologians do form a "trajectory" to which at least one wing of the Reformation may claim inheritance. It is therefore entirely justifiable to examine the reading of the plain sense of these three theologians together.

I will be working with an understanding of the notion of "plain sense" informed by Loewe, Frei, Tanner and Williams. The term "plain sense" will therefore serve to indicate a normative, justifiable or convincing reading offered by the exegete at hand, and the arguments each reader uses to authorize such a reading will be analyzed to fill out the notion of "plain sense" for that exegete. The terms "plain sense," "literal sense," "simple sense," and "verbal sense" will be used interchangeably in accordance with the usage of the exegete examined. However, while I see these terms as overlapping to a certain extent, my understanding is that they often can point to distinguishable reading strategies. Of course, the inadequacy of the terms and the imprecision with which they are used lends to the confusion over what might be meant by the category of "plain sense."

The suggestion that I want to make in the following analysis is that our authors are working with two constraints on "plain sense" reading. One of these constraints we will call verbal sense, by which we will mean something close to what Michael Fishbane refers to with the term *peshat*:

And so the *Peshat* focuses on the givenness and autonomy of the text, on its independence from the words of interpretation. The words of the text are all that we have. The first task of teaching and interpretation is then, to take this 'inscription,' this text, seriously. It is the starting point and precondition of all interpretation. This means recognizing the essentially dualistic relationship the interpreter has with the text. Its words are not his words, nor its thoughts his own—at least not initially... The *Peshat* constitutes the entire received text: the total text and not its component parts. This is the surface text

as it presents itself to us 'literally;' it is not the text as a series
of historical and/or editorial strata.[54]

Thus, verbal sense refers not only to the sense or senses indicated by the lexical units on the page, but also to the textual fixity of the lexical units themselves as the author, or traditioning editors who have erased their own footprints behind them, have arranged them. Reading the verbal sense cannot therefore entail parsing a text into smaller hypothetical traditions or editorial units, ascribing different hypothetical sources to them and thereby avoiding the engagement of the text as a whole. This is not to say that source and form criticism, for example, are "out-of-bounds," but simply to say that they do not directly expound the verbal sense.[55]

The other constraint we will call Ruled reading, that is, the hermeneutical application of the Rule of Faith. As we have argued of the Rule of Faith, so we can also say of Ruled reading that it indicates a prior "take" on the subject matter and plot of the Christian story such that the doctrines of creation and redemption are able to be held together. This prior understanding of the subject matter of scripture drives Ruled reading to embrace some interpretations and to reject others. As the Rule of faith draws a circle around a wide set of possible claims about Jesus and his relation to God and to the world and also rejects other such claims, so the Rule of faith in its hermeneutical application draws a circle around a wide set of diverse interpretations of scriptural texts and rejects others which rub raw against the Rule of Faith.[56]

It will be shown that the theologians to be examined negotiate between these two constraints of verbal sense and Ruled reading, each with different emphases, different motivations and different interpretive results. Depending upon the way in which the theologian at hand negotiates between these two constraints, "plain sense" may therefore encompass what we might have called "figural" reading as well as "literal" in a distinct mix for each theologian. In this respect, we will see that plain sense readings may extend beyond verbal sense.

Notes

1. This is the phrase used to translate Aquinas' *circumstantia litterae*. Cf. *De Pot.* 4.1.r; 4.2.r; Bruce Marshall, "Absorbing the World: Christianity and the Universe of Truths," in *Theology and Dialogue: Essays in Conversation with George Lindbeck* (Notre Dame, IN: University of Notre Dame Press, 1990), 101, n. 38; David S. Yeago, "The New Testament and the Nicene Dogma: A Contribution to the Recovery of Theological Exegesis," *Pro Ecclesia* 3 (1994): 161; Eugene F. Rogers, Jr., "How the Virtues of the Interpreter Presuppose and Perfect Hermeneutics: The Case of Thomas Aquinas," *Journal of Religion* 76 (1996): 74.

2. Included here, of course, are the texts of the Apocrypha. I will be using the term "Old Testament" with full knowledge of the alternative proposals. See, for example, James A. Sanders, "First Testament and Second," *Biblical Theology Bulletin* 17 (1987): 47–9; Christopher Seitz, "Old Testment or Hebrew Bible: Some Theological Considerations," *Pro Ecclesia* 5 (1996): 292–303. "First Testament" gives the impression that the New Testament as "Second Testament" is somehow secondary. However, as will become clear throughout the study, for the three theologians to be examined here, the New Testament might be more aptly described as hermeneutically primary, or even prior in some respects. The term "Hebrew Scriptures" is misleading, for this term technically includes the Talmud. Even the term "Hebrew Bible" is inadequate, for the Hebrew Bible can be argued to be in fact a different book from the Christian Old Testament, with a different canonical ordering and different titles of individual books. Readers will please forbear the use of the traditional term; no slight whatsoever either to the authority or religious value of the "Old Testament" is intended.

3. For a still much-consulted but often misleading introduction to the problem of Christian readings of the Old Testament, see James Samuel Preus, *From Shadow to Promise: Old Testament Interpretation from Augustine to the Young Luther* (Cambridge: The Belknap Press, 1969).

4. The phrase "the Christian tradition" is not used here to indicate the hegemony of those who "won" to define what Christianity was or was to become, e.g. Walter Bauer, *Orthodoxy and Heresy in Earliest Christianity* (Philadelphia: Fortress, 1971) and Daniel J. Harrington, "The Reception of Walter Bauer's *Orthodoxy and Heresy in Earliest Christianity* During the Last Decade," *HTR* 73 (1980): 289–98. For thoughtful theologically-based rejections of Bauer's thesis, see Thomas

A. Robinson, *The Bauer Thesis Examined: The Geography of Heresy in the Early Christian Church* (Lewiston: Edwin Mellen, 1988) and Daniel L. Hoffman, *The Status of Women and Gnosticism in Irenaeus and Tertullian* (Lewiston: Edwin Mellen Press, 1995). A more theologically satisfying attempt than Bauer, see H. E. W. Turner, *The Pattern of Christian Truth: A Study in the Relations Between Orthodoxy and Heresy in the Early Church* (London: A. R. Mowbray, 1954). By the phrase "the Christian tradition" I mean simply the process of handing down of Christian teaching as well as the content of that teaching itself. Therefore, I understand the phrase to indicate both "change and continuity, not only in conflict but also in agreement"; Jaroslav Pelikan, *The Emergence of the Catholic Tradition*, The Christian Tradition: A History of the Development of Doctrine (Chicago: University of Chicago Press, 1971), 7.

5.   This complexity is also apparent in the rabbinic reading of plain sense, or *peshat*. Consider the observation which J. Z. Lauterbach makes of the Tannaitic rabbis: "a distinction between '*peshat*' as the literal sense of Scripture and '*derash*' as the interpretation and derivation could not have been made in antiquity for the simple reason that the Tannaim believed... that their '*derash*' was the actual sense of scripture, and therefore '*peshat*'." See *The Jewish Encyclopedia* IX, 652f., cited in Raphael Loewe, "The 'Plain' Meaning of Scripture in Early Jewish Exegesis," in *Papers of the Institute of Jewish Studies, London*, ed. J. G. Weiss (Jerusalem: Magnes Press, 1964), 178, n. 189.

6.   Cf. the still-useful C. H. Dodd, *According to the Scriptures: The Substructure of New Testament Theology* (London: Nisbet & Co., 1952) and Richard B. Hays, *Echoes of Scripture in the Letters of Paul* (New Haven: Yale University Press, 1989).

7.   Robert M. Grant, "The Place of the Old Testament in Early Christianity," *Interpretation* 5 (1951): 186–202.

8.   "The upshot of this ruled use of the New Testament stories was of course bound to entail the expropriative rules for the interpretation of Jewish scripture which we have noted, and all three cases of the procedure—shadow and reality, prophecy and fulfillment, metaphorical type and literal antitype—came to present modern Christian biblical reading with two enormous problems..." This could be taken to mean either that it *results* in the two problems, or that it *necessitates* that these two problems *be confronted*. While I think Frei actually wanted to say the second, the first is what he appears to be saying. See Hans W. Frei, "The 'Literal Reading' of Biblical Narrative in the Christian Tradition: Does It Stretch or Will It Break?" in *The Bible and the Narrative Tradition*, ed. Frank

McConnell (New York: Oxford University Press, 1986), 47. For an illuminating comparison of the biblical hermeneutics of Frei and Barth, see David E. Demson, *Hans Frei and Karl Barth: Different Ways of Reading Scripture* (Grand Rapids: Eerdmans, 1997).

9. On the Rule of Faith, see William Countryman, "Tertullian and the Regula Fidei," *The Second Century* 2 (1982): 208-27; Eric F. Osborn, "Reason and the Rule of Faith in the Second Century AD," in *The Making of Orthodoxy: Essays in Honor of Henry Chadwick*, ed. Rowan Williams (Cambridge: Cambridge University Press, 1989), 40-61; Paul M. Blowers, "The 'Regula Fidei' and the Narrative Character of Early Christian Faith," *Pro Ecclesia* 6 (1997): 199-228; Bengt Hägglund, "Die Bedeutung der 'regula fidei' als Grundlage theologischer Aussagen", *Studia Theologica* 12 (1958): 1-44; Ellen Flesseman-Van Leer, *Tradition and Scripture in the Early Church*, (Assen: Van Gorcum, 1953); Henri Blocher, "'The Analogy of Faith' in the Study of Scripture," *Scottish Bulletin of Evangelical Theology* 5 (1987): 17-38.

10. François Louvel, "Appendix 3," in *Les Ecrits Des Pères Apostliques* (Paris: Editions du Cerf, 1963), 491-2. Louvel points to these early examples in Ignatius' *Letter to the Ephesians* 7.2: "There is one Physician, who is both flesh and spirit, born and yet not born, who is God in man, true life in death, both of Mary and of God, first passible and then impassible, Jesus Christ our Lord." Again in 18.2: "For our God, Jesus the Christ, was conceived by Mary by the dispensation of God, as well of the seed of David as of the Holy Spirit..." and in 19.1: "And the virginity of Mary, and her giving birth were hidden from the Prince of this world, as was also the death of the Lord..." In Ignatius' *Letter to the Trallians* 9.1-2 Louvel notes the following expansion: "Be deaf, therefore, when anyone speaks to you apart from Jesus Christ, who was of the family of David, and of Mary, who was truly born, both ate and drank, was truly persecuted under Pontius Pilate, was truly crucified and died in the sight of those in heaven and on earth and under the earth; who also was truly raised from the dead, when his Father raised him up, as in the same manner his Father shall raise up in Christ Jesus us who believe in him, without whom we have no true life." In Polycarp's *Letter to the Philippians* 2.1-2 Louvel finds even more direct use of scripture (1 Peter 1:13, 21; Ps 2:11; Phil 3:21, 2:10; Acts 10:42; 2 Cor 4:14, etc.): "Wherefore girding up your loins serve God in fear and truth, putting aside empty vanity and vulgar error, believing on him who raised up our Lord Jesus Christ from the dead and gave him glory, and a throne on his right hand, to whom are subject all things in heaven and earth, whom all breath serves, who is coming as the Judge of the living and of the

dead, whose blood God will require from them who disobey him. Now he who raised him from the dead will also raise us up if we do his will, walk in his commandments and love the things which he loved..." These translations are from Kirsopp Lake, *The Apostolic Fathers, Vol. 1*, Loeb Classical Library (Cambridge: Harvard University Press, 1912), 6.

11. See Irenaeus' *Against Heresies* 1.22.1: "The rule of truth which we hold is that there is one God Almighty, who made all things by His Word, and fashioned and formed, out of that which had no existence, all things which exist." This translation is from A. Cleveland Coxe, *The Apostolic Fathers with Justin Martyr and Irenaeus*, The Ante-Nicene Fathers: Translations of the Writings of the Fathers Down to A.D. 325 (Grand Rapids: Eerdmans, 1884). See also 4.53.2, 5.20.1. Cf. Joseph F. Mitros, "The Norm of Faith in the Patristic Age," *Theological Studies* 29 (1965): 444–71. See also Tertullian's *Against Praxeas* 3: "...the Rule of faith withdraws the simple [who are the majority of believers] from the world's plurality of gods to the one only true God; not understanding that, although He is the one only God, He must yet be believed in with His own oikonomia." And later in 9: "Bear always in mind that this is the rule of faith which I profess: by it I testify that the Father, the Son, and the Spirit are inseparable from each other..." The translation used here is from A. Cleveland Coxe, *Latin Christianity: Its Founder, Tertullian*, The Ante-Nicene Fathers: Translations of the Writings of the Fathers Down to A.D. 325 (Grand Rapids: Eerdmans).

12. *Concerning the Veiling of Virgins* 1. The translation here is from A. Cleveland Coxe, *Fathers of the Third Century*, eds. Alexander Roberts and James Donaldson, The Ante-Nicene Fathers: Translations of the Fathers Down to A.D. 325 (Grand Rapids: Eerdmans, 1885). See also Countryman, "Tertullian," 209; Blowers, "Regula Fidei."

13. Tertullian, *Prescription Against the Heretics*. Translation by S. L. Greenslade, ed., *Early Latin Theology: Selections from Tertullian, Cyprian, Ambrose and Jerome* (Philadelphia: Westminster Press, 1956), 39–40.

14. Countryman, "Tertullian", 223.

15. Loewe, "Plain Meaning," 141–2.

16. Ibid., 155.

17. Ibid., 157–9.

18. David Weiss Halivni, *Peshat and Derash: Plain and Applied Meaning in Rabbinic Exegesis* (New York: Oxford University Press, 1991), esp. ch. 3. Halivni suggests that the understanding of *peshat* as simple meaning was introduced by the medieval exegetes and was therefore not operative in the Talmudic period. He offers a definition of the Talmudic

understanding of *peshat* as "contextual meaning". His work is based on
the thesis of Sarah Kamin, "Rashi's Exegetical Categorization With
Respect to the Distinction Between *Peshat* and *Derash* According to His
Commentary to the Book of Genesis and Selected Passages from His
Commentaries to Other Books of the Bible," *Immanuel* 11 (1980): 16–
32. This in turn is based on her dissertation which is available only in
Hebrew. Kamin argues that a distinction between *peshat* and *derash* did
not develop with Rashi but with Rashi's grandson, Rashbam. Readers
should be aware that the strategy in the present study is the inverse of
Kamin's. That is, while she holds Rashi up to her own definition of the
distinction between *peshat* and *derash*, and then determines that he had
no such distinction, I will be attempting in the present study to uncover
each theologian's own understanding(s) of "plain sense" as evident in the
practice of exegesis rather than imposing my own definition.

19. Loewe, "Plain Meaning", 183.
20. Ibid.
21. Ibid., 181.
22. Kathryn E. Tanner, "Theology and the Plain Sense," in *Scriptural Authority and Narrative Interpretation*, ed. Garrett Green (Philadelphia: Fortress, 1987), 60.
23. Tanner, "Theology and the Plain Sense", 63. She quotes Charles Wood, *The Formation of Christian Understanding: An Essay in Theological Hermeneutics* (Philadelphia: Westminster Press, 1981), 40 ff. and 116 ff., who understands the literal sense as that "normally acknowledged as basic [by the community] regardless of whatever other constructions might also properly be put upon the text..., [that] sense whose discernment has become second nature to the members of that community."
24. Tanner, "Theology and the Plain Sense," 63, quoting Loewe, "Plain Meaning," 181.
25. This is my example, not Tanner's. She points to the historical case of "the oral tradition of rabbinic Judaism," and to appeals to tradition in counter-Reformation arguments. See p. 77, n. 23. I am extending her historical example to the present day Orthodox Jewish communities which understand themselves to be the descendants and inheritors of rabbinic Judaism.
26. Here Tanner seems to bleed her own definition of plain sense with something like "straightforward sense." For example, in speaking apparently of applied sense, she says: "These senses are as much what the text itself says, then, as the plain or obvious sense." Tanner, "Theology and Plain Sense," 71.
27. Karlfried Froehlich, "'Always to Keep the Literal Sense in Holy Scrip-

ture Means to Kill One's Soul': The State of Biblical Hermeneutics at the Beginning of the Fifteenth Century," in *Literary Uses of Typology*, ed. E. Miner (Princeton: Princeton University Press, 1977), 28ff.

28. Tanner, "Theology and Plain Sense," 72-3.

29. Ibid., 65.

30. Rowan Williams, "The Literal Sense of Scripture," *Modern Theology* 7 (1991): 121-34. Williams is using these terms differently from the usage of other scholars, e.g. Brevard Childs. Childs has used "diachronic" to connote the methods of historical reconstruction of Israel's development and "synchronic" those of canonical criticism, and in his recent book has reformulated the terms such that the canonical includes a diachronic dimension. Brevard S. Childs, *Biblical Theology of the Old and New Testaments: Theological Reflection on the Christian Bible*, 1st ed. (Minneapolis, Minn.: Fortress Press, 1993), 104. While for Williams, the *diachronic* is related to plain sense reading, for Childs, both diachronic and synchronic are.

31. Williams, "Literal Sense," 125.

32. Nicholas Lash, "Performing the Scriptures," in *Theology on the Way to Emmaus* (London: SCM Press, 1986), 37-46.

33. Williams, "Literal Sense," 127.

34. Williams, "Literal Sense," 132. There seems to be something missing in the last sentence here; I have recorded it as published.

35. Frei, "'Literal Reading'," 46.

36. John Dominic Crossan, ed., *Semeia 4: Paul Ricoeur on Biblical Hermeneutics* (Missoula, Mont.: Scholars Press, 1975), 32, cited in Frei, "'Literal Reading'," 48.

37. Frei, "'Literal Reading'," 50. In a note here he points to an example in David Tracy, *Blessed Rage for Order: The New Pluralism in Theology* (New York: Seabury Press, 1975), 206, 102-15.

38. Frei, "'Literal Reading'," 50. He continues on the following page, "If the general theory of hermeneutics is to stand, it must persuade us that its appeal to a second naïveté and to a hermeneutics of restoration constitutes a genuine option between reading with first naïveté on the one hand and on the other reading with that 'suspicion' which regards the linguistic 'world,' which text and reader may share, as a mere ideological or psychological superstructure reducible to real or true infrastructures, which must be critically or scientifically adduced."

39. Frei, "'Literal Reading'," 50.

40. Hans W. Frei, *The Eclipse of Biblical Narrative: A Study in Eighteenth and Nineteenth Century Hermeneutics* (New Haven; London: Yale University Press, 1974), ch. 5.

41. "The factuality or non-factuality of at least some of these [Biblical] narratives, important as it is no doubt in a larger religious or an even more general context, involves a separate argument from that concerning their meaning." Frei, "'Literal Reading'," 62-3.

42. Certainly Frei is not unaware of, nor does he hide from his readers, the potential weaknesses of his suggestions. While for our purposes it will not be necessary to outline these, the reader may consult Frei, "'Literal Reading'," 63ff.

43. Frei, "'Literal Reading'," 68-9. See also *Eclipse*, 34: "The occurrence character and the theme or teleological pattern of a historical or history-like narrative belong together. Interpretation or the gathering of meaning is in no sense a material contribution on the part of the interpreter or a unique perspective he might represent. Without this conviction to govern the figural reading of a sequence, it becomes a totally arbitrary forcing together of discontinuous events and patterns of meaning." One could point to the coherence between the Rule of faith and what Frei calls the "theme or teleological pattern" of the history-like narrative of the Gospel.

44. Ibid., 68.

45. Frei, "'Literal Reading'," 71-2. Here he is quoting George A. Lindbeck, *The Nature of Doctrine* (Philadelphia: Westminster, 1984), 113-16.

46. Frei, "'Literal Reading'," 74-5.

47. Frei in fact does not test his theories on anything but the Gospel narratives. For an example of this, cf. Hans W. Frei, *The Identity of Jesus Christ: The Hermeneutical Bases of Dogmatic Theology* (Philadelphia: Fortress Press, 1975). Indeed, the fact that his theory has not engaged reading of biblical texts other than Gospel narratives can be argued to be one of its major weaknesses.

48. James Barr, "Literality," *Faith and Philosophy* 6 (1989): 422. See also James Barr, "The Literal, the Allegorical, and Modern Biblical Scholarship," *JSOT* 44 (1989): 17 and Paul R. Noble, "The Sensus Literalis: Jowett, Childs, and Barr," *Journal of Theological Studies* 44 (1993): 1-23.

49. There are few exceptions to this statement, and the exceptions are such that they only serve to prove the case. See Brevard S. Childs, "The Sensus Literalis of Scripture: An Ancient and Modern Problem," in *Beiträge Zur Alttestamentlichen Theologie: Festschrift Für Walther Zimmerli* (1977), 80-93; Charles Scalise, "The 'Sensus Literalis': A Hermeneutical Key to Biblical Exegesis," *Scottish Journal of Theology* 42 (1989): 45-65. These attempt to sketch a theology of the plain sense,

but in their very brevity they raise more questions than they can answer. There are a few studies which focus on a particular exegete's understanding of the plain sense. For example, see Dan G. McCartney, "Literal and Allegorical Interpretation in Origen's Contra Celsum," *Westminster Theological Journal* 48 (1986): 281-301; Rogers, op. cit; David M. Hay, ed., *Both Literal and Allegorical: Studies in Philo of Alexandria's Questions and Answers on Genesis and Exodus*, Brown Judaica Series (Atlanta: Scholars Press, 1991). One of the most interesting studies for our purposes, which does not directly engage any of the theologians in our trajectory and is more literary than theological in scope, is Thomas H. Luxon, *Literal Figures: Puritan Allegory and the Reformation Crisis in Representation* (Chicago: University of Chicago Press, 1995). There are also some helpful examinations of *peshat*, or the Jewish understanding of plain sense. In addition to Loewe, see Kamin, "Rashi's Exegetical Categorization"; Chaim Cohen, "Elements of *Peshat* in Traditional Jewish Bible Exegesis," *Immanuel* 20-21 (1986-87): 1-36; Yeshayahu Maori, "The Approach of Classical Jewish Exegetes to *Peshat* and *Derash* and Its Implications for the Teaching of Bible Today," trans. Moshe J. Bernstein, *Tradition* 21 (1984): 40-53; Uriel Simon, "The Religious Significance of the Peshat," *Tradition* 23 (1988): 41-63; Mark Lockshin, "Tradition or Context: Two Exegetes Struggle with *Peshat*," in *From Ancient Israel to Modern Judaism, Vol. 2*, ed. E. Frerichs J. Neusner, N. Sarna (Atlanta: Scholars Press, 1989), 173-86; Halivni, *Peshat and Derash*; Benjamin Gelles, *Peshat and Derash in the Exegesis of Rashi* (Leiden: Brill, 1981).

50. This is the understanding behind Halivni, *Peshat and Derash*. See also Loewe, "Plain Meaning," Tanner, "Theology and Plain Sense." I do not, however, go so far as David Dawson's identification of meaning, and thus literal or plain sense, as a "thoroughly rhetorical category." See David Dawson, *Allegorical Readers and Cultural Revision in Ancient Alexandria* (Berkeley: University of California Press, 1992), 7-8 "My use of phrases like 'literal sense'...is not intended to indicate any essentialization or reification of meaning, or to suggest that texts somehow 'possess' meaning the way individuals 'possess' property... 'Meaning' is thus a thoroughly rhetorical category... Consequently, although the 'literal sense' has often been thought of as an inherent quality of a literary text that gives it a specific and invariant character (often a 'realistic' character), the phrase is simply an honorific title given to a kind of meaning that is culturally expected and automatically recognized by readers."

51. See, e.g., Gregory Allen Robbins, ed., *Genesis 1-3 in the History of*

Exegesis: Intrigue in the Garden (Lewiston/Queens: Edwin Mellen Press, 1988); Frank Egleston Robbins, *The Hexaemeral Literature: A Study of the Greek and Latin Commentaries on Genesis* (Chicago: University of Chicago Press, 1912); J. C. M. Van Winden, "'In the Beginning': Some Observations on the Patristic Interpretation of Genesis 1:1," *Vigiliae Christianae* 17 (1963): 105–21; Paul Vignaux, ed., *In Principio: Interprétations Des Premiers Versets de la Genèse* (Paris: Etudes Augustiniennes, 1973).

52. In a formal sense this plays on Bouwsma's "two Calvins", the Calvin of the Tradition of the Church and the Calvin of Humanism. William J. Bouwsma, *John Calvin: A Sixteenth Century Portrait* (Oxford: Oxford University Press, 1988).

53. Rudolf Smend, "Nachkritische Schriftsauslegung," in *Parrhesia: Karl Barth Zum Achtzigsten Geburtstag* (Zürich: EVZ Verlag, 1966), 215–37.

54. Michael Fishbane, "The Teacher and the Hermeneutical Task: A Reinterpretation of Medieval Exegesis," *JAAR* 43 (1975): 712–13.

55. Here I should note that what some call literal sense is what I mean by the narrower category of verbal sense. Verbal sense is just one of the constraints which I find in my analysis of plain sense readings here. Cf. Francis Watson, *Text and Truth: Redefining Biblical Theology* (Edinburgh: T & T Clark, 1997), 123–4: "The literal sense of the biblical texts comprises (i) verbal meaning, (ii) illocutionary and perlocutionary force, and (iii) the relation to the centre... To grasp the verbal meaning and the illocutionary and perlocutionary force of a text is to understand the *authorial intention* embodied in it. Authorial intention is the principle of a text's intelligibility, and cannot be detached from the text itself... A text's verbal meaning, illocutionary and perlocutionary force, and relation to the centre precede and transcend the additional meanings or significances it may acquire as it is read in different communal contexts. *Objective interpretation* concerns itself with the primary and determinate aspects of a text's existence."

56. As was the case with our own use of the phrase verbal sense overlapping with other uses of the phrase literal sense, so also is this true of our use of the phrase Ruled reading. Thus, we find Gene Rogers picks out three distinguishable senses of "literal" in Thomas Aquinas, intentional, narrative, and communal. The latter two we might categorize as Ruled reading. See Rogers, "Virtues of the Interpreter," 66.

Chapter Two:
Augustine's Understanding
of the Literal Sense of Scripture
in De Genesi ad litteram

The Search for Literal Interpretation of Genesis 1-3

In biblical exegesis, whether pre-critical or critical, the interpreter's fundamental understanding and attitudes about the nature of the text and the purpose of interpretation may often be more important than any specific "methods" used. This is true of Saint Augustine's interpretation of scripture, for his basic convictions set the program for his exegesis. He understands the biblical text to be inspired and therefore assumes that it bears the voice and will of God. This is one way of understanding his dictum, "I believe in order that I might understand," for it indicates that understanding the treasures that lie in scripture requires the gift of faith. In fact, for Augustine it is the seeking that is in some respects more important than the actual understanding, for he assumes that full understanding will not be gained during this earthly life. These attitudes about scripture and its reading imply a "preferential hermeneutical option" for the Christian. That is, the non-Christian can at best only *under*interpret scripture, and will without the gift of faith fail to receive scripture's full benefits. This means that for Augustine the act of reading scripture and Christian formation cannot be split apart. Reading scripture can foster Christian formation, while Christian formation enriches and aids the understanding of scripture.

In Augustine's pre-Christian stage, he rejected Christianity partly because of what he deemed to be the obscurity of Scripture, particularly in the Old Testament. Augustine had found the Bible distasteful because of the "immorality" of the people of Israel and because he deemed the Bible to be literature of an inferior class when compared with the classics on which he was nourished. Since Ambrose's allegorical sermons on the Old Testament allow Augustine to break through beyond his Manichean rejection of the Bible, it is fair to say that allegory is the key which opens the scriptures to Augustine.[1] Paul's statement that God chooses the simple to confound the wise (1 Cor 1:27) becomes programmatic for Augustine's understanding of the Old Testament, and he comes to believe that what he had previously considered obscurity and coarseness in the Bible is more profound than even the wisdom of the classical authors he had esteemed far beyond Scripture.

While allegorical interpretation did indeed enable Augustine to accept Christian scripture, he does nevertheless still value "literal" interpretation, for allegorical interpretation does not rule out the possibility or the necessity of attempting to keep to the letter. We therefore see the tension within which Augustine reads the Bible: his understanding of the Bible as inspired allows and indeed necessitates allegorical interpretation, but his understanding that the Bible speaks of the same continuity of time and space within which he lives requires literal reading as well.[2]

At the heart of his exploration of why and how one seeks to unfold the literal sense of scripture are his reflections on the Genesis creation and fall narratives. He returns to the opening chapters of Genesis again and again over the course of his lifetime. The first attempt to expound them, *De Genesi contra Manichaeos*, was written in 388/389 before his ordination to the priesthood but after his return to Africa. In this work, he uses allegorical interpretation in an attempt to refute the Manichean literal interpretation of the Old Testament which rejected the linking of the doctrines of creation and redemption required by the Rule of Faith and the catholic canon of scripture.[3] Augustine later regarded this early work as too allegorical and therefore ineffectual at convincing the Manicheans of the error of their ways.[4] He decided that focussing on the literal or narrative meaning of the plainer passages of scripture would generally be the more fruitful approach in apologetics.[5] Even so, he held that multiple levels of meaning can coexist without necessarily conflicting or contradicting each other.

Later, in 393, he attempted to interpret Genesis "according to the letter" in *De Genesi ad litteram imperfectus liber*,[6] but was not entirely satisfied with this unfinished work either.[7] He tried later in *De Genesi ad litteram*, written between 404 and 420, to focus on a more literal approach.[8] In this work he attempted to uphold the integrity of the biblical narrative as record of both history and prophecy, and it is this work which will occupy most of our attention when we turn to Augustine's exegesis of Genesis 1–3.[9] The irony of his work on Genesis is this: while it is allegorical interpretation which in part opened to him the Hebrew scriptures, he realizes that allegorical interpretation alone is not sufficient to win the Manichees to the "orthodox" faith.

Since Augustine's work on Genesis begins with his commentary directed against the Manichees, even at the outset his writing on Genesis is polemically driven. And even throughout his complete commentary on Genesis, *De Genesi ad litteram*, he refers to "some interpreters" who have erred in their ways whom he seeks to correct. When he attempts to correct these readers, he often resorts to the Rule of Faith to guarantee an understanding of the text which does not violate the catholic faith. Thus, even in his mature commentary, those who "distort" the faith are always within his peripheral vision, and he is still concerned to refute them even if the commentary is not directed to them specifically but rather to the faithful at large.

When speaking in *De Genesi ad litteram* about his earlier commentary on Genesis against the Manichees, he says that he rejects the Manichean interpretation of the Old Testament not simply because of its material content, but because the Manichees hold nothing but contempt for the Old Testament. His intent in that work, was to give as much plain or proper exposition as possible, but he finds this not always possible.

> At that time I did not see how all of Genesis could be taken in the proper sense, and it seemed to me more and more impossible, or at least scarcely possible or very difficult, for it all to be so understood. But not willing to be deterred from my purpose, whenever I was unable to discover the literal meaning of a passage, I explained its figurative meaning as briefly and clearly as I was able, so that the Manichees might not be discouraged by the length of the work or the obscurity of its contents and thus put the book aside.[10]

He then restates his defense of allegorical interpretation which he had offered in *De Genesi contra Manichaeos*, and he then lays out his purpose for the fresh attempt in *De Genesi ad litteram* to expound the plain sense:

> Now the Lord has wished that I should look at and consider the same matter more thoroughly, and I believe that according to His will I can reasonably hope that I shall be able to show how the book of Genesis has been written with a proper rather than allegorical meaning in view.[11]

In this later work, therefore, he does not turn away from his former concern to refute the Manichees, but he simply tries to take a more refined attempt in presenting his concern. While the Manichees are no longer his sole sparring partner here, he is clearly still seeking to "apologize" for the book of Genesis and the orthodox doctrine of creation, only now he does so with more diligence to expound the letter of the text. For the most part in this later commentary, the polemic is broadened to cover any interpretation that violates the Rule of Faith and the literal sense of scripture. Both of these are not to be understood for Augustine in starkly contrasting terms, nor even as distinct hermeneutical guidelines. Indeed, the interplay between the Rule of Faith and literal sense is extremely important in Augustine's *De Genesi ad litteram*.

Augustine's Exegetical Principles

Before turning our attention to Augustine's treatments of the creation and fall narratives, it will be helpful to sketch a general picture of his exegetical theory as laid out in *De doctrina christiana*,[12] not only because the principles he enumerates here are influential on his *De Genesi ad litteram*, but also because they are important for the entire tradition in the West after him, including, of course, Calvin and Barth. Begun in 396 but not completed and published until 427, *De doctrina christiana* represents his mature view on the interpretation of scripture. Books 1 and 2 treat the "secular" as well as theological training necessary for interpretation. Book 3 focuses on hermeneutics and Book 4 concentrates on the application of interpretation in preaching.

His fundamental commitment to embrace the Biblical text as inspired influences his entire exegetical program, extending even to his choice of canon and text. It is of course this issue which is at the heart of Augustine's difficulty in accepting Jerome's work at translating what will become (parts of) the Vulgate from the *Hebraica veritas*.[13] Augustine considers the Septuagint to be uniquely inspired and authoritative for the church, and Jerome's translation in supplanting it would wreak havoc with the prayer and worship of the Church.[14] Augustine retains the Septuagint as the Christian Old Testament not only because he deems it to be catholic and apostolic,[15] but also because he accepts as true the legend of its providential and inspired production.[16] It is apparent from Augustine's exegetical principles set forth in *De doctrina christiana* that he felt no immediate constraint to fix a pure and hence authoritative text in the modern critical sense; for him, the ultimately authoritative text is the Septuagint because it is uniquely inspired.

Because the biblical text is inspired, it is therefore divinely "arranged" to bear communication(s) from the Divine to humanity. Thus, the text is to be read with respect to the hermeneutical guidance of the Rule of Faith, which sets the parameters for the outer limits to this "message."[17] To this Rule, longstanding within Christian reading of the Bible by his time, Augustine adds the Rule of Charity, for he understands the goal of this Divinely communicated text to be the building in us love of God and neighbor. The Rules of Faith and Charity thus function as "controls" on interpretation, excluding as improper those interpretations which either contradict the inseparability of the doctrines of creation and redemption (the Rule of Faith) or which do not nourish in the reader love of God and neighbor (the Rule of Charity). Most often these Rules do not therefore prescribe a "correct" interpretation, but rather serve to draw a circle around an array of allowable interpretations from which the interpreter may choose. In fact, Augustine states that any interpretation which does not lead to the building up of love of God and of neighbor is simply a *mis*understanding or *under*interpretation of the text: the interpreter "does not yet understand as he ought."[18] In fact, since scripture builds faith, hope and love, if one already has a firm grasp on these, it is conceivable that one would have no need of Scripture except to instruct others.[19] Of course, Augustine's assumption is that one never reaches this point in one's earthly life; the Bible is therefore seen to be an inexhaustibly interpretable text. This means that the interpreter should not have to doubt his or her own abilities in interpreting the text as long as he or she "is bent on making all understanding of scripture to bear upon these three graces."[20] Since understanding scripture's bearing upon these three graces is the sole purpose of interpretation, one need not feel constrained to find a single meaning in the text for a plurality of meanings by definition may be found.

Indeed, the variety of interpretations a single text may have (provided the two criteria of faith and charity are met) does not denigrate or detract from Scripture, but rather underscores its richness and its divinely inspired quality.[21] Interpretations which might be seen as "mistakes" or "eisogesis" by a modern critic's understanding of exegesis (e.g. reading the story of the Good Samaritan as an allegory of the Christian life) are allowable in Augustine's plan as long as the Rules of Faith and Charity are not contradicted. Augustine now comes to see the obscurities and difficulties in scripture as part of the divine plan and as such they serve to spur the reader on to greater understanding.[22] While the "plainer passages satisfy our hunger, the more obscure ones stimulate our appetite" to learn more.[23] This classically trained scholar who formerly thought the Bible an inferior work and later comes to regard it as a challenge to his intellect, now understands this challenge to be divinely arranged in order to subdue pride, the root of sin. Therefore, even the act of reading the Bible, with the proper goal set ahead of one, can be part of the redemptive process. In approaching scripture, therefore, one must adopt an attitude of teachableness and receptivity to the divine nurture of faith, hope and love through the Word. Exegesis is, to be sure, an exercise of the mind, but it also edifies the soul; in Augustinian terms, it is both a matter of loving as well as knowing.

In order to discern the obscurities of scripture from the plainer passages, Augustine makes the distinction between two types of signs, natural and conventional.[24] Natural signs "lead to the knowledge of something else," as the appearance of smoke leads one to the knowledge that there is fire. Conventional signs are exchanged by living creatures in order to show feelings and thoughts, just as the dove's coo is a sign that it is calling for its mate. Conventional signs are what compose language, and words are the encoding of this kind of sign. The signs we have in Scripture are therefore conventional signs.

Of these conventional signs, Augustine distinguishes between proper and figurative signs. An example of a proper sign would be the word *bos*, which refers to the animal known as "ox" in English. Augustine then points to Paul's interpretation of a figurative sign, for Paul implies that the word "ox" in Dt 25:4 refers not so much to the beast of burden at all, but to the preacher, for "is it for oxen that God is concerned?" (1 Cor 9:9). It is this type of figurative sign which obscures scripture. The interpreter must beware of taking figurative expressions literally,[25] for a "carnal understanding" will result. Presumably Augustine means here an interpretation which does not meet the criteria of faith and charity. Augustine says that in order not to be in bondage to signs, one must know what the sign signifies, or at least be able to recognize that it is a figurative and not a proper sign, and admit ignorance regarding its referent.[26]

To test whether a sign is figurative or proper, Augustine relies again on the rules of faith and charity. If something in the text is taken literally, but it cannot be referred either to "purity of life [charity] or soundness of doctrine [faith]," it must be taken figuratively.[27] In other words, one should try to interpret by uncovering the literal or proper meaning first, but if that does not accord with faith and charity, figurative interpretation must be sought. For example, in speaking of the stories told in the Old Testament, he recommends this approach:

> ...though the authors of them are praised, (their actions) are repugnant to the habits of the good men who since our Lord's advent are the custodians of the divine commands; let (the interpreter) refer the figure to its interpretation but let him not transfer the act to his habits of life.[28]

Thus we can via figurative interpretation render less offensive the Old Testament stories which seem abhorrent to our sense of morals and thereby remove the unnecessary scandal of their actions. Yet, it must be noted that in speaking of the immoral actions of the people of the Old Testament (which, it will be remembered, stood as one of Augustine's major obstacles in accepting the Christian faith), Augustine does not merely allegorize them away or indicate that they need not trouble us. The incomprehensibly barbaric actions of the saints of old are not to be simply passed off as discordant with faith in Jesus Christ, nor are they dismissed as though "non-historical." This is because these people were chosen of God to bear the faith and from them is descended the Christ. According to Augustine, we need to read these events, important in their own right, as lessons to teach us humility, presumably lest we Christians consider ourselves better than the "saints of old."[29]

Augustine recommends a knowledge of the Biblical languages to aid in the discernment between figurative and proper signs, as he says, "on account of the diversities among translators."[30] The oddity in this is that Augustine had no knowledge of Hebrew whatsoever, and only towards the end of his life did he gain a very little knowledge of Patristic Greek. It seems that the most we can say for his linguistic skills is that he knew a few words of Punic, which he recognized as a North African cognate of Hebrew.[31] Thus, while he admits that knowledge of the Biblical languages is a remedy for ignorance, he is not able to avail himself of that knowledge to strengthen his own interpretation. For example, in his treatment of Galatians 6:2 and Galatians 6:5, Augustine says that the two verses do not contradict each other as they may appear to do because they refer to different types of burdens. The Latin translation makes this interpretation less easily defensible than would the Greek text, for the Latin translates both $\beta\alpha\rho o$ of 6:2 and $\phi o\rho^?\iota o\nu$ of 6:5 as *onus*. Had Augustine known the distinction in Greek, this would have strengthened his case.[32]

Augustine stresses in addition to Biblical languages that a broad and general education will be of much help to the interpreter. This of course is not surprising coming from Augustine, the teacher of rhetoric.[33] However, what is surprising is that at the time of his ordination, Augustine's theological education and his knowledge of the Bible were slim indeed. In fact, he had to request time off from his bishop Valerius in order to study the Bible in preparation for his priestly responsibilities.[34] Despite this, it is clear that even at this early date he insisted on the linking of study of the Bible with prayer and the life of the community of faith. In other words, while he recommends a broad education as helpful in the interpretation of scripture, he does not assume that the "liberal arts" can replace basic familiarity with scripture.[35]

Even while Augustine embraces knowledge from many different areas in his interpretation, scripture is not held hostage to this but is "self-interpreting." This is not to say that one need not think in order to read scripture, but that scripture itself has its own rules for reading. Augustine recommends drawing examples from plainer passages to shed light on the obscure ones, in order to "remove all hesitation in regard to doubtful passages."[36] It follows from this that the literary context of the passage must also be considered.[37]

Because of this self-interpreting nature of scripture, "author intentionality", the uncovering of which Augustine clearly understands to be an important goal in interpretation, cannot be the ultimate arbiter of textual meaning.[38] If an interpretation is supported by the testimony of another passage of scripture and by the rules of faith and charity but seems to contradict the author's intention, then according to Augustine it can be determined that "the Holy Spirit foresaw the different interpretations."[39] The implication is that the intention of the Divine Author may be different from the intention of the human writer. Both are important, but the former is of greater concern for the Christian interpreter, and it is Divine intentionality which is bound up in the Rules of Faith and Charity.

Also integral to Augustine's interpretive guidelines is the application of what one learns from the reading of scripture. The fourth book of *De doctrina christiana* therefore focuses on the "means of communicating our thoughts to others". Its very inclusion in this work is evidence of Augustine's concern to bind together what we might call interpretation and homiletics, biblical studies and pastoral theology. In this fourth book, Augustine describes the qualities which will benefit the preacher, and he recommends the biblical authors themselves as the best models for preaching. The goal of homiletics, according to Augustine, is to "bring home the truth to the hearer so that he may understand it, hear it with gladness, and practice it in his life."[40] Again, it is clear that the goal of exegesis for Augustine is broader and farther reaching than mere textual explication, for it extends to the shaping of Christian lives and communities.

In order to gain a clearer understanding of what Augustine means by the "literal," "proper," or "historical" sense, we must turn to his exegesis itself. Apart from *De doctrina Christiana*, if one were interested in his hermeneutical theory one would look for example at *On the Spirit and the Letter*, which was written in 412 during the same period of writing as *De Genesi ad litteram*. But our interest is in seeking hermeneutical assumptions as they become evident "at work" in interpretation itself. Therefore, we will need to look at instances of actual exegesis, where the rubber meets the road, so to speak. An

examination of Augustine's mature and most extensive "literal" commentary
on Genesis, *De Genesi ad litteram*, will help us here.

Literal vs. Allegorical

As we have seen, the biblical text for Augustine does not always speak
univocally, but rather can speak on different levels of meaning simultaneously.
The two levels of broad categories of meaning which Augustine seeks to interpret are referred to alternately as the "literal" and "figurative" or
"allegorical," the "proper" and "symbolical," the "historical" and
"prophetic." In *De Genesi ad litteram* he states that scripture is to be
explained under both "aspects," the literal and allegorical.[41]

> In the case of a narrative of events, the question arises as to
> whether everything must be taken according to the figurative
> sense only (*secundum figurarum*), or whether it must be
> expounded and defended also as a faithful record of what hap-
> pened (*secundum fidem rerum gestarum*). No Christian will
> dare say that the narrative must not be taken in a figurative
> sense (*figuraliter*).[42]

He follows this statement by pointing to Paul's use of the Exodus and Numbers narratives in 1 Cor 10:11 and of Gen 1:24 in Ephesians 5:32 to substantiate his claim that figurative interpretation must be allowed.[43] However,
Augustine also states elsewhere that his purpose in this particular commentary
is to interpret the proper sense of the beginning of the Genesis narrative.[44]

Throughout the commentary, these two levels of the literal and the
allegorical vie for attention. Even so, the modern reader at first glance may
think there is very little in the way of "literal" interpretation here at all.
However, the reader must put aside any preconceived notions of what the
terms "literal" and "allegorical" might mean, or Augustine may appear to be
talking nonsense. Instead we must let Augustine's understanding of these
terms emerge from his exegetical conclusions. Augustine's discussion of the
different ways of interpreting Paradise in Book 8 of *De Genesi ad litteram*
provides an excellent example of his use of the terms "literal" and
"allegorical" and their alternatives:[45]

Literal	Allegorical
corporeal (*corporaliter*) corporeal (*corporaliter*)	spiritual (*spiritualiter*) signifies something else (*aliquid aliud significat secundum id*)
style proper to history (*genere locutionis rerum gestarum*)	style proper to allegory (*genere locutionis figuratarum rerum*)
literal sense (*ad litteram*)	figurative sense (*futurorum res ipsae gestae*)
proper sense (*in expressionem proprietatis*)	figurative sense (*figurata significatione*)
" "	signs of spiritual realities (*spiritalium naturarum*)
" "	[signs of] future events (*rerum futurarum*)
material sense (*corporaliter intellecta*)	

The spiritual meaning, allegorical meaning, and prophetic meaning overlap and fall into one broad category, while the proper meaning, literal meaning, historical and corporeal meaning overlap and fall into another category. One could in turn subdivide each category further. Literal/proper either indicates a) an "event" that happened in the past or b) a material thing, place or person. Figurative/allegorical either indicates a) an "event" that will happen (prophetic) or b) a material thing, place or person's ontological participation in the being of God.

Augustine opens his commentary *De Genesi ad litteram* by noting that both the Old and the New Testaments are to be read according to both the allegorical and literal senses.

In all the sacred books, we should consider the eternal truths that are taught, the facts that are narrated, the future events that are predicted, and the precepts or counsels that are given. In the case of a narrative of events, the question arises as to whether everything must be taken according to the figurative sense only, or whether it must be expounded and defended also as a faithful record of what happened. No Christian will dare

say that the narrative must not be taken in a figurative sense.
For Saint Paul says: 'Now all these things that happened to
them were symbolic.' And he explains the statement in
Genesis, 'And they shall be two in one flesh,' as a great
mystery in reference to Christ and to the Church.[46]

Clearly in his concern for seeking out the literal sense in this particular commentary he does not intend to disparage figurative exegesis. On the contrary, he says that no Christian can deny its importance. This is especially the case for the reading of the Old Testament, which the Church generally takes to mean more than just what the surface structure of the text indicates.[47]

Part of the distinction between the literal meaning and the figurative meaning becomes clear in Augustine's discussion of the separation of light from darkness in Gen 1:4. At one point he suggests an interpretation which would imply that the creation of evening signifies the sin of rational creatures while the creation of morning signifies their renewal. He objects to this interpretation, however, on the grounds that it is an

allegorical and prophetical interpretation, a thing which I did
not set out to do in this treatise. I have started here to discuss
Sacred Scripture according to the plain meaning of the historical facts, not according to the future events which they
foreshadow.[48]

He then suggests that evening can be understood according to the literal sense as the end of each work accomplished in creation, while morning is an indication of the work to follow. It is clear that he wants to distinguish between the literal sense and figurative sense; the literal sense refers to the "history" or present of the narrative and the figurative refers to the future events foreshadowed.

He contrasts figurative and literal interpretation when discussing the Psalm verses "Who made the heavens in understanding... He established the earth above the water" (Psalm 136:5-6) within the larger consideration of Gen 1:6-8. He offers both figurative and literal interpretations of the Psalm verses. From the figurative interpretation one gets the impression that "figurative" indicates a one-to-one correspondence in meaning. The heavens refer to the "tranquil in understanding of truth," while earth refers to the "simple faith of children...an unshakable assent founded on the teaching of the prophets and the Gospels, the faith that is made firm by baptism."[49] This figurative interpretation is thus an attempt to make sense of God's creation of the earth above the water by which the "heavens" of Gen 1 are something other than sky, and the earth is something other than, say, land formations. The literal interpretation, however, takes the earth above the water to be the tops of caves overhanging the ocean waters. This explains away the difficulty Augustine has in imagining the earth above the waters without introducing symbols or figures. Here "literal" means taking the words to refer in their usually accepted way, while "figurative" means taking the words to refer in a secondary way, by which the word signifies something other than its conventionally accepted referent.

Elsewhere, Augustine indicates that he understands "literal" to mean "obvious to everyone from the testimony of the senses."[50] This he suggests while trying to reconcile the stretching out of heaven like a skin (Ps 104:2) with current scientific theory that the heavens are shaped like a vault above the earth. He refers the reader to what he calls his allegorical interpretation of the Psalm verse in Book 13 of the *Confessions*. There he reads Ps 104:2 in conjunction with Is 34:4, Rev 6:14, and Gen 3:21.

> And who but you, our God, Made for us the firmament, that is, our heavenly shield, the authority of your divine Scriptures?...You know, O Lord, how you clothed men with skins when by sin they became mortal. In the same way you have spread out the heavens like a canopy of skins, and these heavens are your Book, your words in which no note of discord jars, set over us through the ministry of mortal men.[51]

This beautifully illustrates how allegorical interpretation involves an imaginative linking of the words of the text with "signifieds" other than their normally accepted ones. The heavenly canopy is the manuscript of Scripture stretched taut. The clothing of the earth with the stretching out of the firmament is like the merciful clothing of Adam and Eve after their sin. The literal interpretation which he offers, however, reconciles the vault and the skins in a more straightforward way:

> Both the skin and the vault perhaps can be taken as figurative expressions; but how they are to be understood in a literal sense must be explained. If a vault can be not only curved but also flat, a skin surely can be stretched out not only on a flat plane but also in a spherical shape. Thus, for instance, a leather bottle and an inflated ball are both made of skin.[52]

Here, the literal interpretation simply tries to take the words in their conventional sense, or the "sense obvious to everyone."

Another passage which helps us see how Augustine understands the relationship between the literal and figurative senses occurs in his discussion of the
days of creation. Speaking of the creation of spiritual light and the creation of
the angels, he explains to his readers that these interpretations must not be dismissed as only figurative or allegorical. Of course, the problem of the creation
of the angels first arises logically for Augustine because elsewhere the Bible
speaks of angels, but nowhere in the creation narratives does it tell us when
they were created. Augustine therefore offers the interpretation of "Let there
be light" to include the creation of the angels.[53] He continues:

> These interpretations, of course, are different from our
> ordinary understanding of light in the material sense. But it is
> not true that material light is literally 'light' and light referred
> to in Gen is metaphorical 'light.' For where light is more
> excellent and unfailing, there day also exists in a truer sense.[54]

Here "literal" is clearly being distinguished from "material" and "ordinary."
The "truer sense" of light in the Gen narrative is not the "material" light but
the "metaphorical" light. The (so-claimed) non-figural interpretation which
takes the morning to be the rising of angelic knowledge to the praise of the
Creator, and the evening to be the angelic gazing down on creatures after con-
templating the Creator, is the "truer" sense of the light in the creation story.
Here Augustine is making an ontological claim that the understanding of light
as angelic knowledge is "truer" than the material understanding of light
because angelic contemplation is unchangeable. This is thus an example of
Augustine's ontology playing a role in distinguishing between the categories of
literal and figurative. In fact, this causes the distinction between the two
categories to begin to blur. This continues as he follows this with a comment
that appears almost as if out of nowhere:

> Christ Himself is not called the Light in the same way as He is
> called a stone: He is literally the Light but metaphorically a
> stone.[55]

Apparently he is referring to the Gospel texts John 8:12, "I am the light of the
world," and Mark 12:10 and parallels which quote Psalm 118:22 as a
reference to Jesus, "The stone which the builders rejected has become the head
of the corner." Although Augustine does not openly state this, it seems that

there are (at least) two possible assumptions at play here. He may be saying that Christ is literally Light because He names Himself thus but is metaphorically a stone because this prophecy is applied to Him by others. Or, Augustine may possibly be saying that Christ is literally Light since the second person of the Trinity, the Word, is active in creation ("And God said, 'Let there be light.'"), but Christ is metaphorically a stone since "stone" is less of a controlling metaphor for the identity of the second person of the Trinity in the catholic faith. Later, Augustine parses the distinction this way: Christ is literally the Stone anointed by Jacob but figuratively he is the Stone rejected by the builders. This, he says, is because the first refers to "an event that really happened" (Jacob really anoints the stone at Bethel in the story of Gen 35) whereas the second is a "proclamation by a prophet who was foretelling only events to come."[56] Augustine seems to feel that he is clear enough, for he does not explain himself but simply drops the comment rather casually. Again, as with the previous example there seems to be a slippage in the use of the term "literal," for here the interpretation that Christ is literally Light is grounded more in Augustine's ontology than in any verbal indicator in the text. Christ is literally the Light because He is the Word by which God creates the light.[57]

In his discussion of how the serpent was the most subtle of beasts, we see again an interesting way of distinguishing the proper meaning from the figurative sense of words. Augustine says that it is only in a figurative sense that the serpent is called "the most subtle" or "the most wise" (*prudentissimus; sapientissimus*) of creatures.[58] The literal or proper use of the word, he says, is usually in reference to God or to the angels. When the words *prudentissimus* and *sapientissimus* are used with reference to creatures, they are used only figuratively or by extension:

> In the proper meaning of the word, 'wisdom' (*sapientia*) is normally taken in a good sense referring to God or the angels or the rational soul; but we speak of wise bees or ants because their works suggest an imitation of wisdom.[59]

The proper or plain sense of "wisdom" is in its reference to goodness, and in Christian terms, to God as the highest good. Since words are a matter of convention, their use will change from language to language, and their meaning will alter with their use. Thus, the interpretation one can justifiably argue for may change depending upon the language in which one reads the text.

But it is really a misuse of words to speak of wisdom
(*sapientia*) in an evil creature, and of cunning (*astutia*) in a
good one. In the proper sense and in ordinary usage, at least
in Latin, men are called wise (*sapientes*) in a good sense,
whereas cunning men (*astuti*) are understood to have evil in
their hearts. Hence, some translators, as we can see in a large
number of manuscripts, have translated the idea rather than the
word into Latin, and thus have chosen to call this serpent more
cunning (*astutiorem*) than all the beasts rather than wiser
(*sapientiorem*) than all. I leave it to experts in Hebrew to say
what the proper meaning of the word is in that language and
whether in that language men may be called wise and be
understood to be wise in a bad sense not by a misuse, but by
the proper use, of the word.[60]

In his discussion later of the verse in which it describes the eyes of Adam
and Eve being opened when they ate the fruit of the tree of life, Augustine
questions how their eyes could have been closed in the first place. If they
were created with eyes closed, how could Adam see the beasts and birds in
order to name them? How could he have seen Eve to be able to declare "Bone
of my bones and flesh of my flesh?" And how could Eve have seen the tree
and concluded that it was "pleasing to the eyes and a delight to behold?"
Augustine remarks that one cannot read about Adam and Eve's eyes being
opened and take the word "opened" in its proper sense. But then he goes on
to argue from the basis of other scripture passages that "one should not take
the whole passage in a figurative sense on the basis of one word used with a
transferred meaning" (*figurate*).[61] He points to Luke's narrative of the
Emmaus Road when the apostle's eyes were opened to the identity of the risen
Christ in the breaking of the bread (Lk 24:31).

St. Luke does not mean that they were walking with their eyes
closed, but simply that they were unable to recognize Him. In
the Gospel text as well as in our passage in Genesis there is no
question of a narrative with a figurative meaning, although
Scripture has used a word in a transferred sense in speaking of
'opened eyes' which were already literally open, meaning that
they were opened to see and recognize what they had not formerly noticed... [As for Adam and Eve] casting their eyes on
their bodies, they felt a movement of concupiscence which they
had not known. It was in this respect, then, that their eyes

were opened to that to which they had not been open before, although they were open to other things.[62]

The word "opened" is not to be taken literally but on the basis of "transferred meaning," or (presumably in this case) metaphor.[63] However, metaphorical usage of the word does not prevent a "literal" interpretation of the passage as a whole. Indeed, the interpreter is still obliged to seek the literal meaning in spite of the use of metaphor within the passage.[64]

Augustine makes a distinction in reading the literal sense between the words of the human author of scripture and the words which are spoken by God within that narrative. This is clear in his comments on the curse in Genesis 3. While the entire curse itself is spoken by God, the words which indicate that God speaks demand their own way of being read.

> The words 'The Lord God said to the serpent' are the only words of the writer and they are to be taken in the proper sense. It is true, therefore, that these words were spoken to the serpent. The rest of the words are God's words, and they leave the reader free to decide whether they are to be understood in the proper or figurative sense, in accordance with what I said in my introductory remarks at the beginning of this book.[65]

There seems, therefore, to be a qualitative difference in reading when one comes to the words written by the human author as opposed to the words which the human author attributes to God. The words of the narrator must be taken according to their literal sense as is fitting to the narrative, for "the reliability of the writer and the truth of the narrative demand only that we do not doubt that the words were spoken." However, it is up to the reader's discretion to determine whether the words spoken by God within the narrative should be taken properly or figuratively. He determines that the words spoken to the serpent are to be taken figuratively:

> For in these words the tempter is described as he will be with respect to the human race. For the human race began to be propagated only when this sentence was pronounced, apparently against the serpent but in reality against the Devil.[66]

The words of the curse are spoken by God within the narrative, not by the narrator, and therefore are to be interpreted figuratively because God speaks to all who read the text through his address of the serpent. Again, we see Augustine's ontology and doctrine of God taking the front seat in his interpretation.

After arguing for the figurative meaning of the curse, Augustine then goes on in the next chapter to consider its literal meaning. He suggests that the "literal" meaning of the portion of the curse directed to Eve is her domination by Adam.[67] Yet he also refers to his earlier figurative interpretations of the words of the curse.[68] While he tries to interpret according to the letter, he is again and again drawn to figurative interpretation. Indeed, at times the two overlap because, as he says, "we must safeguard the prophetic meaning...[which] is foremost in God's intention."[69] Ultimately, the text is not a fanciful story meant to amuse but communicates God's voice, instructs in faith, and nourishes in charity. Because of this, the intention of God as "author" must be taken into account. However, this divine author complicates the distinction between the categories of literal and figural for Augustine.

From the preceding discussion, it is apparent that for Augustine there is indeed a discernible distinction between the notions of "literal" and "allegorical." Yet, even while the two levels are distinct, they are not necessarily mutually exclusive. It is this interpenetration of the two which makes his "literal" interpretation often seem far from what we might otherwise understand to be literal.[70] The two levels are only mutually exclusive when the literal sense admits absurdity and thus impugns the authority of scripture, or when it violates the Rules of Faith and Charity.[71] When this happens, the search for the literal sense must be abandoned and the text must be taken figuratively alone. Agaësse puts it this way:

> Nous aboutissons donc à cette conclusion paradoxale et pourtant inévitable que chercher le sens littérale, c'est dépasser l'immédiat de la lettre, tout en s'y référant toujours, pour en dégager le sens méta-physique, ce mot étant pris en son acception étymologique de 'au-delà de la nature,' puisque l'acte créateur qui donne naissance au monde ne peut être connumeré parmi les événements créés. Il ne s'agit donc pas d'une réflexion religieuse que, tout en intégrant les analyses et les démarches philosophiques susceptibles d'éclairer la révélation elle-même, prend pour point de départ la parole de Dieu et s'y ressource toujours en s'éfforçant de la déchiffrer à la lumiere de la foi.[72]

There does seem to be a distinction for Augustine between what we will call plain sense and the "letter," because plain sense does not necessarily take the letter *au pied de la lettre* or "literally". This is because plain sense reading is a religious activity, not merely a literary activity alone, and entails basic presuppositions about the text and about God. These two aspects of Augustine's plain sense reading, reading the text as sacred text and as text *qua* text, will be examined in the remainder of this chapter. Since the first generally takes precedence for Augustine, we will begin by looking at his plain sense reading as a religious activity. Here we will see how and to what extent Ruled reading shapes plain sense interpretation. Within this subsection we will examine the role of the Rules of Faith and Charity as they bear on interpretation in *De Genesi ad litteram*, the use of prooftexting, and the function of Augustine's understanding of textual "accommodation." Next, we will look at examples of his plain sense reading as it is constrained by verbal sense and literary categories. Within this subsection we will examine Augustine's assessment of the text's capacity to refer historically, his understanding of verbal sense and authorial intention in interpretation, his assessment of the hermeneutical role of narrative structure, and his use of extra-biblical explanatory "narratives." We will then be in a better position to draw some conclusions regarding Augustine's understanding of the literal sense in his exegesis in *De Genesi ad litteram*.

Sacred Text and Ruled Reading

The Function of the Rules of Faith and Charity

We have seen that while Augustine reads the Bible as polysemic or open to interpretations on many levels of meaning at once, there are indeed limits to polysemy. One such limit to the polysemy for Augustine is, of course, the catholic faith: the different readings of any given text must conform to the Christian faith as understood and passed down by the Church. Thus the Rule of Faith functions as the final arbiter on various possible interpretations and imposes limits on polysemy:

> In matters that are obscure and far beyond our vision, even in
> such as we may find treated in Holy Scripture, different inter-
> pretations are sometimes possible without prejudice to the faith
> we received. In such a case, we should not rush in headlong

and so firmly take our stand on one side that, if further progress in the search of truth justly undermines this position, we
too fall with it. That would be to battle not for the teaching of
Holy Scripture but for our own, wishing its teaching to conform to ours, whereas we ought to wish ours to conform to
that of Sacred Scripture.[73]

This would indicate that Augustine understands the "teaching of Holy Scripture" to be coextensive with the teaching of the Church, and the teaching of
the Church with that of Holy Scripture. Therefore the Rule of Faith can be
used, as we have seen, as the test which excludes "improper" interpretations
but does not prescribe specific interpretations, for "different interpretations are
sometimes possible without prejudice to the faith we received." Indeed, the
Rule of faith will be more important than determining the author's intention,
which itself is of no small account. After pointing to the importance of considering the author's intention, and then to the importance of the context of
scripture, Augustine says that if these are not clear,

at least we should choose only that which our faith demands.
For it is one thing to fail to recognize the primary meaning of
the writer, and another to depart from the norms of religious
belief.[74]

Indeed, whenever scripture seems to speak against the rule of faith, it is then
that it speaks "metaphorically":

Now to think of God as forming man from the slime of the
earth with bodily hands is childish. Indeed, if Scripture had
said such a thing, we should be compelled to believe that the
writer had used a metaphor rather than that God is contained in
the structure of members such as we know in our bodies...But
anyone in his right mind understands that the name of a bodily
member has been used in these passages for the power and
might of God.[75]

The Rule of Faith, it can be argued, does not negate the necessity for
literal reading; rather, abiding by the Rule of Faith is part and parcel of reading the literal sense for Augustine. In his discussion of God's breathing of the
soul into Adam, Augustine rejects the Manichees' interpretation that

understands the soul to be of the same substance as God. He rejects it first on the basis of the Rule of Faith:

> We should be cautioned to reject this opinion as opposed to the Catholic faith. For we believe that the nature and substance of God, which is in the Trinity, as many believe but few understand, is absolutely unchangeable. But who doubts that the soul can be changed for better or worse? Hence, it is sacrilegious to suppose that the soul and God are of one substance. For this simply amounts to believing that He is changeable.[76]

While the Manichees' interpretation contradicts the Rule of Faith and therefore is to be rejected, one is still left with the words of the text which indicate that God breathed into Adam's face. In *De Genesi ad litteram* Augustine is determined not only to rule out "deviant" interpretations on the basis of the Rule of Faith, but more self-consciously on the basis of the letter of the text. Augustine's text read "[God] breathed into his face the breath of life, and man was made a living being." He therefore says that the very word used makes it clear that the soul is not part of God's substance; it is the verb "breathed" which is at issue and not the noun "breath."[77] And so, says Augustine, "We might say that the breath of God is not the soul of man but that God, by breathing forth, made the soul of man."[78] In this instance we see that the verbal sense of the text itself contains the same clues as the Rule of Faith in this instance, and the two concur. However, when they do not, presumably the Rule of Faith would trump the verbal sense.

The Rule of Charity also comes to play a significant role in *De Genesi ad litteram*, for it too sets limits to polysemy. The broadest function of a given interpretation in Augustine's exegesis of Genesis 1–3 is apologetic and catechetical in nature.

> The shame (of giving nonsensical interpretations) is not so much that an ignorant individual is derided, but that people outside the household of the faith think our sacred writers held such opinions, and, to the great loss of those for whose salvation we toil, the writers of scripture are criticized and rejected as unlearned men. If they find a Christian mistaken in a field which they themselves know well... how are they going to believe those books in matters concerning the resurrection of the dead, the hope of eternal life, and the kingdom of heaven,

when they think their pages are full of falsehoods on facts
which they themselves have learnt from experience and the
light of reason?[79]

Since Scripture was written for the nourishing of the faithful, it should be read
with that goal ever in mind.[80] Interpretation should uphold the authority of
scripture, which in turn upholds the catholic faith.[81] Indeed, scripture does
not record every detail, but only those details which are "important not only
for a knowledge of what had happened but also for the foreshadowing of what
was to be," that is, for literal and figurative interpretation, so that the reader
might neither refuse to approach the Christian faith nor, having accepted, deny
it.[82] Therefore, the posture that accompanies interpretation which seeks this
goal is a "restraint that is proper to a devout and serious person and on an
obscure question to entertain no rash belief."[83] This patience which is needed
for interpretation is exhorted time and again by Augustine[84] and he himself
will frequently make an attempt at an interpretation but hold final judgment at
bay if another more convincing interpretation arises.[85] In his concern for
apologetically-driven biblical interpretation, Augustine himself curbs any
desire to set up his own interpretation as the decisive solution, while allowing
the Rules of Faith and Charity to limit textual polysemy. Thus, while the
literal reading for Augustine does not understand the text to open itself to an
infinite number of interpretations, neither does it necessitate, much less allow,
the fixing of a single justifiable interpretation.

We therefore see how the Rules of Faith and Charity set the inner and
outer parameters for interpretation, necessitating an understanding and acceptance of textual polysemy while at the same time insisting on the limits of this
such that the text is not an infinite regression of signifieds and signifiers.
Moreover, these rules set the agenda for how Augustine construes the text's
overall message, goal or subject matter of the text. This in turn shapes his
attempt to read the text according to its letter. Examples of the impact which
Augustine's preconceptions of the subject matter of the text have on his reading of the plain sense are not hard to find. One such place in his commentary
De Genesi ad litteram is in his discussion of the words "In the beginning" and
how they indicate a reference to the Son, the second person of the Trinity.[86]
Clearly he approaches the text with the understanding that God is triune,
Father, Son and Holy Spirit. He also understands from John's gospel that God
created the world through the Word, and that the Word was in the Beginning.
He also understands from the catholic faith that God is eternal and not under
the limits of time.[87] Therefore, he understands "in the beginning", the first
phrase of the Bible, to speak of the second person of Trinity. While this is by

no means a novel interpretation for Augustine's day, it indicates the extent to which the understood or preconceived thrust of the text bears on its reading.[88]

Likewise, Augustine is concerned to stress in his interpretation of the words "God said, 'Let there be...'" that God does not speak these words as a human would, but that this is an immaterial utterance of God in his eternal Word.

> God in His eternity says all through His Word, not by the sound of a voice, nor by a thinking process that measures out its speech, but by the light of Divine Wisdom, coeternal with Himself and born of Himself.... There is mention of the Son, who is also the Word, where Scripture declares: "God said, 'Let there be...'"[89]

Thus, countering possible interpretations that would understand God to speak as a human with a voice, Augustine chooses to show how the text can be read as indicating the Second Person of the Trinity.

Again, Augustine takes the Trinity to be represented in the creation narrative. The words "In the beginning" are understood to refer to the Son, the word "God" to the Father, and the Spirit of God stirring over the waters to the Holy Spirit.[90] He also considers the Trinity to be implied in the words "And God said,'Let us make mankind according to our image and likeness'..." It is not so much the text itself but the orthodox understanding of the Trinity which generates this interpretation. Yet even so a close reading of the text is crucial in backing the proposed interpretation:

> I must briefly point out the importance of the fact that in the case of the other works it is written, "God said, 'Let there be...'" whereas here it is written, "God said, 'Let us make mankind to Our image and likeness.'" Scripture would indicate by this plurality of Persons the Father, Son and Holy Spirit. But the sacred writer immediately admonishes us to hold to the unity of the Godhead when he says, "And God made man to the image of God." He does not say that the Father made man to the image of the Son, or the Son made him to the image of the Father... The fact that here Holy Scripture says "to the image of God," whereas above it says "to Our image," shows us that the plurality of Persons must not lead us into saying, believing or understanding that there are many gods, but rather that we must accept the Father, Son and Holy

Spirit as one God. Because of the three Persons, it is said "to
Our image;" because of the one God, it is said "to the image
of God."[91]

While this interpretation may appear to the modern reader to be theologico-
eisogesis, or even "allegorical" interpretation, one cannot dispute the fact that
Augustine's reading here is intimately close to the text, carefully investigating
verbal meaning. Clearly, however, the catholic understanding of the subject
matter of the text guides his interpretation.

Another example of Augustine's reading that is highly controlled by a
prior grasp of the "subject matter" of scripture is the interpretation of God's
rest on the seventh day. Augustine's first concern when dealing with this
verse is to emphasize that God does not rest because of fatigue: "we must first
drive from our minds all anthropomorphic concepts."[92] We must not, argues
Augustine, interpret this verse to indicate that God needs rest after the work of
creation as a mortal would need rest after work, for this would violate the
catholic understanding of God.

What other interpretation is left, therefore, unless we
understand that God gave rest in Himself to the rational beings
He had created, among whom man is included, that is, that
after their creation He gave them this rest by the gift of the
Holy Spirit... For as we are justified in saying that God does
whatever we do by His operation within us, so we can rightly
say that God rests when by His gift we rest.[93]

Augustine reads this verse to speak of God's rest not as a break won after
tiring work, but as God's gift of our rest in Him. But Augustine is not content
to leave the matter thus; he says that he feels compelled despite the merits of
this interpretation to press on and inquire exactly how it is that God could have
rested, because that is what the text says plainly that God did after the sixth
day. He admits at this point that the previous interpretation he offered to the
effect that "God rests when by His gift we rest" is not according to the letter,
but is figurative, for "it is clear that in revealing to us the fact of His own rest
He has admonished us to hope to find our rest in Him."[94] It speaks of future
things, our future rest for which we wait hopefully. While he does not use the
terms "literal" or "figurative," this reference to our hope indicates the
prophetic thrust of this interpretation. He says that just as we cannot read the
words "God created..." to indicate that we ourselves have created something

among these works by a creative power given us by God, so the words "God rested..."

> ought not to be taken to mean our rest, which by His gift we shall attain, but primarily His rest, that of the seventh day when His works were completed. Thus, we must first point out the facts as reported by Holy Scripture and then, if necessary, indicate whatever figurative meaning they may have. It is, of course, correct to say that we shall rest after our good works, just as God rested after His. But for this reason it is also right to demand that, after our discussion on the works of God, which are obviously His, we now investigate the repose of God, which is clearly His own.[95]

Augustine understands the figurative reading he offered to be appropriate; however, it is not the figurative meaning which he had set out to uncover but rather the literal meaning. The literal meaning is not sought first because it is more "true" or more "fitting" than the figurative, but simply because it is the proper order of interpretation first to set out the literal meaning and then to indicate whatever figurative meaning may be gleaned from the foundation of the literal meaning.

Then, in seeking the "literal meaning" of the words "God rested," Augustine juxtaposes this verse with John 5:17, "My Father works even until now, and I work." Augustine asks how the truth is found in both texts, which (he implies) appear to contradict each other. He notes that the words of John 5:17 were spoken by Jesus to those who complained when he did not observe the Sabbath, ordained in remembrance of God's rest on the authority of the Genesis verse which Augustine is attempting to interpret literally. Even though attempting to interpret according to the letter, he again embroils himself in figurative interpretation. He says that Sabbath observance was prescribed of the Jews

> to foreshadow what was to be and to symbolize the spiritual rest that God by the mystery of this sign, using His own repose as an exemplar, promised to the faithful who perform good works. Our Lord Jesus Christ Himself, who suffered only when He wished, also confirmed the mystery of this repose by His own burial. For it was on the Sabbath day that He rested in the tomb, and He passed this whole day in a kind of holy leisure after He had finished on the sixth day all His

works...He used this very word 'finish' when He said 'It is
finished'...Is it a matter for wonder, therefore, if God, wishing
in this way also to foreshadow the day on which Christ was to
rest in the sepulcher, rested on one day from all His works,
although after that He would work the unfolding of the progress of the ages? Thus the Gospel text is true that says, 'My
Father works even until now.'[96]

Thus, Augustine begins his attempt at reading according to the letter by bringing in a verse from the Gospel of John which deals with similar subject matter:
the rest and work of God. He then links thematically the Sabbath observance
of the Jews with the spiritual rest that God promises at the end time, and God's
rest after creation, Christ's rest in the tomb, and in the next chapter with
Christian baptism. This chain of foretelling and confirming of prophecy is
capped by the identifying of God's rest after creation as a prophecy or foreshadowing of Christ's rest in the tomb. This then is used to reconcile the two
verses of Genesis and John and to substantiate the claim that the work of God
continues.

Augustine presses the question further: If God rested from creation in that
no new creatures were made, how does God work continuously in his
governing and sustaining all of creation? Augustine here attempts to remain
close to the letter by arguing that this question could pose a problem if John
5:17 had read "He works now." In that case, the continuation of God's work
could be questioned. But according to John's gospel Jesus says "even until
now," which indicates that God has worked from the moment of creation
onward. Augustine concludes this lengthy attempt at uncovering the literal
sense:

Therefore, we understand that God rested from all the works
that He made in the sense that from then on He did not produce any other new nature, not that He ceased to hold and
govern what He had made. Hence it is true that God rested on
the seventh day, and it is also true that He works even until
now.[97]

Running throughout this attempt to interpret God's sabbath rest is, of course,
the assumption that scripture does not contradict itself,[98] and undergirding the
entire section is the catholic understanding of God as eternal and unchanging.
God cannot "rest" as we rest, partly because it is not in God's nature to tire,
and partly because if God were to rest heaven and earth would perish.[99] It is

the doctrine of God that drives this whole section, and the concern to interpret according to the letter follows this. This becomes particularly clear when Augustine sets out two salient points:

> First, God did not find joy in a period of time devoted to rest as one might after toil as he comes to the long-sought end of his efforts; and secondly, the words of Holy Scripture, which rightly possess supreme authority, are not idle or false when they say that God rested on the seventh day from all the works that He made, and because He rested upon it He made it holy.[100]

The first point entails an argument based on Augustine's doctrine of God, and the second point entails an argument based on his understanding of the authority of the letter of the biblical text, and these points are made in order of their interpretive priority.

Thus we see how the Rules of Faith and Charity function both formally and materially. Formally, accepting the Rules of Faith and Charity necessitates the corresponding insistence on both inner and outer parameters for interpretation which embraces a range of justifiable interpretations which can be neither rigidly fixed nor infinitely indeterminate. Materially, the Rules function to sketch a broad understanding of the subject matter of the text, which informs literal reading in matters of doctrine.

Prooftexting

As we saw in our examination of Augustine's exegetical principles, he understands scripture to be at a certain level "self-interpreting." His use of prooftexting, or the use of different canonical passages to shed light on others, is an important aspect of his literal reading, and can be understood as an outgrowth of Ruled reading. While it would be a tedious and not an altogether fruitful task to catalogue the instances in which Augustine resorts to prooftexting in order to arrive at a literal reading, throughout his exegetical work in his commentary *De Genesi ad litteram*, this is clearly an important hermeneutical device.[101]

One example of this is in his discussion of the creation of Adam according to the image of God. Augustine identifies this image as the "reason or mind or intelligence."[102] He blends two New Testament texts to back up his claim:

> Hence Saint Paul says, 'Be renewed in the spirit of your mind,
> and put on the new man, who is being renewed unto the
> knowledge of God, according to the image of his Creator.' By
> these words he shows wherein man has been created to the
> image of God, since it is not by any features of the body but
> by a perfection of the intelligible order, that is, of the mind
> when illuminated.[103]

Instead of arguing on the basis of the Genesis text alone for this interpretation,
Augustine regards the use of these New Testament texts to reinforce his point
as a literal interpretation of the Genesis text. The New Testament texts thus
inform the interpretation of the Genesis story.

Another more extended example is in his discussion of the narrative of
the creation of the world in six days. This poses a theological problem for
Augustine: how can a God who is beyond time work within the confines of
time? The narrative also poses a hermeneutical problem: how can it be reconciled with the verse from Sirach, "God created all things simultaneously?"[104]
Augustine's solution to these problems is to propose that God in effect accommodates the narrative to our understanding.

> [God], who created all things together, simultaneously created
> these six days, or seven, or rather the one day six or seven
> times repeated. Why then, was there any need for six distinct
> days to be set forth in the narrative one after the other? The
> reason is that those who cannot understand the meaning of the
> text, 'He created all things together' cannot arrive at the mean-
> ing of Scripture unless the narrative proceeds slowly step by
> step.[105]

Thus Augustine interprets the six days of creation both in harmony with the
Sirach text and in line with the theological assertion that God is not within
time but beyond it in eternity. This he does by bringing these texts together
and offering the suggestion that the six days are a necessary part of the narrative for the sake of the reader for whom and to whom scripture accommodates
itself.

Yet later he states that he would not have to appeal to the Sirach text at
all (as he did earlier) in order to assert that God created all things
simultaneously, for the narrative of creation tells us this itself. Gen 2:4–6
indicates according to Augustine's text that

after day had been made, then God made heaven and earth and every green thing of the field... Hence, I do not now appeal to another book of Holy Scripture to prove that God created all things together. But the very next page following the first narrative of creation testifies to this when it tells us, 'When day was made, God made heaven and earth and every green thing of the field.' Hence, you must understand that this day was seven times repeated, to make up the seven days.[106]

The summing up of the narrative at this point in Genesis 2 itself indicates that everything was created simultaneously after day was made. Therefore, Augustine contends, one may assume that God made one day which was repeated without lapse of time.[107] While he did not reach this interpretation without the aid of the Sirach text, he argues that the Genesis text alone apart from the Sirach text supports his interpretation. Ultimately, Augustine's "literal" reading adds to the narrative an element which was at least not patent and at most missing in the verbal sense, that is, the sevenfold repetition of the one day of creation.

Again, when discussing the nature of Adam's body, Augustine poses several questions. Was the created body a natural, physical body (*corpus animale*) such as ours which needs nourishment and is prone to fatigue, disease and death? Or was Adam's body a spiritual body (*corpus spirituale*) such as we expect in the resurrection, which neither needs nourishment nor is prone to fatigue, disease and death?[108] Augustine turns to Paul's discussion of the resurrection in 1 Corinthians 15, and using this determines that Adam was given a natural body. What we are to receive in the resurrection is not a regaining of what was lost in Adam, but "something much better."

Taking off with this idea of finding something much better, he then turns to consider the Parable of the Prodigal Son. He points to other interpreters who read this to indicate that what was lost will be found, and that what Adam lost in the fall we can anticipate to gain in the resurrection. This interpretation operates under the assumption that Adam first had a natural body but when he was placed in Paradise he was changed, just as we will be in the resurrection. Augustine counters this:

This change, to be sure, is not mentioned in Genesis. But wishing to harmonize the biblical texts on both points, namely the fact of the natural body of Adam and the fact of the renewal of our bodies mentioned in many texts of Sacred

Scripture, they are convinced that this is a necessary conclusion.[109]

Clearly, therefore, Augustine does not consider what he himself is doing to be a harmonizing of texts, while those "other interpreters" do indeed harmonize texts. This is because Augustine claims that he is looking for the plain meaning, while he sees the other interpreters as settling for a figurative interpretation of Paradise in which the trees and their fruits are to be taken as symbols of something other than actual trees and fruits which would produce food for natural, material bodies.[110] The problem with their interpretation is not the fact that they read Genesis through other texts and vice versa, which Augustine clearly practices, but rather that they "read in" elements which are neither in the narrative nor supplied in Ruled reading. Thus, these other readers do not search for the literal sense while reading the texts in light of each other. According to Augustine's understanding of what they are doing, the other exegetes harmonize texts while he does not understand himself to do so.

Textual "Accommodation"

As mentioned above in the examination of Augustine's consideration of the narrative of the six days of creation, he understands Scripture to speak in such a way as to stoop to the level of human understanding and facilitate its own interpretation by its very manner of presentation: "The narrative of the inspired writer brings the matter down to the capacity of children."[111] This, as we shall see in the next chapter, influences Calvin's practice of interpretation. Augustine's use of this concept of accommodation occurs often in conjunction with the attempt to understand scripture according to the Rule of Faith.[112]

Augustine's understanding of scripture's capacity to accommodate itself makes a statement about his own doctrine of scripture and about God's providence at work in its very inscription. It also makes a statement about his understanding of the readers' relationship to scripture's divine Author. When discussing the meaning of the six days of creation read in conjunction with Sirach 18:1, "God created all things together," Augustine explains

Perhaps Sacred Scripture in its customary style is speaking
with the limitations of human language in addressing men of
limited understanding, while at the same time teaching a lesson
to be understood by the reader who is able.[113]

The implication is that human language is itself limited in its capacity to express divine realities, and scripture itself takes on those limitations in order to address humans who themselves are of limited capacity in understanding.[114] Scripture bends itself to the limitations of human language and human understanding, accommodating itself not only in its inscription but also in its being read. Augustine warns that those of limited understanding should not presume to be able to interpret scripture without the aid of those of greater understanding. Still, because of the "effectiveness" of scripture, even those of limited understanding can hope to make progress. Scripture in fact is described as a mother who helps her toddler learn to walk:

> If you cannot yet understand it, you should leave the matter for the consideration of those who can; and, since Scripture does not abandon you in your infirmity, but with a mother's love accompanies your slower steps, you will make progress. Holy Scripture, indeed, speaks in such a way as to mock proud readers with its heights, terrify the attentive with its depths, feed great souls with its truth and nourish little ones with sweetness.[115]

Scripture is thus an active force on the reader and is not an inert collection of data for the interpreter to shape at will. Rather, scripture shapes the reader both in understanding, in faith and in love.

We have seen, then, how Ruled reading sets the parameters for the understanding of both the material content and formal function of scripture. Ruled reading supplies the prior grasp of the overall subject matter of the text and its function to form in readers a "catholic" understanding of God and attendant virtues. It sets up in the reader expectations of how the text functions to interpret itself and to accommodate itself to the meager capacities of the reader.

At the same time, literal reading for Augustine cannot rely on Ruled reading alone. Understanding the Bible as text *qua* text acts as a counterweight to understanding it as sacred text, pulling the reader's attention to verbal meaning and literary features. It is to this that we now turn.

"Historicity," Textuality and Literal Sense

Historical Referentiality of the Text

While Augustine's understanding of the Bible as inspired sacred text calls for a corresponding understanding of polysemy and therefore necessarily entails interpretations on multiple levels, his understanding of the biblical text as describing and referring to time and space requires reading the text according to its "literal sense." Augustine regards Genesis to be, in terms of "genre," historical narrative. Because Genesis is written in a style "proper to history," it must be read as a "literal narrative of events":

> The narrative in these books is not written in a literary style
> proper to allegory, as in the Canticle of Canticles, but from
> beginning to end in a style proper to history, as in the Books
> of Kings and the other works of that type. But since those his-
> torical books contain matters familiar to us from common
> human experience, they are easily and readily taken in a literal
> sense at the first reading... But in Genesis, since there are
> matters beyond the ken of readers who focus their gaze on the
> familiar course of nature, they are unwilling to have these mat-
> ters taken in the literal sense but prefer to understand them in a
> figurative sense. Accordingly, they assume that history, that
> is, the literal narrative of events that happened (*historiam, id*
> *est rerum proprie gestarum narrationem*), begins at the point
> where Adam and Eve, dismissed from Paradise, were joined in
> sexual union and begot children... In answer to this I say that
> the creation of natures narrated here is something unfamiliar,
> because it is the creation of things for the first time.[116]

The genre or literary style of Genesis itself demands interpretation first according to history, or what Augustine might have called in this case the literal sense of the text, before engaging in allegorical interpretation. Adam in Genesis is to be understood as a man who lived a certain number of years, fathered many children, and died as all humans die. Augustine acknowledges that Paul's treatment of Adam as the type of the One to come takes Adam to signify more than merely the individual of the creation narrative. Even so, here in Genesis Adam is to be understood as a man, a character, a "historical" Adam. Paradise, likewise, is "simply a place, that is, a land where an earthly man would live."[117] The genre into which Genesis falls, then, as historical narrative, is to be read first according to the literal sense, "so that the meaning of the historical events (*res ipsae gestae*) in relation to the future may also be subsequently drawn from them."[118] The literal sense therefore is not to supplant figure, prophecy or allegory as Augustine alternatively refers to them, but the literal sense is to be sought first in this case especially because of the literary genre of Genesis itself.

This entails reading the text not only as repository of timeless truths about God, not only prophecy of future events, not only a story in which we place ourselves which shapes our moral lives, but also a record of occurrences which are reported to have happened to people within time and which are accepted by the Christian community as "real."

> In all the sacred books, we should consider the eternal truths that are taught, the facts that are narrated (*quae facta narrentur*), the future events that are predicted, and the precepts or counsels that are given.[119]

Augustine wants to make it clear that, while spiritual reading of the biblical text is necessary, one must not allow allegorical interpretation to render the things and events of the biblical stories unrecognizable. For example, he insists that while Sarah and Hagar signify the two covenants in Galatians 4:24–26, "yet they were two women who actually existed."[120] He speaks of the world of "material reality" represented in the biblical text:

> All these events signified something other than what they were, but none the less they themselves existed in the world of material reality (*sed tamen etiam ipsa corporaliter fuerunt*). And when they were narrated by the sacred historian, they were not set forth in figurative language, but rather in a narrative of events that prefigured what was to come.[121]

The biblical text is not to be read simply as containing ciphers which point to realities other than what they appear to be on the surface. On the contrary, the surface or "letter" of the text can be trusted to speak of the world in which we live. The letter of the narrative can prefigure realities yet to come, but these realities do not destroy the power of the letter of the narrative to speak meaningfully of and to refer to the world of "material reality." Thus, Christ is indeed the Lamb immolated on the Passover, yet the Passover was not just a story but a "real act" (*sed etiam faciendo*) and the lamb was "truly a lamb, and it was slain and it was eaten; and although this was something that really happened (*et tamen eo vero facto*), something else was prefigured by it."[122]

Augustine does not presume, however, to argue that the entire biblical text refers to the world of "material reality" in the same way. For example, he distinguishes the story of the immolation of the Passover Lamb in its historical referentiality from that of the story of the Fatted Calf in Luke 15.

> In the latter case the narrative itself is a narrative of figures or types; it is not a matter of a figurative meaning of events that really happened. The narrator was not the Evangelist but the Lord Himself, although the Evangelist did state that the Lord told the parable. Thus, what the Evangelist told did happen: the Lord did speak these words. But the narration told by our Lord was a parable, and in this kind of narrative one is never expected to demonstrate that events told in the story literally happened.[123]

Here we see how genre makes a difference in the text's interpretation. The distinction between the genres of the historical narrative and parable is a necessary although not sufficient key to determining the degree to which the text is able to refer historically. In part, according to Augustine, the interpretation turns on distinguishing the text's genre (historical narrative vs. parabolic narrative) and in part on identifying the narrator. The parabolic narrator is Jesus himself, and the parable is part of his teaching. While one is to trust that the Lord did speak these words, one is neither expected to believe nor to demonstrate that the "events in the story literally happened." The narrating itself is what "literally happened."

Augustine follows with another example such as this in which the historicity of a text is important, but this time distinguishing the text's genre is not key. He links the story of Jacob's dream and Psalm 118. Christ, says Augustine, is both the stone which pillowed Jacob's dream in Gen 28 with the stone of stumbling from Psalm 118. While Christ is signified by both of these "stone" texts, there is a different reason given for each text:

> Christ is the Stone anointed by Jacob, and the Stone rejected by the builders, which has become the head of the corner. But in the first case there is reference to an event that really happened, whereas in the second case an event is foretold in figurative language. The former was an account of a past

event written by a historian, but the latter was a proclamation
by a prophet who was foretelling only events to come.[124]

Here Augustine does not point to a difference in genre to account for the difference in these texts' ability to refer historically. He could have argued, for
example, that the reason they differ in this respect is because the first is from a
narrative and the second from psalmic material, but he does not do this.
Instead he argues that the Genesis text depicts an event that occurred within
time past, while the Psalm text depicts an event which had not yet happened at
the time of its composition. The first text refers historically to a past event
(i.e. Jacob) as well as prophetically to a future event (i.e. Christ) because it
"really happened" (*in rebus gestis factum est*), whereas the second is only an
event foretold, the rejection of Christ by the Jews. The difference lies not in
the texts themselves but in their respective location in time in relation to that
which they depict or to which they refer.

In *De Genesi contra Manichaeos*, Augustine had discussed the four rivers
of paradise according to their allegorical meaning. There he demonstrated how
they represent the virtues of prudence, fortitude, temperance and justice.[125]
But in *De Genesi ad litteram* he sets out immediately to argue that the four
rivers are "true rivers, not just figurative expressions without a corresponding
reality in the literal sense, as if the names would signify something else and
not rivers at all."[126] The thrust of the discussion regarding the four rivers in
this later text is to argue that the account in Genesis is historical in genre, not
prophetic alone, and that the narrative refers to a geographical location which
existed in time and space and yet has a figurative meaning which does not
obscure or obliterate its literal reference. He insists that, unlike the manner in
which one would read a parable, nothing in this Genesis text prohibits the
reader from understanding it first as "true historical realities," but rather
demands this:

> We can, therefore, follow with simplicity the authority of
> Scripture in the narration of these historical realities, taking
> them first as true historical realities, and then search for any
> further meaning they may have.[127]

The historical referentiality of the text, that is, the understanding that the
events narrated occurred in time and space, plays a large role in the determination of the literal sense, and it is this "historical" quality which allows the text
to function figuratively. In discussing Gen 2:19–20 in which Adam names the
animals, Augustine reflects that

> There seems to me to be a prophetic meaning in what took
> place; but none the less it did take place, so that with the
> occurrence of the event established we are free to seek its
> figurative meaning....Hence, I have no doubt that this all hap-
> pened for the sake of some prophetic meaning, but none the
> less it really happened.[128]

Even though this text does have a prophetic meaning, Augustine declares that
he is not seeking to "examine prophetic mysteries but to interpret the narrative
as a faithful history of events that happened" (*rerum gestarum fidem ad proprietatem historiae*).[129] Again later, he declares that his purpose in writing this
commentary is not to "unfold hidden meanings but to establish what really
happened" because, as he says of the interrogation of Adam and Eve by God in
the garden, the account was written down precisely because it took place in
order to be recorded truthfully for the instruction of the faithful.[130]
Augustine argues that if it were not recorded truthfully, it could not instruct,
and thus we would not benefit from the text in our understanding of the true
nature of the disease of pride. The text's ability to teach is contingent upon its
trustworthiness to depict events faithfully.

In the following chapter where Augustine discusses God's curse on the
serpent, he makes a distinction in the historical referentiality of the different
parts of the text, somewhat as he did with regard to Jesus' parable of the
Prodigal Son. The words of the curse itself are God's words and therefore
possibly either figurative or literal. However the words of the writer, "The
Lord God said to the serpent," are to be taken in what Augustine calls the
proper sense. The proper sense of this phrase, implies Augustine, indicates
that the curse itself was indeed spoken: "The reliability of the writer and the
truth of his narrative demand only that we do not doubt that the words were
spoken."[131]

Again, in his discussion of the garments of skin and the condemnation of
Adam's pride, the claim that this actually took place is important to reading
the literal meaning of the account for Augustine. While he says that a symbolic meaning is intended to be understood by the clothing of Adam and Eve
after the fall, nevertheless they were actually clothed.[132] He then goes on to
say:

> I have often said, and I do not hesitate to say it again and
> again, that we must demand of the author of a historical narra-
> tive that his account contain the events that actually occurred
> and the words that were actually spoken. Now in considering

an event, we ask what happened and what it signifies; and in
like manner, in considering words, we ask what was said and
what it signifies. For we must not take as figurative the fact
that something was said, whether what is said has a figurative
or literal meaning.[133]

Again, interpreting Adam's and Eve's expulsion from Paradise, Augustine
argues that while this has a "symbolical meaning," that is, excommunication
from the Church and the wretched life of the sinner, still that symbolical meaning does not erase or disvalue the literal meaning of the passage, which is
simply that Adam and Eve were sent out from Paradise. "This action actually
took place, but it also has a symbolical meaning..."[134] He does not attempt
to prove how this happened or that it happened, but the fact that one is to
accept that the event did indeed occur is taken up as part of what it means to
read the literal sense. The literal sense can then serve as a springboard for
seeking a symbolic sense, but the symbolic sense cannot allow the interpreter
to reject the claim of the "having happened-ness" of the event narrated.

Verbal Sense and Authorial Intention

While the understanding of direct historical referentiality of the text
demands literal reading for Augustine, it is verbal sense itself which bears
literal meaning, at least in part. That is, the literal sense is not confined to
verbal sense alone.

Even in a literal interpretation one cannot take the words 'He
established the earth above the water' to mean that in nature a
mass of water was placed underneath a mass of earth to support
it.[135]

Augustine implies that since this is a physical impossibility in the natural
world, it cannot be the literal sense of the passage. This shows that verbal
sense does not automatically render literal sense for Augustine. This is not to
say, however, that verbal sense is disregarded as unimportant in Augustine's
interpretation. In fact, Augustine's interpretation is at times so close to the
words of the text that the modern reader often fails to sympathize with his concerns or even to understand what he is worrying over in a passage. It is in part
his understanding of the text as divinely inspired that makes every word significant for him and thus pushes him to literal interpretation. Because the text

is inspired, no word or turn of phrase may be left unexamined if the reader is to understand the text. Because there is no textual dross in Holy Scripture, verbal meaning is of extreme significance.

The search for verbal meaning for Augustine therefore begins to look very odd from the perspective of the modern reader. At times Augustine goes to great lengths performing grammatical and lexical gymnastics in order to attempt to explicate verbal meaning, often coming to an apparently small conclusion for the amount of effort expended. For example, he struggles to understand what might be meant by the terms "beasts," "herds," "quadrupeds" and "creeping things" in Gen 1:24–25. He asks whether these terms refer to four classes of animals designated by the four nouns, or if three classes of animals are designated by the triple use of the term "according to their kind."[136] This investigation is necessary for Augustine since, because scripture contains no extraneous details, each word is significant. Even though, after some discussion of the matter, he does not arrive at a neatly identifiable "meaning," he does not consider his preceding investigation worthless.[137]

Again, the text Augustine uses leaves open some questions regarding Gen 2:15. Augustine thus asks what or whom is to be cultivated and guarded in Genesis 2:15, "And the Lord God took the man whom He made and placed him in Paradise to cultivate and guard it." Seeking the meaning of the terms "cultivate" and "guard," Augustine asks from whom Adam would have guarded Paradise.[138] That is, he attempts through an examination of the verbal sense to answer a question which he considers the text itself to raise. His possible answers to the question may seem to suggest an oblique rather than plain sense reading to modern interpreters. He concludes that Genesis 2:15 indicates that God cultivates and guards man, not that man cultivates and guards Paradise:

> Perhaps we should say that what man cultivated in the earth by
> the art of agriculture he guarded or preserved within himself
> by discipline. I mean that just as the soil which he tilled
> obeyed him, so he would dutifully render to his Lord, who had
> given him the command, the fruit of obedience, not the thorns
> of disobedience... another possible meaning for these
> words...that is, God was to cultivate man and guard him.[139]

Augustine is not engaged here in transferring meaning or linking in one-to-one correspondence the words of the narrative with extra-narrative realities. The verbal sense of the verse itself (in his text) leaves open the possibility of this interpretation, and thus demands the investigation.

Clues to verbal meaning for Augustine are found in such devices as parallelism and the repetition of words and phrases. This is particularly true if one "stanza" of the repeated biblical phrase drops a word or phrase.[140] Using this strategy, Augustine identifies in the formulaic series of the first chapter of Genesis, *"Fiat...et sit factum...fecit Deus... et vidit Deus quia bonum"* ("let there be...and so it was done... And God made...And God saw that it was good") four "stages" of creation. He then notes that at Gen 1:9 the repetition of the first stage (*Fiat*) is lacking. Instead of the usual "Let there be..." the text reads "Let the waters be gathered." Augustine struggles with what this break in the formulaic series could indicate and concludes that the water and land is of a "lower order" than the form which the heavens had been given. The break in the formula indicates for Augustine a distinction in the created order described in the verse, such that the waters and the land are "more corruptible and nearer to formlessness" than are the heavens.[141]

Again, Augustine notes that the phrase "the Lord God" is not used in the narrative before Gen 2:15. He points out that up to this point the word "God" alone appears, and he sets out to seek the significance of this.[142] Modern exegetes, of course, tend to credit the different names for the deity to the theory of different sources in the narrative's composition. Since the word *Elohim* is used in the Hebrew text of the first narrative from Gen 1:1 to 2:4a, this section is said to be derived from the Priestly tradition or "P" source. Since the word *Yahweh* is used in the second narrative from Gen 2:4b to 3:24, this section is said to be derived from the Yahwist tradition or "J" source. While the problem of the different names for the deity is thus noted in modern exegesis, the matter of its significance is usually left unaddressed. Here is one of the major differences between modern and ancient exegetes: for moderns, offering a theory of different sources is generally deemed sufficient explanation of this aspect of the text.[143] However, while Augustine does not posit different authorship for the two accounts, he searches further for what might possibly be the significance of the change in the divine name.

> Here we should observe a fact which I think has a lesson for us and calls our attention to something important...This account was written for man, not for the angels or other creatures, and it was to remind him how important it is for him to recognize God as his Lord, that is, to be obedient under His rule rather than to live uncontrolled and abuse his freedom...the author did not want to put this expression earlier but rather to save it

for that part of the narrative where God would put man in Paradise to cultivate and to guard him... For God does not need our service but we need His rule so that He may cultivate and guard us.[144]

Thus the change in the Divine name in the narrative is a "grain of sand" which brings forth the pearl of interpretation. Augustine understands this verbal change in the text to be no random fluke; rather, the text was thus arranged by the Divine Author to instruct readers in obedience to God.

This brings up the matter of authorial intention. As Augustine interprets the Bible, is he interested in seeking the intention of the author, whether human or divine? Some have answered this by saying that it is not the human author's intention which interests Augustine, but rather the intention of the Holy Spirit. However, the argument that seeking (human) authorial intention is not a concern for Augustine's interpretation cannot reasonably be sustained.[145] While it is true that it does not carry the hermeneutical weight it would for a modern such as Schleiermacher, assessing the author's intention is indeed an important factor in plain sense reading for Augustine in his *De Genesi ad litteram*.

For example, when adjudicating between several possible interpretations, Augustine suggests choosing the one which "appears as certainly the meaning intended by the author."[146] When the author's intended meaning is not clearly recognizable, the next guide one must use to determine which interpretation is the most fitting is that which is, not surprisingly, "in keeping with the context of scripture and in harmony with faith."[147] If the context of scripture is not helpful one must choose only that interpretation "which faith demands."[148] Augustine is quite clear, however, that determining authorial intention, while important, is not a facile task:[149]

> If reason should prove an opinion unquestionably true it will still be uncertain whether this sense was intended by the sacred writer...If the general drift of the passage shows the sacred writer did not intend this teaching, the other, which he did intend, will not thereby be false, but true...We shall still have to enquire whether he could not have meant something else besides...it will not be clear which of the two meanings he intended.[150]

One of the most important points to note here is that, for Augustine, seeking the author's intention does not entail fixing on a single interpretation, for the author may well have intended more than one interpretation. Multiple interpretations are allowable if they are all supported in the context of the passage's plain sense as a whole, for the ultimate authorship of the text is Divine.[151] Nevertheless, part of seeking verbal meaning for Augustine is the inquiry into what the human author may have meant or seems to have been trying to say by the words and constructions chosen.

Narrative Structure

Along with verbal meaning and authorial intent, another textual guide in literal reading for Augustine is the context of the passage or text as a whole. We might call this inquiry into the narrative structure of the text, how the parts of the story hold together. An example of this is his puzzling over the two accounts of the creation of Adam, Gen 1:27ff and Gen 2:7ff, and how these different accounts might be related to each other.[152]

His first hypothesis is that the later narrative is a recapitulation of the first. However, then he points out how the later text is more than simply a summing up of the argument to that point in the text. The Genesis 2 account includes God's bringing forth trees, he notes, which is different from God's work of the third day and is more like God's present work in governing creation.[153] His second hypothesis is therefore that God created all living beings "potentially and in their causes"[154] in the first creation account of the six days and that the second account explains God creating them in their visible forms.

Augustine then moves from this working hypothesis to examine the interpretation that would understand the text to say that the male was made on the sixth day and the female made later. Augustine then rejects this interpretation. Why? Because scripture says explicitly regarding the sixth day "Male and female He made them."[155] He then considers the interpretation that understands the two accounts to indicate that it was only the souls of the two which were made on the sixth day, with the bodies to be created later. This he also rejects, because scripture says that God finished his work on the sixth day.[156] Besides this, argues Augustine, since the only distinction between male and female is with respect to the body, this interpretation would be impossible, as is clear from the narrative element that food is given on the sixth day for the nourishment of their bodies.

Since for Augustine the claim that this text is part of sacred Scripture entails the correlate claim that there can be no contradictions either within this text or between this text and another scriptural text, he takes the narrative as a whole. That is, he sets out assuming that the text makes sense, or rather, assumes that the role of the reader is to show *how* it makes sense. In this example, Augustine examines many different interpretations, but rejects them as violating the letter of the narrative. He feels that the interpretation on which he finally settles respects the narrative flow of the whole text.

> There can be no doubt, then, that the work whereby man was formed from the slime of the earth and a wife fashioned for him from his side belongs not to that creation by which all things were made together, after completing which God rested, but to that work of God which takes place with the unfolding of the ages as He works even now.[157]

Attention to the flow of the narrative understood as a seamless whole thus guides plain sense reading for Augustine.

A correlate to attention to narrative structure in guiding literal reading for Augustine is the degree to which the text is silent. In other words, Augustine also pays attention to what the text does *not* say. Augustine constantly asks himself why such-and-such a detail is omitted by the sacred writer. Such questions then call for explanations in which he attempts to offer a plain sense reading to fill in the gap. For example, he notes that while (his text of)[158] Genesis 1 depicts God as acknowledging the goodness of each creative act, it does not indicate that God sees this at the creation of man.[159] This omission is telling, according to Augustine:

> Perhaps the explanation is that God, knowing man was going to sin and not remain in the perfection of the image of God, wished to say of him, not in particular but along with the rest, that he was good, thus hinting what would be... Man, therefore, before the fall, was good even when considered separately from the rest, but instead of declaring so, Scripture said something else foreshadowing the future.[160]

One might object to this reading on the basis of the lack of indication in the narrative that God knew "man was going to sin...," but Augustine clearly bases this interpretation on a close reading of the text, or at least a close reading of a seeming textual flaw or gap. It is in part this kind of close reading which makes Augustine's plain sense reading seem rather oblique to the modern reader, but Augustine clearly does not see it that way.[161] There are important textual clues to plain sense reading for Augustine in the repetition, alteration and omission of narrative elements. Often those places where the text fails to speak are highly instructive, even according to the literal sense.

Extra-Biblical "Narratives": Pagan Wisdom and the Interpreter's Reason

In addition to the immediate narratival context of the text itself, we find that the larger "narratives" of pagan wisdom and of the readers' personal experience or reason can inform the literal reading of the text for Augustine. Remember Augustine's famous advice from *De Doctrina Christiana* recommending the use of pagan knowledge in the interpretation of scripture, which he justifies by pointing to the story of the fleeing Hebrew slaves being told to plunder the Egyptians' gold.[162] One way to look at this of course is to conclude that Augustine advocates a quasi-modern stance toward the relationship between biblical interpretation and secular knowledge, such that the Bible should be read "like any other book." This would be true to the extent that Augustine did read the Bible "like any other book," exposing it to the challenges of secular knowledge. Yet for Augustine the Bible is also *not* "just like any other book" at all, and interpreting the Bible must take this into account.

> When [detractors of scripture] are able, from reliable evidence, to prove some fact of physical science, we shall show that it is not contrary to our Scripture. But when they produce from any of their books a theory contrary to Scripture, and therefore contrary to the Catholic faith, either we shall have some ability to demonstrate that it is absolutely false, or at least we ourselves will hold it so without any shadow of a doubt. And we will cling to our Mediator, in whom are hidden all the treasures of wisdom and knowledge, that we will not be led astray by the glib talk of false philosophy or frightened by the superstition of false religion.[163]

Clearly, for Augustine secular knowledge cannot contradict or overturn a Ruled interpretation of scripture, and when it *appears* to, Christians are to show how it actually *does not* do so. But no matter the case, Christians are not to argue with pagans on the basis of the authority of scripture. Non-Christians are not bound by Ruled reading, and any argument based on the authority of scripture will not be convincing to them. On the contrary, such argumentation may only discredit the faith.

Let no one think that, because the Psalmist says, 'He established the earth above the water,' we must use this testimony
of Holy Scripture against these people who engage in learned
discussions about the weights of the elements. They are not
bound by the authority of our Bible; and, ignorant of the sense
of these words, they will more readily scorn our sacred books
than disavow the knowledge they have acquired by unassailable
arguments or proved by the evidence of experience.[164]

The thrust of Augustine's argument about the use of secular knowledge in biblical interpretation, therefore, is apologetic, pragmatic, and logical.   The
Christian should not argue on the basis of scripture against the claims of pagan
science in part because strategically it is not useful to seek to convince detrac-
tors on the basis of something they do not accept.   More importantly, if the
pagan discounts the Christian's argument this will discredit the Catholic faith
and drive the pagan further away from Christianity, much to the detriment of
the pagan's soul.

Yet for Augustine, secular knowledge does make claims on the interpretation of scripture such that extra-biblical "narratives" or construals of reality
must be taken into account.   They can be used to back a specific interpretation.[165] They can also be used to rule out certain interpretations.   For example, the phrase "He established the earth above the water" cannot be taken to
mean that a mass of water supports a mass of earth above it; this is, Augustine
implies, a physical impossibility.[166] Therefore, even in a literal interpretation
the words cannot be read to mean that God established the earth above the
water in this sense.   Augustine suggests that a literal interpretation might
understand the earth above the water then to signify the

...promontories that tower over the water, whether on con-
tinents or on islands; or again, the roofs of caverns that rest on
solid supports and overhang the waters below.[167]

The literal interpretation, therefore, is not to contradict secular knowledge so
long as this is possible without compromising the authority of scripture, which
is "greater than all human ingenuity."[168]

Some of Augustine's reflections on the six days of creation even seem to
indicate that the laws of arithmetic govern the work of God. Augustine notes
that six is the first perfect number because it corresponds to the sum of its factors, and that God accomplished the works of creation in six days, the perfect
number.[169] Interestingly enough, he does *not* say that six is the perfect num-

ber because God created the world in six days. Rather, says Augustine, God accomplished the works of creation in six days because six is a perfect number. Even if these works did not exist, he claims, six would still be a perfect number. Furthermore, if six had not been a perfect number, God would not have perfected creation in six days.[170] Here it appears that Augustine is saying that God is bound by the laws of arithmetic even within the act of creation itself. Of course, since Augustine would consider God to be the author of the laws of arithmetic, God is here simply following his own rules, so to speak.

Augustine does distinguish between what he deems true science and false science. What he might call "true science" is that established by "scientific observations" (*experimenta documentorum*) or proofs derived from specific cases.[171] Astrologers are an example of false science with their "so-called scientific observations."[172] It is this type of pagan "knowledge" that must be scrupulously avoided by the Christian. However, he admits that this is ultimately not because of the astrologers' lack of "scientific observations" but for their "headstrong impiety" which distorts the Rule of faith:

> With such talk they try to undermine even the foundations of
> our belief in prayer, and with headstrong impiety they treat
> evil-doing that is justly reprehensible as if God were to blame
> as the Maker of the stars, and not man as the author of his own
> sins.[173]

Augustine thus charges the knowledge of astrologers with being the work of evil spirits.[174] They must be avoided especially when they tell the truth, for then the Christian risks consorting with demons.[175] Clearly, Christians are not to attempt to attend to all pagan knowledge in the interpretation of scripture; some is worth our attention while other pagan knowledge is demonic when it violates the faith of the Church.

This delicate balance of authorities is clearly illustrated in Augustine's discussion of the form and shape of heaven in Book 2, Chapter 9 of *De Genesi ad litteram*. He acknowledges here that many scholars debate the shape of heaven, but he then points out that the writers of scripture do not engage in such debate.[176]

> ...such subjects are of no profit for those who seek beatitude,
> and what is worse, they take up very precious time that ought
> to be given to what is spiritually beneficial.[177]

Here he sets up the discussion of secular debates regarding the shape and form of heaven by immediately relativizing their importance. This is because the reading of scripture for Augustine must serve the specific function of upbuilding the reader in faith and love, and whatever does not drive the reader to these goals is not worth one's time. Here we see the Rule of Charity making an observable impact on his reading of the literal sense. However, just because they may be a waste of time, he cannot easily recommend ignoring secular debates, for indeed the very

> credibility of Scripture is at stake...and there is danger that a man uninstructed in divine revelation, discovering something in Scripture or hearing from it something that seems to be at variance with the knowledge he has acquired may resolutely withhold his assent in other matters where Scripture presents useful admonitions, narratives or declarations.[178]

While the debates of pagan scholars may be spiritually unprofitable to readers of scripture, to ignore them would be to risk an opportunity to permit Scripture to speak to those outside the faith. Here again the concern is apologetic.

Even still, Augustine does not want to let his readers think that the authorities of Scripture and secular scholarship are merely "incommensurable." He flatly states that as regards the subject of the form and shape of heaven, the sacred writers "knew the truth, but ...the Spirit of God, who spoke through them, did not wish to teach men these facts that would be of no avail for their salvation."[179] The writers of scripture knew the answer to the debates raised by secular scholarship, according to Augustine, but were withheld by the Holy Spirit from raising the issues because of the lack of profit it would bring to scripture's readers. The sacred writers knew more than the secular authorities and more than they themselves disclose.

But then Augustine turns to the problem of whether or not the theories of secular scholarship are opposed to the witness of scripture regarding the form of heaven. When secular scholars are able to prove undeniably their theories, it is then the task of the Christian interpreter to show that the statements of Scripture are not opposed to secular conclusions.[180] Regarding passages of scripture which seem to contradict each other, such as Ps 104:2 and Is 40:22, Augustine does have advice for us. In his Old Latin text, these passages respectively indicate that the heavens are stretched out like skin and suspended like a vault. He adds, however, that

it is also necessary that both of these passages should not contradict the theories that may be supported by true evidence, by
which heaven is said to be curved on all sides in the shape of a
sphere, provided only that this is proved.[181]

Again, not only does scripture not contradict itself, it should not contradict the
"theories that may be supported by true evidence." Augustine illustrates how
this is to be done with Ps 104:2 and Is 40:22 and the theory of the spherical
nature of the heavens:

If a vault can be not only on a flat plane, a skin surely can be
stretched out not only on a flat plane but also in a spherical
shape. Thus, for instance, a leather bottle and an inflated ball
are both made of skin.[182]

The task of the interpreter therefore is to read the text such that there are no
contradictions within the larger context of scripture itself, and then to seek to
bring the interpretation of scripture in line with secular knowledge for
apologetic purposes. If this last maneuver is not possible, assumedly
Augustine would have to resort to his statement made earlier to the effect that
pagan theories cannot contradict scripture, and when they appear to do so they
are clearly false.[183] However, here he does not have to do this because he has
been able to bring the text in line with the theories of pagan knowledge.

Likewise, the extra-biblical "narrative" of the interpreter's reason can
inform the reading of the plain sense within certain limits. First, regarding the
limits to this, Augustine does not assume that scripture must speak in a way
consonant with our everyday experience. On the contrary, it often will not do
so, and when this is the case, our experience should not dictate how scripture
is to be interpreted. Rather, the words of the text themselves will instruct us
how to read. Clearly the six days of creation are not like the days with which
we are familiar, Augustine argues, for scripture itself according to his text says
"When day was made God made heaven and earth and all the grass of the
field" (Gen 2:4-5). Augustine points out how this comes in the narrative
order *before* the sun was made, which is narrated on the fourth day. But how
could the sun be created on the fourth *day*, if there was previously no sun to
define "day" and differentiate it from "night?" Therefore, he reaches the conclusion that the six "days" of creation are not like the days we know from our
experience. This he claims not on the basis of reason or experience but on the
basis of what he understands to be the literal sense of scripture itself.[184]

Augustine considers the interpretation of those who argue that, since the first creation account in Genesis is not parallel to our experience, historical narrative begins only at the point of the expulsion of Adam and Eve from Paradise and no earlier. He finds this interpretation unnecessary. Just because we cannot imagine now God creating the world such as is narrated in Genesis 1 and 2, this is no reason to discard Genesis 1 and 2 from the pile of "historical" accounts.[185]

> Surely we are not to believe that God did not make the world because He does not make worlds today, or that He did not make the sun because He does not make suns today...[186]

Our experience or imagination of the possible cannot dictate what may or may not be a literal reading. This "believability" principle comes up again, in the context of discussing the creation of woman as a helper for man. Here Augustine states that if there had been no transgression which had merited the punishment of death, the man and woman would have reproduced sexually but without "the tumultuous ardor of passion and without any labor and pain or childbirth."[187] Here the "believability" of his interpretation is questioned by those who point to post-fall sexuality. Augustine responds by saying that one should not disbelieve that which experience fails to teach. When defending his position against those who, he says, think it is untenable because they look only at "the ordinary course of nature as it is after man's sin and the punishment he received," he states that:

> ...we ought not to be in the number of those who accept only what they have been accustomed to see. For one could not reasonably doubt that such a privilege as I have described could have been given to a person who lived an obedient and holy life, especially if there is no doubt that the garments of the Israelites were kept in their original condition so that through forty long years they showed no wear.[188]

Here he uses an instance described in scripture which defies "the ordinary course of nature": in Deuteronomy 29:5 Moses tells the people that God has protected them so thoroughly that even their clothes suffered no wear during the forty years in the desert. Augustine uses this to back up his claim that "the ordinary course of nature" cannot confine God's activity nor should it dictate the interpretation of scripture. Seeing should *not* necessarily be believing.

Thus his interpretation regarding the pre-fall nature of sexuality and reproduction, so he deems, should stand, or at least, may stand.

Indeed, the "believability" of scripture itself is ultimately dependent for Augustine not on reason but on the faith of the church.[189] This is particularly clear in his discussion of the difficulties in the story of the creation of Eve. Augustine acknowledges that unbelievers consider the events of the creation of Eve from Adam's rib, and also its typological link, the Virgin Birth of Christ, to be unbelievable. He does not argue for their "believability" or rationality of the places in scripture where these are indicated, but simply says that believers "have no doubt" and "firmly believe" that God created through these means. This belief is part of the total pattern of the Christian faith. Those who are not Christians who do not hold the total pattern of the faith find these "events" of the creation of Eve and the Virgin Birth untenable. Yet Christians are to trust that scripture speaks "believably." Therefore, if one of the accounts is credible, indeed is an article of faith in the creed, then its typological link should be as well:

But for believers, why should the account of the conception of Christ be accepted in the literal sense and the account of the creation of Eve be accepted only in a figurative sense?[190]

Within the whole of the Christian faith, each is just as "believable" as the other. However, it is not reason that renders them believable but the Christian faith itself which does.

For Augustine, the interpreter's reason and experience serve to aid in the investigation of scripture within the bounds of a faithful reading. Even if our experience of the world and our reason, that faculty which according to Augustine distinguishes humanity from beasts,[191] should give a contradictory witness to scripture, they cannot trump scripture's authority. The role of reason in determining the literal sense of a passage is generally to confirm or support the teaching of the Church. The two can in fact work together: "Catholic faith declares and right reason teaches that there could not have existed any matter whatsoever unless it came from God."[192] Even so, the authority of reason is necessarily trumped by that of scripture when the two are in conflict: "the authority of scripture in this matter is greater than all human ingenuity."[193]

Thus we see how the extra-biblical "narratives" or construals of reality, whether those of pagan wisdom or the interpreter's reason and experience, can and must come to play in the reading of the literal sense of scripture. While Ruled reading can overturn interpretations which may seem reasonably plain to the interpreter, or according to the canons of pagan wisdom, such interpretations must at least be considered for apologetic purposes. Ruled reading must always be allowed the power to overturn readings which it "rules" out.

Conclusion

We have seen how Augustine's understanding of Genesis 1–3 as both part of a sacred text and as "historical" narration generates two forces which impinge on each other in his reading of the literal sense. The understanding of the text as bearing meaning on more than one level depends partly on the supporting assumption that it is divinely inspired. Thus the text can and must be read on both the literal and allegorical levels because it conveys both human and divine authorial intent. The role of tradition as played out in the Ruled reading not only generates polysemy but also poses a limit to polysemy, because the text cannot be read in contradiction to the catholic faith. Therefore, the function of plain sense reading of the biblical text is, for Augustine, closely wed to both intra-communal and extra-communal apologetics. Augustine's theological presuppositions shape the questions which he poses the text and exclude certain interpretations via the Rule of Faith, but in his concern for the "literal sense" he clearly does not allow this exclusively to determine his interpretations. The verbal sense of the text wields its own impact on interpretation and it too places limits on the text's polysemy. Verbal sense anchors literal reading and thus restricts allegorical reading, for it is on the basis of the literal sense that one can and must authorize doctrine.

Notes

1. See *De civitate Dei* 11.19. Henceforth abbreviated *DcD*. The translation used will be Marcus Dods, trans., *The City of God*, in *The Nicene and Post-Nicene Fathers of the Christian Church*, by Aurelius Augustine, ed. Philip Schaff (Grand Rapids: Eerdmans, 1978). See also J. Patout Burns, "Ambrose Preaching to Augustine: The Shaping of Faith," in *Collectanea Augustiniana: Augustine, "Second Founder of the Faith,"* eds. Joseph C. Schnaubelt and Frederick Van Fleteren (New York: Peter Lang, 1990), 373-86.
2. E.g. *DcD* 15.27 and 16.37 where the historical or literal sense and the allegorical sense are not considered to be alternatives to one another but are held together.
3. On Augustine's use of the Rule of faith to link the doctrines of creation and redemption with particular regard to the *de Trinitate*, see Jaroslav Pelikan, "Canonica Regula: The Trinitarian Hermeneutics of Augustine," in *Collectanea Augustiniana: Augustine, 'Second Founder of the Faith,'* eds. Joseph C. Schnaubelt and Frederick Van Fleteren (New York: Peter Lang, 1990), 329-43. Pelikan points to Augustine's statement of the Rule of faith in *De Trinitate* II.1.2: "We hold most firmly, concerning our Lord Jesus Christ, what may be called the canonical rule [*canonica regula*], as it is both disseminated through the Scriptures and has been demonstrated by learned and Catholic handlers of the same Scriptures, namely, that the Son of God is both understood to be equal to the Father according to the form of God in which He is, and less than the Father according to the form of a servant which He took."
4. Henceforth abbreviated *DGncMan*. The translation used will be Roland Teske, trans. and annot., *Saint Augustine on Genesis: Two Books on Genesis Against the Manichees and On the Literal Interpretation of Genesis: An Unfinished Book*, Fathers of the Church (Washington, D.C.: Catholic University America Press, 1991).
5. Of course, this raises the logical question as to why Augustine himself could have been convinced by allegorical reading as to the truth of the Gospel. As far as I know, he never fully addressed this question.
6. Henceforth abbreviated as *DGnLImp*. The translation used will be Teske, *Saint Augustine on Genesis: Two Books on Genesis Against the Manichees and On the Literal Interpretation of Genesis: An Unfinished Book*.
7. *Retractions* 1.17, 1.18.
8. Henceforth abbreviated as *DGnL*. The translation used will be John Hammond Taylor, trans. and annot., *St. Augustine: The Literal Meaning*

of Genesis, Ancient Christian Writers: The Works of the Fathers in Translation (New York: Newman Press, 1982). Books 10 and 11 of this work are generally dated after 412 since they reflect Pelagian issues, and according to Epistle 143, written in 412, Augustine is still at work on the commentary. See P. Agaësse, "L'exégèse 'Ad Litteram'," in *La Genèse Au Sens Littéral en Douze Livres*, Bibliothèque augustinienne: Oeuvres de Saint Augustin (Paris: Desclée de Brouwer, 1972), 25-31. Elizabeth A. Clark argues for an earlier end-date. Cf. Elizabeth A. Clark, "Heresy, Asceticism, Adam and Eve: Interpretations of Genesis 1-3 in the Later Latin Fathers," in *Genesis 1-3 in the History of Exegesis: Intrigue in the Garden*, ed. Gregory Allen Robbins (Lewiston/Queens: Edwin Mellen Press, 1988), 117-20. Cf. also R. J. O'Connell, *The Origin of the Soul in St. Augustine's Later Work* (New York: Fordham University Press, 1987).

9. Books 11-13 of his *Confessions* contain allegorical interpretation of the creation and fall narratives of Genesis as do books 11-14 of the *City of God* (417-418).

10. *DGnL* 8.2.5. Taylor, *Literal Meaning of Genesis*, vol. 1, 35-6.

11. Ibid.

12. Henceforth abbreviated *DDC*. The translation used will be John Shaw, trans., *On Christian Doctrine*, in *Nicene and Post-Nicene Fathers, Vol. 2*, by Aurelius Augustine, ed. Philip Schaff (Grand Rapids: Eerdmans, 1979). If one translates "doctrina" as "culture," one begins to understand Augustine as setting the Bible up as the cornerstone of a new Christian culture, the classical text for education within this culture. Cf. Peter Brown, *Augustine of Hippo* (Berkeley: University of California Press, 1969), 26-34.

13. It is generally accepted that what we know as the Vulgate draws greatly on but is not identical to Jerome's translation. Cf. H. F. D. Sparks, "Jerome as Biblical Scholar," in *Cambridge History of the Bible, Vol. 1*, eds. P. Ackroyd and C. Evans (Cambridge: Cambridge University Press, 1970), 518-19.

14. *DDC* 2.8. While Augustine recognizes Jerome's work, he is never fully able to accept this version translated from Hebrew texts.

15. Augustine indicates that he follows the principles of catholicity and apostolicity in upholding the authority of the Septuagint in *DDC* 2.8.12.

16. He favors the Septuagint version of the Old Testament because it is inspired, for it is one voice in seventy translators. *DDC* 2.15, 22; *DcD* 15.13, 14; 18.42, 43; F. van der Meer, *Augustine the Bishop: The Life and Work of a Father of the Church*, trans. Brian Battershaw and G. R. Lamb (New York: Sheed and Ward, 1961), 343-44. However,

Augustine relies on a Latin translation because of his lack of skills in Greek. The Latin version he prefers is the Itala, for it "keeps closer to the words without prejudice to clearness of expression." *DDC* 2.15. He is referring here most probably to the Vetus Latina, a fourth century northern Italian translation prior to Jerome's Vulgate. The provenance of this text has been a matter of some debate. See J. N. Birdsall, "The New Testament Text", in P. R. Ackroyd and C. F. Evans, *The Cambridge History of the Bible*, Volume 1: From the Beginnings to Jerome (Cambridge: Cambridge University Press, 1970), 372.

17. See *DcD* 15.7, 26, from the section written in 418.
18. *DDC* 1.36.40.
19. *DDC* 1.39.43.
20. *DDC* 1.40.44.
21. E.g., *DcD* 11.32. In fact, a diversity of interpretations is even useful as long as the translation itself is not wrong. Cf. *DDC* 2.12.
22. "...in order to [subdue] pride by toil and [prevent] a feeling of satiety in the intellect which generally holds in small esteem what is discovered without difficulty." *DDC* 2.6.7.
23. *DDC* 2.6.8.
24. *DDC* 2.1.
25. *DDC* 3.5. But cf. also *DcD* 16.2: "So in this prophetic history some things are narrated which have no significance, but are, as it were, the framework to which the significant things are attached."
26. *DDC* 3.9.
27. *DDC* 3.10.
28. *DDC* 3.22.
29. Referring to 1 Cor 10:12, he urges "that we might tremble at the saying of the apostle, 'Therefore let anyone who thinks that he stands take heed lest he fall'." *DDC* 3.23.
30. *DDC* 2.11.
31. As far as we know, of all the early church Fathers only Jerome and Origen could read Hebrew. Augustine does note that Punic shares some words with Hebrew, such as בַאל. See R. C. Trench, "Augustine as Interpreter of Scripture," in *Exposition of the Sermon on the Mount Drawn from the Writings of Saint Augustine* (London: Macmillan and Co., 1869), 16.
32. Cf. Trench, "Augustine as Interpreter of Scripture," 2.
33. This is or course a common element in the education of Augustine and Calvin, for both were trained as rhetoricians.
34. "Perhaps there are some counsels in the sacred books—indeed it is certain that there are—which, if the man of God understands and accepts, will

enable him to perform his duties to the Church, or at least keep a clear conscience in a wicked world so that, living and dying, he lose not that life for which alone meek and gentle Christian hearts long. But how can this be done except, as our Lord Himself says, by seeking, asking and knocking, that is by prayer, study and penitence? It was with this end in view that I sought through my brethren to obtain from your dear and venerable kindness some little time—say until Easter—and to theirs I now add my personal appeal." Ep. 21:4, cited in Gerald Bonner, "Augustine as Biblical Scholar," in *The Cambridge History of the Bible, Volume 1*, eds. P. Ackroyd and C. Evans (Cambridge: Cambridge University Press, 1970), 541.

35. On the contrary, Augustine found useful and recommended to others the memorizing of entire passages of scripture in order to saturate the mind with it. This is borne out in his own Confessions, the text of which is laced with scripture, above all the Psalms. This, of course, is presumably the result of saying the Daily Office. Cf. *DDC* 2.9.14.

36. Here we see Augustine's influence on the Reformer's maxim, *scriptura sui ipsius interpres*, for obscure passages are to be interpreted by those which are clearer. *DDC* 2.9; 3.26.

37. *DDC* 3.2.

38. "For thus we learn the salutary lesson, that our aim should be nothing else than to ascertain what is the mind and intention of the person who speaks." *De Consensu Evangelistarum* 2.12.29. Translation in S. D. F. Salmond, trans., *Harmony of the Gospels*, by Aurelius Augustine, Nicene and Post-Nicene Fathers (Grand Rapids: Eerdmans, 1978).

39. *DDC* 3.27.

40. *DDC* 4.5.

41. *DGnL* 1.1.2.

42. *DGnL* 1.1.1. Taylor, *Literal Meaning of Genesis*, vol. 1, 19.

43. Of course, Augustine assumes Pauline authorship of Ephesians.

44. E. g. *DGnL* 8.2.5: in comparing his commentary *DGncMan* with his present project in *DGnL*, Augustine says, "And now the Lord has wished that I should look at and consider the same matter more thoroughly, and I believe that according to His will I can reasonably hope that I shall be able to show how the Book of Genesis has been written with a proper rather than an allegorical meaning in view." Cf. *DGnL* 9.12.22; 11.36.49.

45. *DGnL* 8.1.4; cf. also 9.14.24, where he opposes the categories of "foreshadowing of future events" with "events that actually happened," the "allegorical" with the "proper" meaning. Cf. also *DGnL* 1.17.33-34.

46. *DGnL* 1.1.1. Taylor, *Literal Meaning of Genesis*, vol. 1, 19. He justifies the use of figurative interpretation on the basis of New Testament reading of the Old Testament also in his *DGncMan* 2.2.3.

47. E.g. *De Utilitate Credendi* 9.

48. *DGnL* 1.17.34. Taylor, *Literal Meaning of Genesis*, vol. 1, 39. *"Sed haec allegoriae propheticae disputatio est, quam non isto sermone suscepimus. Instituimus enim de scripturis nunc loqui secundum proprietatem rerum gestarum, non secundum aenigmata futurarum."*

49. *DGnL* 2.1.4.

50. *DGnL* 2.9.22. *"...omnium sensibus patet."*

51. *Confessions* 13.15.16. The translation of R. S. Pine-Coffin, trans., *Saint Augustine: Confessions* (Baltimore: Penguin Books, 1961) used here is smoother than that in the *NPNF*.

52. *DGnL* 2.9.22. Taylor, *Literal Meaning of Genesis*, vol. 1, 60.

53. Christopher J. O'Toole, *The Philosophy of Creation in the Writings of Saint Augustine* (Washington, DC: Catholic University of America Press, 1944), 34–49.

54. *DGnL* 4.28.45. Taylor, *Literal Meaning of Genesis*, vol. 1, 135.

55. *DGnL* 4.28.45. Taylor, *Literal Meaning of Genesis*, vol. 2, 136. Here again Augustine speaks of metaphor as though it were under the rubric of figure.

56. Cf. *DGnL* 8.4.8.

57. It is along these lines that Bertrand de Margerie speaks of "la doctrine augustinienne de l'unipluralité du sens littéral." Pointing to Augustine's discussion in *De Trinitate* 9.7.12–8.13 he says: "En somme, l'unipluralité du sens littéral présuppose l'unité de l'Eglise et celle de l'humanité, l'unité même de la Trinité: dans chacun de ces cas, c'est aussi d'une unipluralité qu'il s'agit." Bertrand de Margerie, *Introduction à l'Histoire de l'Exégèse*, 3 volumes (Paris: Le Cerf, 1980), vol. 3, 83–4.

58. *DGnL* 11.2.4. Augustine notes that some Latin manuscripts read the latter as opposed to the former. The variants of the Old Latin text read *sapientior, prudentior, astutior, sapientissimus, prudentissimus*, while the Vulgate reads *callidior*. Taylor, *Literal Meaning of Genesis*, vol. 2, 287, n. 8.

59. *DGnL* 11.2.4. Taylor, *Literal Meaning of Genesis*, vol. 2, 135. Here we see clearly Augustine's influence on Aquinas' biblical hermeneutics.

60. *DGnL* 11.2.4. Taylor, *Literal Meaning of Genesis*, vol. 2, 136.

61. *DGnL* 11.31.41.

62. *DGnL* 11.31.41. Taylor, *Literal Meaning of Genesis*, vol. 2, 163–4.

63. For an example of understanding metaphor under the rubric of figure, see *DDC* 3.16.24.

64. Again, we see the influence on Thomas' biblical hermeneutics.
65. *DGnL* 11.36.49. Taylor, *Literal Meaning of Genesis*, vol. 2, 169. The "introductory remarks" to which he refers are presumably in 11.1.2: "One may expect me to defend the literal meaning of the narrative as it is set forth by the author. But if in the words of God, or in the words of someone called to play the role of a prophet, something is said which cannot be understood literally without absurdity, there is no doubt that it must be taken as spoken figuratively in order to point to something else. It must not be doubted that the statement was made, a fact which the reliability of the writer and the promise of the commentator demand." Taylor, *Literal Meaning of Genesis*, vol. 2, 134–5.
66. *DGnL* 11.36.49. Taylor, *Literal Meaning of Genesis*, vol. 2, 170.
67. *DGnL* 11.37.50: "...it is not by her nature but rather by her sin that woman deserved to have her husband for a master. But if this order is not maintained, nature will be corrupted still more, and sin will be increased." The "literal" meaning of the part of the curse that is directed at Eve is her domination by Adam.
68. Cf. *DGncMan* 2.17.26–2.18.28: "For the term 'chest' signifies 'pride' because the strong drives of the soul rule there. The term 'belly' signifies 'carnal desire' because that part of the body is recognized as softer..."
69. *DGnL* 11.38.51. Taylor, *Literal Meaning of Genesis*, vol. 2, 171.
70. E.g. *DGnL* 2.1.4; 2.9.22; 8.7.13.
71. *DGnL* 5.19.39; 9.12.22; 11.1.2.
72. P. Agaësse, "L'exégèse 'Ad Litteram'," 40.
73. *DGnL* 1.18.37. Taylor, *Literal Meaning of Genesis*, vol. 1, 41.
74. *DGnL* 1.21.41. Taylor, *Literal Meaning of Genesis*, vol. 1, 45.
75. *DGnL* 6.12.20. Taylor, *Literal Meaning of Genesis*, vol. 1, 192.
76. *DGnL* 7.2.3. Taylor, *Literal Meaning of Genesis*, vol. 2, 4.
77. *DGnL* 7.1.1: "*Flavit in faciem eius flatum vitae, et factus est homo in animam viventem.*"
78. *DGnl* 7.3.5. Taylor, *Literal Meaning of Genesis*, vol. 2, 5.
79. *DGnL* 1.19.39. Taylor, *Literal Meaning of Genesis*, vol. 1, 43.
80. *DGnL* 1.20.40, 2.10.23.
81. *DGnL* 9.12.22.
82. *DGnL* 5.8.23.
83. *DGnL* 2.18.38.
84. E. g. *DGnL* 3.12.20. He is especially blunt in *DGnL* 5.3.6: "If you yet cannot understand it, you should leave the matter for the consideration of those who can..."
85. E.g. *DGnL* 4.21.38; 4.28.45: "Whoever, then, does not accept the mean-

ing that my limited powers have been able to discover or conjecture but seeks in the enumeration of the days of creation a different meaning which might be understood not in a prophetical or figurative sense, but literally and more aptly, ...let him search and find a solution with God's help." See also 9.1.1: "Now, if anyone thinks that a different solution of this problem should be offered, I ask only that he give careful attention to all the points I have considered in arriving at my opinion; and if he will then be able to set forth a more probable theory, I must not only not oppose him but must even congratulate him."

86. *DGnL* 1.4.9. Of course, it can be argued that this reading of בראשׁת is not so strange when one considers that Prov 8:22, itself an ancient interpretation of Gen 1:1, renders αρχη as σωφια, probably an indication of the unusual use בראשׁת of to render "in the beginning."

87. "God does not work under the limits of time by motions of body and soul, as do men and angels, but by the eternal unchangeable, and fixed exemplars of His coeternal Word and by a kind of brooding action of His equally coeternal Holy Spirit." *DGnL* 1.18.36. See also *DcD* 11.6: "For if eternity and time are rightly distinguished by this, that time does not exist without some movement and transition, while in eternity there is no change, who does not see that there could have been no time had not some creature been made, which by some motion could give birth to change...? Since then, God, in whose eternity is no change at all, is the Creator and Ordainer of time, I do not see how He can be said to have created the world after spaces of time had elapsed..."

88. Cf. Theophilus of Antioch, *Ad Autolycum* 2.10, Origen, *In Genesim homiliae* 1.1, Marius Victorinus, *Liber de generatione divini Verbi* 27. Jerome allows this interpretation but points out that the Hebrew text cannot be read literally this way; *Liber hebraicarum quaestionum in Genesim* 1.1. Taylor, vol. 1, 225–226, n. 19.

89. *DGnL* 1.4.9. Taylor, *Literal Meaning of Genesis*, vol. 1, 23.

90. *DGnL* 1.6.12; cf. also 1.39.53; 2.6.10; 2.7.15; 3.19.29.

91. *DGnL* 3.19.29. Taylor, *Literal Meaning of Genesis*, vol. 1, 95.

92. *DGnL* 4.8.15.

93. *DGnL* 4.9.16. Taylor, *Literal Meaning of Genesis*, vol. 1, 114. Cf. *DcD* 11.8.

94. *DGnL* 4.10.20.

95. *DGnL* 4.10.20. Taylor, *Literal Meaning of Genesis*, vol. 1, 116.

96. *DGnL* 4.11.21. Taylor, *Literal Meaning of Genesis*, vol. 1, 116–17.

97. *DGnL* 4.12.23. Taylor, *Literal Meaning of Genesis*, vol. 1, 118.

98. E.g. *DGnL* 5.8.23.

99. *DGnL* 4.12.22.

100. *DGnL* 4.14.25. Taylor, *Literal Meaning of Genesis*, vol. 1, 120.

101. For a few interesting examples of Augustine's use of prooftexting in *DGnL* see 2.1.4 (Ps 135.5-6; Gen 1:7); *DGnL* 3.1.1. (Ps 148:4-5; Gen 1:20-23); *DGnL* 4.3.7 (Wisd 11:21; Gen 2:2); *DGnL* 4.14.25 (Lk 10:38-42; Gen 2:2); *DGnL* 6.8.13. (Mt 28:20; Jer 1:5; Heb 7:9-10; Gen 1:27-29); *DGnL* 9.10.16. (Rom 7:22-25; Gen 2:17).

102. *DGnL* 3.20.30.

103. *DGnL* 3.20.30. Taylor, *Literal Meaning of Genesis*, vol. 1, 96. Cf. Eph 4:23, Col 3:10. Of course, in Augustine's day the Pauline authorship of Ephesians and Colossians was not disputed.

104. Sirach 18:1; *DGnL* 4.33.52-4.35.56.

105. *DGnL* 4.33.52. Taylor, *Literal Meaning of Genesis*, vol. 1, 142.

106. *DGnL* 5.3.5-6. Taylor, *Literal Meaning of Genesis*, vol. 1, 149-50. For a discussion of Augustine's version of this text, see P. and A. Solignac Agaësse, trans. and intro., *La Genèse Au Sens Littéral en Douzes Livres*, Latin Text of Augustine, with French Translation, Bibliothèque Augustinienne: Oeuvres de Saint Augustin (Paris: Desclée de Brouwer, 1972), vol. 48, 668-70.

107. *DGnL* 5.3.6.

108. *DGnL* 6.19.30-6.28.39.

109. *DGnL* 6.20.31. Taylor, *Literal Meaning of Genesis*, vol. 1, 201.

110. *DGnL* 6.21.32.

111. *DGnL* 2.6.13.

112. E.g. *DGnL* 1.14.28; 1.15.30.

113. *DGnL* 5.6.19. Taylor, *Literal Meaning of Genesis*, vol. 1, 157.

114. Cf. Peter Brown's statement on allegory in the ancient world and how Augustine adapts this: "The idea of allegory had come to sum up a serious attitude to the limitations of the human mind, and to the nature of the relationship between the philosopher and the objects of his thought... This was the function which many ancient philosophers had assigned to allegory; it could easily lapse into a justification of effort for effort's sake. Augustine, however, went further: he produced a singularly comprehensive explanation of why allegory should have been necessary in the first place. The need for such a language of 'signs' was the result of a specific dislocation of the human consciousness... for Augustine, it is the outcome of the Fall. For the Fall had been, among other things, a fall from direct knowledge into indirect knowledge through signs." Brown, *Augustine of Hippo*, 260-61.

115. *DGnL* 5.3.6. Taylor, *Literal Meaning of Genesis*, vol. 1, 150.

116. *DGnL* 8.1.2-3. Taylor, *Literal Meaning of Genesis*, vol. 2, 33.

117. *DGnL* 8.1.1.

118. *DGnL* 8.1.2.

119. *DGnL* 1.1.1. Taylor, *Literal Meaning of Genesis*, vol. 1, 19.

120. *DGnL* 8.4.8; "*et Sarra et Agar quamuis duo testamenta significarent, erant tamen etiam quaedam mulieres duae.*"

121. *DGnL* 8.4.8. Taylor, *Literal Meaning of Genesis*, vol. 2, 38.

122. Ex 12:3–11; *DGnL* 8.4.8.

123. *DGnL* 8.4.8. Taylor, *Literal Meaning of Genesis*, vol. 2, 39.

124. *DGnL* 8.4.8. Taylor, *Literal Meaning of Genesis*, vol. 2, 39. "*Christus est et lapis unctus a Jacob et lapis reprobatus ab aedificantibus, qui factus est in caput anguli; sed illud etiam in rebus gestis factum est, hoc autem tantum in figuris praedictum. Illud quippe scripsit narrator rerum praeteritarum hoc praenuntiator tantummodo futurarum.*"

125. *DGncMan* 2.10.13, 14; cf. also Ambrose, *De paradiso*, 3.14, and Philo, *Questiones in Genesim* 1.12. Taylor, *Literal Meaning of Genesis*, vol. 2, 256, n. 40.

126. *DGnL* 8.7.13. "*Vera sint flumina nec figurate dicta, quae non sint, quasi tantummodo aliquid nomina ipsa significent.*"

127. *DGnL* 8.7.13. Taylor, *Literal Meaning of Genesis*, vol. 2, 43. "*Cur non potius auctoritatem scripturae simpliciter sequimur in narratione rerum gestarum res vere gestas prius intellegentes, tum demum quidquid aliud significant perscrutantes?*"

128. *DGnL* 9.12.20, 21. Taylor, *Literal Meaning of Genesis*, vol. 2, 83–5. "*Videtur enim mihi propter aliquam significationem propheticam factum, sed tamen factum, ut re gesta confirmata figurae interpretatio libera relinquatur... Non itaque arbitror dubitandum hoc alicuius propheticae significationis gratia factum, sed tamen factum.*"

129. *DGnL* 9.12.22.

130. *DGnL* 11.35.47. "*Ad hoc ista conscripta sunt, quia et ipsae interrogationes nimirum ad hoc factae sunt, ut et veraciter et utiliter scriberentur, quia, si mendaciter, non utique utiliter, ut advertamus, quo morbo superbiae laborent homines hodie nonnisi in creatorem conantes referre, si quid egerint mali, cum sibi velint tribui, siquid egerint boni.*"

131. *DGnL* 11.36.49. "*...nec aliud ei debet scriptoris fides narrationisque veritas, nisi ne illam dictam fuisse dubitemus.*"

132. In *DGncMan* 2.21.32, Augustine suggests that the clothing of Adam signifies death. This was also the interpretation of Gregory of Nazianzus, Gregory of Nyssa, Methodius, and Epiphanius. For complete citations, see J. Pépin, "Saint Augustin et le Symbolisme Néoplatonicien de la Vêture," *Augustinus Magister: Congrès International Augustinien* 1 (1954): 301.

133. *DGnL* 11.39.52. Taylor, *Literal Meaning of Genesis*, vol. 2, 172. "*Hoc*

enim, quod saepe dixi nec me saepius piget dicere a narratore rerum
proprie gestarum exigendum est, ut ea narret facta esse quae facta sunt et
dicta esse quae dicta sunt. Sicut autem in factis quaeritur, quid factum
sit et quid significet ita in verbis, et quid dictum sit et quid significet.
Sive enim figurate sive proprie dictum sit, quod dictum esse narratur,
dictum tamen esse non debet putari figuratum."

134. *DGnL* 11.40.54, 55.

135. *DGnL* 2.1.4. Taylor, *Literal Meaning of Genesis*, vol. 1, 48.

136. *DGnL* 3.11.16.

137. Cf. *DGnL* 3.12.20: "It may be enough to observe at this point that the
phrase 'according to his kind' was not used in the case of the man
because only one was created and from him woman was made."

138. *DGnL* 8.10.19–23. The Old Latin text which Augustine uses here reads
ut operaretur et custodiret; the object of the verbs is not specified.
Augustine notes correctly that the Greek text has a pronoun in the accusa-
tive case (εργαζεσθαι αυ˚ον και φυλασσειν), but he feels this leaves an
ambiguity. The pronoun could function in one of two ways: either as the
object of the two infinitives, referring to Paradise, or as their subject,
referring to Adam. Taylor, *Literal Meaning of Genesis*, vol. 2, 257, n.
50, 51.

139. *DGnL* 8.10.20, 23. Taylor, *Literal Meaning of Genesis*, vol. 2, 47–8.

140. For example, regarding Gen 1:3, he asks, "Can it be also that light is not
created through the Son? Here there is no repetition at all. The writer
might have put it this way: 'And God said 'Let there be light,' and so it
was done. And God made the light, and He saw that it was good.' Or at
least he might have described it as he did the gathering of the waters, so
as not to say, 'God made the light,' but only to repeat the statement,
'And God said, 'Let there be light,' and so it was done; and the light was
made; and God saw that the light was good.' But there is no repetition
here." *DGnL* 2.7.15. The variant on the formula here causes Augustine
to ask what the significance of the alteration of the verbal pattern is.
Although he comes to no decisive conclusion, he plays with the various
verbal combinations the writer *could* have used and their possible meanings in contradistinction to what the writer actually did say. Some other
examples are: the discussion of the significance of the repetition of the
phrase "according to their kind" in *DGnL* 3.12.18–19; the significance of
the words "to you" in the phrase at Gen 3:18 from the curse of the
ground which will now bring forth thorns and thistles, *DGnL* 3.18.28;
the significance of the singular object pronoun "male and female He
made him" at Gen 1:27, *DGnLM* 3.22.34.

141. *DGnL* 2.11.24.

142. The phrase "Lord God" (*Dominus Deus*), in which *Dominus* translates the Hebrew יהוה, first appears in the Vulgate at Gen. 2:4b and occurs also in vv. 5, 7, 8 and 9. The Old Latin text which Augustine followed, however, omits *Dominus* from these verses. Taylor, *Literal Meaning of Genesis*, vol. 2, 258, n. 60.

143. E.g., Hermann Gunkel, *The Legends of Genesis*, trans. Will Carruth (New York: Schocken Books, 1964), 123-44.

144. *DGnL* 8.11.24. Taylor, *Literal Meaning of Genesis*, vol. 2, 49-50.

145. Gilles Pelland, *Cinq Etudes d'Augustin sur le Début de la Genèse* (Montréal: Bellarmin, 1972), 228-9. While Pelland is correct that exegesis for Augustine "ne se réduit pas à une quelconque recherche de type objectif," it is an overstatement to argue that "ce qui compte, ce n'est pas ce que l'hagiographe a pû avoir à l'esprit en écrivant, mais ce que le Maître intérieure, dans les Livres saints, veut bien nous faire entendre des mystères de Dieu..." The texts which Pelland cites argue as well against him as for him here. E.g., cf. *Confessions* 11.3: "If (Moses) were here...I would beg and beseech him to explain those words to me"; 12.18: "All of us who read [the writer's] words do our best to discover and understand what he had in mind"; 12.24: "Whether (Moses) had one of these two meanings in mind when he wrote those words, or was thinking of some other meaning which I have not set down here, I am quite sure that he saw the truth and expressed it accordingly."

146. *DGnL* 1.21.41.

147. *DGnL* 1.21.41.

148. *DGnL* 1.21.41.

149. E.g. *DGnL* 4.1.1: "It is a laborious and difficult task to see clearly the meaning of the sacred writer in the matter of these six days..."

150. *DGnL* 1.19.38. Taylor, *Literal Meaning of Genesis*, vol. 1, 42.

151. *DGnL* 1.19.38. Cf. Taylor, *Literal Meaning of Genesis*, vol. 1, 230 n. 66. He cites *DGnL* 1.21.41, *DDC* 3.27.38 and *Confessions* 12.31.42. He concludes regarding Augustine's view that "a writer can wish that his words will be given several interpretations even though he himself has only one literal meaning in writing them." Cf. also *Confessions* 12.32: "O Lord make clear to us this meaning or any other true meaning that it may please you to reveal, so that whether you disclose to us the one which your servant Moses had in mind or any other which can be extracted from these same words, we shall feed from your hand and not be deluded by error." De Margerie speaks thus of Augustine's understanding of "la polysémie ordonée de Moïse et surtout à l'omniscience aimante et salvifique de l'unique Locuteur divin," de Margerie, *l'Histoire de l'Exegèse*, vol. 3, p. 72.

152. *DGnL* 6.1.1–6.7.12.
153. *DGnL* 6.4.5. Here we see Augustine's idea of the two forms of the providence of God given scriptural backing. Cf. 8.9.17 and the distinction between natural and voluntary providence.
154. *DGnL* 6.5.7.
155. *DGnL* 6.5.8.
156. *DGnL* 6.7.12.
157. *DGnL* 6.3.4. Taylor, *Literal Meaning of Genesis*, vol. 1, 180.
158. Augustine's Old Latin text reads *Et vidit Deus quia bonum est* at Gen 1:8. This phrase is, of course, lacking in the Hebrew texts used by Calvin and Barth. Cf. Taylor, *Literal Meaning of Genesis*, vol. 2, 325.
159. *DGnL* 3.24.36–37.
160. *DGnL* 3.24.37. Taylor, *Literal Meaning of Genesis*, vol. 1, 101–2.
161. Other examples include the following: "It is not unreasonable to suppose that on the completion of the sixth day, after its evening, morning was made not to indicate the beginning of the creation of another creature, as on the other days, but the beginning of that state in which the whole of creation remains and rests in the repose of Him who made it. This repose has no beginning and no end in God; it has a beginning but not an end in creation. For it the seventh day begins with morning, but no evening ends it." Cf. *DGnL* 4.18.32. "For night belongs to day, not day to night, when the holy angels of heaven refer their knowledge of creatures in themselves to the honor and love of Him in whom they contemplate the eternal reasons by which creatures were made. Perfectly united in this contemplation, the angels are one day that the Lord has made, to which the Church will be joined when freed from this pilgrimage, that we also may be glad and rejoice therein." *DGnL* 4.25.42.
162. Cf. *DDC* 2.40: "For, as the Egyptians had not only the idols and heavy burdens which the people of Israel hated and fled from, but also vessels and ornaments of gold and silver, and garments, which the same people when going out of Egypt appropriated to themselves, designing them for a better use, not doing this on their own authority, but by the command of God,... in the same way all branches of heathen learning have not only false and superstitious fancies and heavy burdens of unnecessary toil... but they contain also liberal instruction which is better adapted to the use of the truth and some most excellent precepts of morality; and some truths even in regard to the worship of the One God are found among them..."
163. *DGnL* 1.21.41. Taylor, *Literal Meaning of Genesis*, vol. 1, 45. Cf. Col 2:3.
164. *DGnL* 2.1.4. Taylor, *Literal Meaning of Genesis*, vol. 1, 47–8. Cf. Ps

135:6.

165. E.g. *DGnL* 3.2.3, where Augustine refers to the pagan poet Lucan in support of his own argument.

166. *DGnL* 2.1.4.

167. *DGnL* 2.1.4. Taylor, *Literal Meaning of Genesis*, vol. 1, 48.

168. *DGnL* 2.5.9.

169. *DGnL* 4.2.2, 6. Cf. also *De Trinitate* 4.4.7; *DcD* 11.30.

170. *DGnL* 4.7.14.

171. Cf. *DGnL* 2.17.35 and *Confessions* 7.6.8; Taylor, *Literal Meaning of Genesis*, vol. 1, 238 n. 56.

172. *DGnL* 2.17.35.

173. *DGnL* 2.17.35. Taylor, *Literal Meaning of Genesis*, vol. 1, 71.

174. *DGnL* 2.17.37.

175. Cf. also *DDC* 2.23.35–36.

176. Possible authors and texts Augustine may have had in mind are: Plato, *Timaeus* 33b; Aristotle *De Caelo* 286a 10-12 and 297a8; Cicero, *De republica* 6.17.17 and 6.20.21. Cf. Taylor, *Literal Meaning of Genesis*, vol. 2, 233 n. 25.

177. *DGnL* 2.9.20. Cf. also *DGnL* 2.16.34: "But let those who are strangers to our Father who is in heaven say what they will about the heavens. For us it is neither necessary nor fitting to engage in subtle speculation about the distances and magnitudes of the stars or to give to such an enquiry the time needed for matters weightier and more sublime."

178. *DGnL* 2.9.20. Taylor, *Literal Meaning of Genesis*, vol. 1, 59.

179. *DGnL* 2.9.20.

180. *DGnL* 2.9.21.

181. *DGnL* 2.9.21. Taylor, *Literal Meaning of Genesis*, vol. 1, 59.

182. *DGnL* 2.9.22. Taylor, *Literal Meaning of Genesis*, vol. 1, 60.

183. *DGnL* 1.21.41: "But when they produce from any of their books a theory contrary to Scripture, and therefore contrary to the Catholic faith, either we shall have some ability to demonstrate that it is absolutely false, or at least we ourselves will hold it so without any shadow of a doubt."

184. *DGnL* 5.2.4. Cf. *Confessions* 11.13-27 where this is used to distinguish between measured time existing only from the fourth day and time as motion.

185. *DGnL* 8.1.2-3.

186. *DGnL* 8.1.3. Taylor, *Literal Meaning of Genesis*, vol. 2, 33.

187. *DGnL* 9.3.6; cf. 3.21.33.

188. *DGnL* 9.3.7. Taylor, *Literal Meaning of Genesis*, vol. 2, 74. Cf. Dt 29:5.

189. Note the linking of the "believability" of scripture, the literal sense, and

the Rule of faith. Cf. Starnes: "Augustine stands in the same relation to Scripture as does the modern scientist to nature. Scripture and nature are both regarded as closed, complete and coherent systems in which the natural is held to be fully intelligible in its own terms. The difference is that where Augustine looks for the truth of nature through the medium of Scripture, the modern scientist looks immediately to nature itself. Augustine is confident that the literal sense of Scripture is intelligible because he believes that its words are the word of that principle in whom nature and God are one. The modern scientist has the similar confidence—to which Descartes gave the classic expression—that when nature is held in the form of a clear and distinct idea, God guarantees the conformity of these ideas with nature. This becomes the single principle of all the modern sciences of nature just as the rule of faith in the incarnate world is the single principle of all exegesis." Colin Starnes, "Augustinian Biblical Exegesis and the Origins of Modern Science," in *Collectanea Augustiniana: Augustine, 'Second Founder of the Faith,'* eds. Joseph C. Schaubelt and Frederick Van Fleteren (New York: Peter Lang, 1990), 348.

190. *DGnL* 9.16.30. Taylor, *Literal Meaning of Genesis*, vol. 2, 91.
191. E.g., *DGnL* 3.20.30.
192. *DGnL* 1.14.28. Taylor, *Literal Meaning of Genesis*, vol. 1, 35.
193. *DGnL* 2.5.9. Taylor, *Literal Meaning of Genesis*, vol. 1, 52.

Chapter Three:
Calvin's Understanding of the Literal Sense in his Commentary on the First Book of Moses

Literal Sense and Ruled Reading

As we turn to Calvin's reading of the opening chapters of Genesis according to the literal sense, we find an ease with the text which Augustine did not share. In part because of his understanding of the coherence between the Christian "story" and the story of Israel, Calvin does not have to resort to the exegetical gymnastics which Augustine needs in order to read the text according to the Neo-Platonic narrative of the ascent of the soul. Calvin's greater ease with the Old Testament narratives in general can be seen as both a result of and a contribution to his concentration of his preaching efforts on Old Testament texts.[1]

Calvin's Old Testament commentaries originated as lectures which he delivered in "simple Latin" with no notes and little preparation.[2] His commentary on Genesis is mostly a product of such lecture material, although the beginning chapters may be the result of the work he put into a proper commentary on Genesis which he began in 1550. This effort, however, was interrupted by his work correcting a French translation of the New Testament and there is no evidence that this commentary was ever completed. The lectures on Genesis date from 1550 to 1552, and one of Calvin's secretaries, Nicholas des Gallars, compiled a commentary from the notes which he took at these lectures. This material was then read to Calvin, who would amend and edit it as he saw fit.[3] The commentary on Genesis as we have it was finally published in July of 1554. From this T.H.L. Parker concludes that

> Calvin wrote the first two or three chapters himself, was then held up by his other work, and in the end turned to des Gallars for help, at least to the extent of supplying him with notes of the lectures and of sermons which Calvin had preached before 1549.[4]

How much of the material on which the present study focuses may have been in Calvin's original commentary and how much originated from des Gallar's lecture notes one can only guess, and since it is not important for our purposes here the question shall detain us no longer.[5]

Calvin is well-known for disdaining allegorical interpretation and preferring literal exegesis.[6] One clear example of this harsh view of allegories is found in his comments on Galatians 4. Here he accuses Origen and others of "twisting Scripture...away from the genuine sense." Calvin chalks this up to their apparent judgment that the literal sense is "too meagre and poor and that beneath the bark of the letter there lie deeper mysteries which cannot be extracted but by hammering out allegories." Calvin himself, however, declares that the literal sense is not barren. Scripture's fertility is not to be found in attaching meanings to the literal sense at the whim of the interpreter, but in embracing and holding the simple and natural sense itself.[7] Calvin's attitude toward non-literal reading is in practice, however, not as straightforward as this might make it seem.[8]

Calvin's "literalism" is often related to the influence of humanist interest in authorial intention and natural meaning as opposed to allegorical, and this cannot be disputed.[9] Calvin lived in an age when words and translations were the object of great passion. Yet the question remains: what does "literal" reading entail for Calvin? Why and when is he a critic of allegorical interpretation? Does he treat it simply as a "hermeneutical aberration," and how does he come to read and defend what he finds to be the "simple truth" of the text?

If one were to focus on Calvin's hermeneutical observations on the reading of the plain sense of scripture, one might think of considering his treatise *Against the Libertines*, his consideration of scripture or teaching on the Lord's Supper in the *Institutes*, or his Preface to Chrysostom's Homilies. Certainly these are important as background material to the present study, but the goal here is to examine Calvin's hermeneutical theory as it comes to bear on his exegesis itself.

Unlike Augustine, Calvin does not discuss in any length his own hermeneutical methodology, and therefore does not make explicit systematic reference to his understanding of textual polysemy. This only occurs *in medias res*, in the process of his exegetical remarks. As mentioned above, Calvin's comments on Galatians 4:22 are such an instance in which he acknowledges the richness of scripture but rejects the possibility of its containing "various meanings."

Scripture, they say, is fertile and thus bears multiple meanings. I acknowledge that Scripture is the most rich and inexhaustible fount of all wisdom. But I deny that its fertility consists in the various meanings which anyone may fasten to it at his pleasure. Let us know, then, that the true meaning of Scripture is the natural and simple one [*verum sensum scripturae, qui germanus est et simplex*] and let us embrace and hold it resolutely. Let us not merely neglect as doubtful, but boldly set aside as deadly corruptions, those pretended expositions which lead us away from the literal sense [*a literali sensu*].[10]

Apart from a few places which broach the topic in a theoretical and tangential way, we have little which would help us to understand clearly and directly Calvin's hermeneutical theory on the plain sense of scripture.[11] The following is therefore an attempt to sketch the "theory" from its use in practice in Calvin's exegesis of the first three chapters of Genesis in his 1554 commentary.

Instances abound in his commentary on Genesis of his *ad hoc* statements regarding the merits of his own interpretations for their adherence to the literal sense, the genuine sense,[12] the simple sense,[13] or the "natural treatment of things."[14] He acknowledges that other interpreters do read allegorically, and this he usually disparages:

Thus it has happened that in striving earnestly to elicit profound allegories, they have departed from the genuine sense of the words [*a genuino verborum sensu*], and have corrupted by their own inventions what is here delivered for the solid edification of the pious. But lest we should depreciate the literal sense [*literalis sensu*] as if it did not contain speculations sufficiently profound, let us mark the design of the Holy Spirit...[15]

Calvin's understanding of the notion of the literal sense is sufficiently deep that allegory is deemed unnecessary. He understands allegorical interpretation to be, more often than not, a distortion not only of the text but also of the very "mysteries of God":

I abstain from those allegories which to some appear plausible because as I said at the beginning of the chapter I do not choose to sport with such great mysteries of God.[16]

Even so, there are instances where he clearly sees the text to be speaking on more than merely a verbal level and where he offers figural interpretation, without ever openly suggesting that the search for literal reading of such a text should be abandoned. This phenomenon is generally described by the secondary literature as "typological" reading and is distinguished from allegorical reading, the former being judged as legitimate and the latter being judged a "twisting" of scripture.[17] It will be assumed for the purposes of this study that Calvin's distinction between allegory and typology does not actually reflect a distinction in his exegetical methodology. Rather, it reflects in part his polemic. Any improper reading is termed "allegory" while his proper reading acknowledges "types" or "literal anagogy."[18] However, the distinction is also pinned to two underlying assumptions, firstly, that the biblical text is inspired, and secondly, that the text refers historically such that "what happened" in the narrative exhibits recurring patterns of which certain key "events" are types. While the first assumption he shares with Augustine, the second is more particular to Calvin than to Augustine. Because of Calvin's understanding of a closer bond between the historical referentiality of the text and certain key events which serve as "types," his conception of the Christian narrative is tied more directly to the story of Israel. This means that reading *ad litteram* will not necessarily exclude figural reading, nor will the two be understood as separate "levels" of meaning.

The following, then, is an attempt to organize our discussion of Calvin's understanding of "literal sense" around the terms he uses in his Genesis commentary. The numbers after the English terms on the following chart indicate page references to John King's translation, and those after the Latin terms indicate column references to *Ioannis Calvini Opera Quae Supersunt Omnia* volume 23, of the *Corpus Reformatorum* volume 51:

Allowable	Literal, but not verbal	Disqualified
simple sense (124)		dreams in air (114)
simplex Mosis sententia (44)		*somniarunt in äere*
(37)		
certain and firm (114)		fly in the air (114)
certi vel firmi		*in äere volitare* (48)
		leave the earth (115)
		terra relinquere (48)
visible form (79)		fable (132)
de visibili mundi forma (18)		*fabulare dicant* (48)
	figure (106-7, 117)	
	quid proprie conveniat	
	veteribus figuris (33)	
	not limited to corporeal	
	life (117-18)	
	restringere ad vitam	
	corporalem (39)	
	symbol/external sign (184)	
	obscure figures (141)	
	obscuris figuris (53)	
genuine sense (141)	mixed language (165-66)	subtleties (165)
in genuino sensu (54)	*mixtum sermonem* (68)	*argutiae* (68)
	literal analogy (168-69)	
	vere literalis anagoge (70)	

It is clearly important to Calvin that he advance what he deems to be the "true and simple" meaning of scripture.[19] For example, the term "simple sense" appears at the end of the discussion of the rivers of paradise, during which Calvin has tried to locate geographically these rivers at great effort. After spilling much ink over this passage (Gen 2:10-14), six pages in the English translation, Calvin reaches the following conclusion:

> The simple meaning of Moses is that the garden of which
> Adam was the possessor was well watered, the channel of a
> river passing that way which was afterwards divided into four
> heads.[20]

One might remark that Calvin could have easily stated this "simple meaning"
at the beginning of his exposition of this passage, avoiding much discussion,
especially for one who is apparently so concerned to avoid verbosity and
excessive speculation.[21] There is evidently much at stake here in these verses.

This becomes apparent from his rejection of the allegorical reading of an
adjacent passage, which he says builds a "dream in the air." This he says of
the reading of the clause at Gen 2:8, "And the Lord God planted a garden in
Eden..." which understands the garden symbolically, not as a specific place on
earth. Such allegorical reading must be rejected, says Calvin, because it
renders "the doctrine of Scripture ambiguous and destitute of all certainty and
firmness."[22] Allegorical reading then undermines the reliability of the text
and renders it "ambiguous."[23] The authority of scripture and its use in
proposing and warranting doctrinal arguments are clearly at issue with regard
to the literal sense. Calvin acknowledges that some interpreters allow the
necessity of allegorical reading here, but he himself claims to reject it:

> It may be that some, impelled by a supposed necessity, have
> resorted to an allegorical sense, because they never found in
> the world such a place as is described by Moses: but we see
> that the greater part, through a foolish affectation of subtleties,
> have been too much addicted to allegories. As it concerns the
> present passage, they speculate in vain and to no purpose by
> departing from the literal sense.[24]

Because there is a correspondence between reading according to the letter and
the physical world of time and space, and since that is, according to Calvin,
what the first three chapters of Genesis are "about," one must read according
to the letter or one will read to no advantage.[25] Reading the rivers as
allegories of something else obscures this aspect of the text for Calvin.
Indeed, sometimes Calvin uses the term "allegory" as though it were that
which does not read the text as referring to the "visible world", as if it were
the stuff of imagination.

> For it appears opposed to common sense and quite incredible
> that there should be waters above the heaven. Hence some

resort to allegory, and philosophize concerning angels, but quite beside the purpose. For to my mind this is a certain principle that nothing is here treated of but the visible form of the world.[26]

In this respect, Calvin is opposed to allegorical reading, for it assumes the text to refer obliquely. Reading the text according to its literal sense, then, would presumedly read the text as referring to what it claims to refer to, which is, in this context, the creation of the heavens and the earth. Calvin wants to insist that the narrative is not fable or fantasy, which might require an oblique reading; rather, scripture is perspicuous and speaks plainly. Likewise, Calvin defends the passage which tells of Eve's formation from Adam's rib (Gen 2:22) and says that the text does not speak fantastically: "to profane persons this method of forming woman may seem ridiculous, and some of these may say that Moses is dealing in fables..." However, Calvin insists that the text is speaking plainly.[27]

Nevertheless, Calvin does at times in the material on Gen 1–3 embrace figurative reading.[28] In his comments on God's hallowing of the seventh day (Gen 2:3), Calvin says that the legal ceremony of Sabbath observance shadows forth spiritual rest and is a symbol of sanctification.

Therefore when we hear that the Sabbath was abrogated by the coming of Christ, we must distinguish between what belongs to the perpetual government of human life and what properly belongs to ancient figures, the use of which was abolished when the truth was fulfilled...[29]

But for Calvin, this figurative reading does not eliminate the responsibility for the plain reading of the text. The figuration, fulfilled in Christ, is indeed a temporary function of the Sabbath rest. The "letter" of the rest endures, however, "to the end of the world," even though the figuration be fulfilled.[30] Because of this understanding of prophecy/fulfillment, where fulfillment does not abrogate the figure, literal reading cannot be neglected.

Calvin also approves of the figurative reading of the tree of life (Gen 2:9).

Yet I am not dissatisfied with what has been handed down by some of the fathers as Augustine and Eucherius that the tree of life was a figure of Christ inasmuch as he is the Eternal Word

of God: it could not indeed be otherwise a symbol of life than
by representing him in figure.[31]

Calvin says that he does not restrict the understanding of the word "life" here
to corporeal life, but says that it encompasses also the "chief thing in life,
namely, the grace of intelligence."[32] Thus, figurative readings are allowed
and even encouraged, because here the figurative readings teach of Christ and
his grace. And in his discussion Adam and Eve's expulsion from the garden
and separation from the tree of life (Gen 3:22), Calvin says that this signifies
that

> he shall always be an exile from a happy life...for [God] by
> depriving [Adam] of the symbol takes also away the thing sig-
> nified...God connects life with the external sign...he represents
> nothing to us with false signs but always speaks to us, as they
> say, with effect.[33]

The tree is therefore more than a mere tree, a living organism with leaves,
branches and bark, and yet also more than simply a cipher for something else.
Instead, it is a symbol which participates "ad litteram" in the reality of the
thing signified, namely, the life of Christ.

Again, Calvin engages in figural reading of Gen 3:1 where the serpent is
introduced in the narrative. Calvin argues that from the immediate narrative
context alone nothing more can be inferred than that the first pair was deceived
by the serpent. Still, it is evident from the testimony of scripture as a whole
that Satan is via the character of the serpent introduced and spoken of, for the
prophets "prove that they were well acquainted with the meaning of Moses
when in different places they cast the blame of our ruin upon the devil."[34]
Thus the "meaning of Moses" (*mentem Mosis*) is itself more than the meaning
drawn from the immediate narrative context, and it is even more than the
meaning one might glean from a reading of, for example, the whole of
Genesis, or the whole Pentateuch. The meaning of Moses can be understood
only from a holistic canonical reading. This is simply one of the many examples in which Calvin follows Augustine in allowing scripture to be its own
interpreter.

Calvin then asks why Moses would have used the character of the serpent
to veil the activity of Satan, and says that "the Holy Spirit then purposely used
obscure figures because it was fitting that full and clear light should be
reserved for the kingdom of Christ."[35] The important thing to note here is
that figuration is not merely a method of reading the text for Calvin, but is

ingredient in the writing of the text and in the flow of time, or what Calvin might call "history." The "meaning of Moses" then overlaps with the meaning of the Holy Spirit, and the Holy Spirit's use of figuration is hinged to the theme of accommodation, or the understanding that the Holy Spirit crafts scripture such that it bends to the simple capacities of human understanding.[36]

It is because of this linking of the Holy Spirit's use of figuration and accommodation that figuration is ingredient in "history" for Calvin, for

> the existing age of the Church was so puerile that it was unable to receive any higher instruction. There is therefore nothing absurd in the supposition that they whom, for the time, we know and confess to have been but as infants, were fed with milk.[37]

Calvin uses the image of Moses as the schoolmaster who teaches with age-appropriate tools and techniques. Certainly Galatians 4 and Paul's discussion of the law as a pedagogue to Christ has influenced this discussion, in this instance, as it openly comes into play in the discussion of the accommodation of the angels depicted as cherubim in Gen 3:24.[38] Here we see that a version of "salvation-historical" understanding of the economy of God is wedded to Calvin's hermeneutic. Figuration is ingredient in the story, not merely an additional "reading in," because figure is part of the way the story is accommodated to those in the "puerile age" of the Church. Indeed, Calvin says that "They who have an aversion to this simplicity must of necessity condemn the whole economy of God in governing the Church."[39]

While figurative reading is to this extent necessary for understanding the "meaning" of the text, there is clearly a distinction in Calvin's mind between a valid and useful figurative reading and one which is a violation of proper interpretation. He does use the term allegory to indicate this violation and distinguishes this from "genuine sense": "Thus I understand the name of the serpent, not allegorically as some foolishly do, but in its genuine sense [to refer to Satan].[40] This figurative reading, based on the figurative "writing" of the narrative (and indeed of the "history" itself) by the Holy Spirit, is integral to an understanding of the "genuine sense" of the passage. And the genuine sense of the word "serpent" is Satan! Clearly this reading is not justified on the basis of verbal meaning alone but on canonical/doctrinal grounds. Here, as we saw for Augustine, we see the importance of Calvin's understanding of the biblical text as inspired. Because the text is understood to be divinely inspired or "authored," figuration can be understood as "written in" to the narrative.

Therefore, this figurative reading is not a "reading in" or a twisting of scripture, but is a "literal" reading.

A similar figurative reading is carried through to the passage of the curse of the serpent at Gen 3:14-15. While Calvin says that it is not certain to whom the words of the curse belong, to the serpent or to Satan, it is nevertheless a question worth asking.

> Wherefore many explain this whole passage allegorically, and plausible are the subtleties which they adduce for this purpose. But when all things are more accurately weighed, readers endued with sound judgment will easily perceive that the language is of a mixed character; for God so addresses the serpent that the last clause belongs to the devil.[41]

While Calvin clearly wants to avoid allegorical "subtleties" which distort the literal sense of the text, still he is bound to claim that the text refers in a "mixed" (*mixtum*) way. Despite what he says about the last clause belonging to Satan, it is evident from Calvin's further comments on this passage that he sees the words of the entire curse as directed to the serpent, and the last clause being directed simultaneously also to Satan. In his discussion of Gen 3:15, he says that there will always be enmity between serpents and humans, and that this is simply restated in the last clause, "It shall wound thy head and thou shalt wound its heel." Thus, the words of the last clause are indeed directed to the serpent. But further on he adds:

> Meanwhile we see that the Lord acts mercifully in chastising man, whom he does not suffer Satan to touch except in the heel; while he subjects the head of the serpent to be wounded by him.[42]

The character of the serpent in the immediate narrative and the character of Satan in the larger narrative of the Christian story overlap at this point, and the text becomes polysemic, speaking not only according to the words, but also figuratively. This does not violate the literal sense for Calvin, though, and this is extremely important:

> ...we must now make a transition from the serpent to the author of this mischief himself; and that not only in the way of comparison, for there truly is a *literal anagogy*; because God

has not so vented his anger upon the outward instrument as to
spare the devil, with whom lay all the blame.[43]

This seemingly non-literal reading is based on what Calvin sees to be a "literal
anagogy" between the serpent and Satan.[44]   This is because, we discover
from reading further, God spoke for the sake not of the serpent within the
immediate narrative but for the sake of Adam and his posterity. Indeed, if the
words had been said only for the sake of the serpent, we could draw no hope
from them, which according to Calvin is proper and indeed imperative to do.
Here we see Calvin operating with an implicit Rule of Hope, as we might call
it.   Whereas for Augustine the text must be read such that it upbuilds in
knowledge and love of God and neighbor (the Rules of Faith and Love or
Charity), Calvin seems to be adding the qualification that it must also sustain
us in hope. It is for our upbuilding in hope that these words were passed on
from Adam through to Moses. They are said with respect to humanity that we
might all the more dread our sin, and take consolation in our misery to know
that we are not slaves of Satan.

> I therefore conclude, that God here chiefly assails Satan under
> the name of the serpent, and hurls against him the lightning of
> his judgment. This he does for a two-fold reason: first, that
> men may learn to beware of Satan as of a most deadly enemy;
> then, that they may contend against him with the assured con-
> fidence of victory.[45]

Here Calvin's reading is not far from what Thomas Aquinas would understand
to be allegorical, for God assails Satan *under the name of* the serpent. This is
because the words of God to the serpent were said ultimately for the benefit
not of the serpent, a character within the story, but for humanity, both the
characters within and the readers of the story.
    While Calvin is willing to read a "literal anagogy" here, he at first seems
to stop short of this in his discussion of the word "seed" in Gen 3:15 and its
traditional interpretation as "protoevangelium."   Calvin indicates that he
wishes he could accept the reading which takes the "seed" to refer to Christ,
but he says that this would be to distort the words "too violently... for who
will concede that a collective noun is to be understood of one man only?"[46]
Calvin therefore reads the word to refer to Eve's posterity in general,
"wherefore the sense will be (in my judgment) that the human race which
Satan was endeavoring to oppress, would at length be victorious."[47]
However, referring to Rom 16:20, Calvin then states that the achieving of this

victory is shown to be through Christ, for Paul says, "The Lord shall bruise Satan under your feet shortly." While refusing at the outset to adopt the interpretation which would read the word "seed" to refer to Christ, he implicitly allows this reading through his quotation of Rom 16:20. Therefore what he explicitly disallows on the basis of verbal sense he implicitly allows on the basis of prooftexting such use within scripture itself.[48] Not only does Calvin therefore place great value on scripture's own intracanonical referencing, but he himself also engages in the practice of reading one text in light of another. Interestingly enough, this move is implied in Jerome's comment on Gen 3:15 in his *Quaestiones*.[49]

The preceding analysis, of course, presses the question as to Calvin's definition of literal sense. If this literal sense can be so elastic as to include complex readings, whether described by Calvin as "anagogé," "mixed" reference, or "figure," how "plain" is it really, after all?[50] Clearly he does not want to allow Scripture to become a "wax nose" to be shaped according to the whim of the interpreter.[51] He believes scripture has a definite content which is not violated by, but rather fully explicated by, such "complex" yet plain (or plainly complex!) reading as he advocates here. As we saw was the case with Augustine, Calvin is attempting in his reading of the literal sense to negotiate between verbal sense and his broader understanding of the nature and subject matter of the biblical text. While Augustine tended to lean more heavily on Ruled reading, Calvin claims to lean more heavily on the examination of verbal sense. It will become clear, however, in the following discussion that Calvin's doctrinal commitments strongly influence his reading.

In the remainder of the chapter we will explore Calvin's assumptions about the literal sense by first looking at the aspects of his reading which are influenced by his Humanist training and his focus on verbal and literary matters. This will include his concentration on verbal sense, narrative structure and context, author intentionality, and the role of tradition. Then we will look at the aspects of his literal reading which are constrained by doctrine, or what we have been calling Ruled reading of scripture. This will include his understanding of the historical referentiality of the text and its capacity to accommodate to the reader, his use of prooftexting, the role of the interpreter's common sense, and the role of apologetics, doctrine and the Christian life in literal reading.

Humanist Aspects of Calvin's Literal Reading

Verbal Sense

It is to state the obvious that for Calvin, unfolding verbal meaning is integral to understanding the plain sense of a passage. Lexical meaning, grammar and syntax, which are all elements of verbal meaning, become more important for Calvin than they were for Augustine for an obvious reason: Calvin was a humanist and therefore a linguist.[52] His knowledge of both Greek and Hebrew far exceeded that of Augustine, which, as we saw in the previous chapter was trifling at best.[53] Calvin also read both Latin and French from his youth. He had at his disposal good texts of the Hebrew, Latin, and Greek Bibles, grammars, lexica and concordances, as well as some contemporary commentaries and, of course, works of the Church Fathers.[54]

While the Hebrew text demands most of Calvin's energy and attention, the Septuagint and Vulgate are consulted in addition, and may even be spread in front of him as he speaks.[55] He will on occasion take issue with the translations of both the Vulgate and the Septuagint[56] and he usually offers his own translation of both New and Old Testament passages.

He often refers to the Vulgate as "the ancient interpreter" and sometimes agrees with its choice of translation.[57] For example, he concurs with the translation of Eden as Paradise by the Vulgate "because the Hebrews call highly cultivated gardens פרדסים."[58] At other points, he takes issue with "the ancient interpreter," which he feels is mistaken in translating the proper name Eden as "pleasure." While he agrees that the name was assigned to the garden because of its pleasures, still it is a proper name and as such serves only to distinguish this place from other places.[59] Again, he claims that the Vulgate's translation of the Hebrew is deficient at rendering אשה (woman, Gen 2:23) as *virago*, for the Hebrew refers simply to the female human. Calvin chooses for his translation the (unconventional) term *virissa* to point to the verbal connection between the man (*vir*) and the woman indicated by the Hebrew.[60] In any case, no translation, regardless of its authority granted by tradition or humanist scholarship, is embraced without scrutiny.

Calvin's Genesis commentary is sprinkled throughout with Hebrew and Greek vocabulary. Both in his lectures as in his sermons, Calvin worked from the Greek or Hebrew text and made his own translation as he went along.[61] More often than not, Calvin's knowledge of Hebrew proves itself to be apace with present-day lexica.[62] For example, in commenting on Gen 2:1, "Thus the heavens and the earth were finished, and the host of them," he offers an alternate translation for "host," צבאם . He says that the term could easily be translated "abundance," "copiam." This, according to Calvin, captures one sense of the work צבאם as well as Moses' intention to describe the world as if complete and well supplied.[63] At Gen 2:23, "This is now bone of my bone," Calvin says that the Hebrew word הפעם (*hac vice*, now) indicates that Adam has been lacking something and enforces the sense of crowning anticipation in the creation of Eve. He also observes that the Hebrew word for woman (אשׁה) is a derivative of the Hebrew word for man (אשׁ) and states that this is so in order "that [Adam] might transmit a perpetual memorial of the wisdom of God".[64] Likewise, at Gen 3:1, "Now the serpent was more subtle," Calvin notes that the term ערום can mean either prudent or crafty, and continues from this observation to question whether or not this term is intended in a good or bad sense. From the small word פן (RSV: "lest") at Gen 3:3, Calvin observes that the word generally, although not always, implies doubt, and thus he takes it to indicate that the woman here begins to waver in obedience to the command of God, even before the serpent "openly accuses God of falsehood."[65]

Calvin often notes the different meanings or uses of Hebrew terms, sometimes merely pointing out the various meanings as though to let them each enrich the understanding of the passage at hand.[66] In other instances he will lay out various possible meanings of a word and then argue for his own choice for the particular passage at hand.[67] At Gen 3:6, he notes that the term להשׂכיל (RSV: "to make one wise") can be translated in two distinct ways, "that the tree was desirable either to be looked upon or to impart prudence". He chooses the latter because it better fits the broader narrative context of the temptation of Eve.

Calvin comments on the curse to Eve "I will greatly multiply your pain in childbearing" (Gen 3:16) by expounding the word "pain" in some detail, indicating that it refers to:

> ...les dégoutements, les défaillances, les lassitudes et autres
> fâcheries sans nombre, jusqu'à ce qu'elles soient venues à
> l'enfantement, qui apporte avec soi de terribles tourments...[68]

He then goes on to say that the double expression "pains and conception" is to be understood under the literary device *hypollage*. This then leads one to wonder why, if Calvin recognizes this, does he not translate the phrase something like "pain in childbearing" as does the RSV instead of *dolorem tuum et conceptum tuum*.[69] In any case it is his inquiry into lexical meaning and rhetoric that occupies his attention here.[70]

At various points, however, Calvin argues an exegetical point on the basis of a word which he has not used in his own translation, or which does not appear at all in the text! For example, at "And every plant..." (Gen 2:5) he has translated the word שִׂיחַ *virgultum*, but then argues in his commentary for the translation *planta*.[71] And when he is discussing the phrase "He shall bruise your head and you shall bruise his heel" (Gen 3:15), Calvin notes that the verb may be derived either from שׁיפ or שׁפה. This leads him to say that he thinks that "Moses wished to allude to the name of the serpent, which is called in Hebrew שְׁפִיפוֹן."[72] The remarkable thing about this comment is that in the narrative of Genesis 3, the serpent is הנחשׁ, not שְׁפִיפוֹן! Clearly, then, his concern with verbal meaning is such that it does not disallow a varying amount of freedom with the text.

For Calvin, much in the way of exegetical and theological conclusion hangs not only on verbal sense but also on a text's grammar.[73] At "And Adam called his wife's name Eve because she was the mother of all living" (Gen 3:20), Calvin observes that there are two possible ways to read the verb ויקרא, either as pluperfect or simple past. Calvin reasons that if one reads it as pluperfect, "Adam had called," the sense will be that Adam "had been greatly deceived in promising life to himself and to his posterity from a wife whom he afterwards found by experience to be the introducer of death."[74] If one reads as simple past, it could be read either that Adam is made hopeful by the *protoevangelium* promise of Gen 3:15b, or that Adam is thoughtless, "who being immersed in death yet gave to his wife so proud a name."[75] Calvin then apparently opts for the simple past with this explanation:

> as soon as he had escaped present death, being encouraged by a
> measure of consolation, he celebrated that divine benefit
> which, beyond all expectation, he had received, in the name he
> gave his wife.[76]

The result of this is that Calvin thus portrays Adam, even in his moment of deepest despair and defeat, as thankful to God for the undeserved graciousness bestowed upon him. This whole interpretive chain is generated by an examination of the verb tense.

Noting sentence structure and parallelism is also important for Calvin. In his thoughts on Gen 1:26, "in our image and after our likeness," he differs from the traditional interpretation which sees the words "image" and "likeness" as referring to two distinct entities. The traditional interpretation then tends to question whether the image exists in substance and the likeness in accidents, or the image in endowments God confers on humanity at large, the likeness in gratuitous gifts. Calvin criticizes Augustine in particular for his "excessive speculation" and states that the definition of the image of God should rest on more "stable ground" than these "subtleties" allow. Calvin denies that the words image and likeness refer to distinct entities:

> for when Moses afterwards repeats the same thing, he passes over the likeness and contents himself with mentioning the image...where he twice uses the word image, he makes no mention of the likeness.[77]

Calvin argues on this basis that the use of the two words is simply an example of Hebrew parallelism, and that the second term is added as explanation of the first term such that the likeness simply represents the image of God itself. He also points out that in Gen 5:1 Moses uses the word "likeness" in referring to the creation of Adam without any mention of "image" at all. Here he uses arguments based on syntax and prooftexts to refute a traditional interpretation. This is done not expressly on doctrinal grounds, but because such interpretation does not fit the exegetical data drawn from the larger literary context.

Even still, Calvin is not committed to overturning traditional interpretation for the sake of being a maverick. While it is true, as we have seen, that he sometimes argues from the basis of lexical or verbal meaning to overturn traditional interpretation,[78] sometimes his lexical forays serve to promote doctrinally traditional readings. He claims that the word choice in Gen 1:1 supports a *creatio ex nihilo*. This he warrants by pointing to the use of the verb ברא, which he claims indicates that the world was created from nothing, whereas the use of יצר would have signified to frame or form something from something else.[79]

Again in discussing Gen 1:26, "In our image and after our likeness," Calvin indicates his unease with the interpretation of some which insists on drawing significance from the position of the particles ב ("in") and כ ("after"). While he argues that "the image of God was only shadowed forth in man until he should arrive at his perfection", Calvin does not think that this ever entered the mind of Moses and influenced his choice of ב and כ in their respective positions. He backs up this argument by pointing out that it is doctrinally correct to say that Christ is the only image of the Father, referring to 1 Cor 11:7, "yet the words of Moses do not bear the interpretation that 'in the image' means 'in Christ'."[80] In other words, there are textual controls over doctrinal interpretive conclusions. Something may be doctrinally true but not exegetically supportable by the text at hand.[81]

On the other hand, there are also examples where doctrine and verbal sense both play into the reading of the literal sense. In Gen 1:26, "Let us make man in our image, after our likeness," Calvin notes the tense of the verb (*faciamus*), and says that while it is in the future, "all must acknowledge that this is the language of one apparently deliberating."[82] By pointing to the tense of the verb, Calvin compares this piece of the narrative with the previous narrative and states that until this point God has been presented as commanding, while here God is presented as entering consultation, thus bestowing a "tribute to the excellency of man, that he would, in a manner, enter into consultation concerning his creation."[83] From this he then concludes that

> Christians therefore properly contend from this testimony that there exists a plurality of persons in the Godhead. God summons no foreign counselor, hence we infer that he finds within himself something distinct, as in truth, his eternal wisdom and power reside within him.[84]

While the comment began on noting the verb tense of God's words in Gen 1:26, the end result is doctrinal, in support of an understanding of this passage at the very least alluding to the Trinity. Here verbal sense is shaped by the understood subject matter of the text, the Triune God. Calvin could not have leapt from a note on verb tense to a conclusion regarding a plurality in the Godhead if "literal sense" were not to a degree the conjunction of verbal sense and subject matter. For the most part, however, it is verbal sense which takes the upper hand over Ruled reading for Calvin.

Narrative Structure and Context

Just as Calvin's Humanist training brings examination of verbal sense to the fore, so it also entails a sharper focus on narrative structure than we saw was the case for Augustine. Reading the first three chapters of Genesis as a coherent narrative is clearly an important interpretive strategy in Calvin's reading of the literal sense of the text.[85] Calvin's understanding of the text at hand as a unified narrative, itself theologically determined because God is its "narrator" and "author," results in his noting such literary aspects of the text as thematic repetition, and character and plot development. At times his understanding of the "storied" character of the text allows him to fill in details in such a way that Calvin himself becomes a sort of second narrator of the story. Further, his understanding of the greater narrative context of the story of Israel impinges upon his interpretation of the text, for the story of Israel repeats itself in the life of the (Christian) reader, and thus the words of the text are addressed not only to the characters in the story but also to Calvin and all readers.[86]

At Gen 1:3, Calvin points to narration and character and plot development in noticing that this is the first point where Moses introduces God as speaking. Up to this point, God is presented as though creating the heavens and earth apart from the Word. Then, after reminding himself and his listeners that the Gospel of John records that nothing was made without the Word (Jn 1:3), Calvin goes on to state that God did not put forth his Word until the creation of light, at which point God's wisdom becomes evident.[87] Here the sequence and means of creation as described in Genesis is understood to be hermeneutically significant. Plot development is also shown to be important in Calvin's comment about the placing of the creation of light on the first day while the creation of the sun and moon is left for the fourth day:

> Therefore the Lord, by the very order of the creation, bears witness that he holds in his hand the light, which he is able to impart to us without the sun and moon. Further, it is certain from the context, that the light was so created as to be interchanged with darkness.[88]

God is presented in Calvin's commentary as though a Great Narrator whose story, in the very order of its narration, instructs its readers. Later, when commenting on Gen 1:11 that the plants and trees were created before the sun and the moon, Calvin says that this did not happen by chance, but that "in order that we might learn to refer all things to him."[89] The order of the narration imparts information to the reader, which in turn is intended to nurture in the reader a particular disposition. Here, the order of the creation of Light and the lights teaches us of God's providence, and engenders the attendant dispositions of obedience and gratitude.

Calvin notes instances of repetition within the text, and he generally sees this literary device as serving a particular function. At Gen 1:31, he notes that the repetition of the phrase "and behold, it was very good" is to impress upon us our own hardness to the graciousness of God:

> The repetition also denotes how wanton is the temerity of man: otherwise it would have been enough to have said, once for all, that God approved of his works. But God six times inculcates the same thing, that he may restrain, as with so many bridles, our restless audacity.[90]

At Gen 1:27, "so God created man," he says that this repetition from the
previous verse is not a coincidental detail, but has a purpose.

> ...it is a remarkable instance of the Divine goodness which can
> never be sufficiently proclaimed. And, at the same time, he
> admonishes us from what excellence we have fallen, that he
> may excite in us the desire of its recovery.[91]

He goes on to say that the addition at this point of the words "male and
female" is to commend to us the bond of marriage, which addition he says has
the same force as if to say that man were incomplete by himself. This seems to
be an instance of reading the first creation account in light of the second; Calvin comments that the effect of the narrative in the second creation story is to
show how Adam was incomplete without the companionship of Eve. Indeed,
Calvin himself admits this reading of the first creation account in light of the
second:

> Under these circumstances, the woman was added to him as a
> companion that they both might be one, as he more clearly
> expresses it in the second chapter.[92]

While Calvin understands Genesis to tell the story of the creation of the
world, he yet sees internal narratives beginning, being reiterated, and concluding. He regards Gen 1:31, "And God saw everything," as one of these conclusions. The second account of the creation of Adam is understood to explain
what had been omitted previously, that Adam's body was formed out of the
earth.[93] The verse which introduces the tree of life and the tree of the knowledge of good and evil (Gen 2:9) refers back to the work of the third day (Gen
1:9-13) when the plants and trees were created. When questioning how to
read the verb in Gen 3:20, "And Adam called," Calvin says that "Moses is
accustomed without preserving the order of the history to subjoin afterwards
things which had been prior in point of time."[94]

Not only does Calvin note patterns of repetition as though Genesis were a
novel which takes up and weaves in themes dropped earlier, he also uses the
narrative flow to inform his reading of the plain sense. In commenting on Gen
1:29 "Behold, I have given you every plant... you shall have them as food,"
Calvin treats this not as an isolated statement but as a word of God spoken to
the first pair in the midst of the story of creation, and he thus looks to elements
of this story to interpret the verse. He notes that some interpret this verse as
indicating that humanity was to be content with a vegetarian diet until after the

Flood, at which point meat is explicitly given for food to Noah (Gen 9:3). Calvin remarks that this is not a strong argument, because even before the flood, the earliest people "offered sacrifices from their flocks," and the law of proper sacrifice is to offer to God only that which has been granted for our use. Here he seems to be thinking of Gen 4:4, the sacrifice of Abel. He also notes that Adam and Eve were clothed with skins and concludes that therefore it was not unlawful to kill animals. This, of course, is a reference to Gen 3:21 when God replaces the fig-leaves with garments of skin before expelling the pair from Eden. While Calvin does not use this line of argumentation to insist on the lawfulness of meat-eating even before the Flood, he does say that he thinks that in light of these arguments it is best to assert nothing either positively or negatively on this matter, but rather to recognize that plants were given as food and that by these words, God promises a "liberal abundance which should leave nothing wanting to a sweet and pleasant life."[95] Elements of the whole creation story, indeed at least the first nine chapters of Genesis, are brought to bear on the interpretation of this one verse.

This is clear also in Calvin's refutation of Jerome's interpretation of Gen 2:8, "And the Lord God planted a garden in the east, in Eden." Jerome had understood "in the east" to signify "in the beginning," but Calvin argues that this is clearly wrong because according to the narrative, Cain is said to dwell to the south of Eden. How could he then live in the south of "the beginning?" Calvin wants to underscore the element of the story which assigns the first pair to a distinct place which is, according to Calvin, geographically locatable. He does this by pointing to a detail from further on in the narrative when Cain is driven from the presence of God (Gen 4:16).

Calvin probes for the narrator's voice at Gen 2:24, "Therefore a man shall leave his father and mother..." He wonders if the speaker could be Adam, and the verse thus a continuation of his joyful exclamation "This is now bone of my bones..." at the creation of Eve in the previous verse. He also suggests that Moses (as narrator) is here portraying God (a character in the story) as speaking as a sort of second narrator. Another possibility he mentions is that Moses (as author) has added this statement in virtue of his teaching office.

Calvin's running commentary on the interchange between the serpent and Eve reads more like a novel of intrigue itself than biblical commentary. He notes that "...the craftiness of Satan betrays itself in this, that he does not directly assail the man, but approaches him, as through a mine, in the person of his wife."[96] Again, he says,

Satan now springs more boldly forward; and because he sees a breach open before him, he breaks through in a direct assault...[97]

The characters interact "behind the scenes," so to speak, behind or underneath the surface of the words of the text. Calvin understands them to be moved by emotions and passions not mentioned in the text and to accuse and attack under the cover of the narrative:

When he says 'God doth know,' he censures God as being moved by jealousy, and as having given the command concerning the tree for the purpose of keeping man in an inferior rank.[98]

and again

This impure look of Eve, infected with the poison of concupiscence, was both the messenger and the witness of an impure heart. She could previously behold the tree with such sincerity...but now, after the heart had declined from faith and from obedience to the word, she corrupted both herself and all her senses...[99]

This is a narrative in which we ourselves figure, or are figured as characters on scene, for Calvin flows directly from running commentary on the text to doctrinal exposition without explicitly changing course:

That we are despoiled of the excellent gifts of the Holy Spirit, of the light of reason, of justice, and of rectitude, and are prone to every evil; that we are also lost and condemned and subjected to death is both our hereditary condition and at the same time a just punishment which God in the person of Adam has inflicted on the human race.[100]

and again

...he, who had found a few leaves to be unavailing, fled to whole trees; for so we are accustomed when shut out from frivolous cavils, to frame new excuses, which may hide us as under a denser shade.[101]

We stand in Adam and Eve's place such that there is no difference for Calvin between the "then" of the text and the "now" of his own lecturing, nor is there any unbridgeable gap between what the text said and what the text meant, between its meaning and its significance.

Calvin's understanding of Genesis as a coherent narrative which enmeshes but does not entirely overlap our own narrative is evident also in his attempt to answer the question he asks about Gen 2:17. Here he wonders what kind of death is meant by the command and threat that Adam and Eve must not eat of the fruit of the tree of the knowledge of good and evil for they are warned that when they eat of it, they will die. In order to attempt to understand what this death is, Calvin considers the kind of life from which the pair fell in respect to body and soul. He decides that before the fall, the life of the soul meant the capacity of proper governing of affections, while the life of the body meant freedom from injury and death. Calvin concludes this not on the basis of the verse at hand, or even surrounding verses, but by a broader understanding of the Christian life in general defined by the "outer limits" of sin and grace, creation and redemption. To put this in Augustinian terms, Calvin is using here the Rule of Faith as a hermeneutical guideline. He points out (without citing any particular texts) that scripture elsewhere understands those who are oppressed by sin and the tyranny of Satan to be dead. Then Calvin suggests that since the cause of death is alienation from God,

> the question is superfluous how it was that God threatened death to Adam on the day in which he should touch the fruit, when he long deferred the punishment. ...For then was Adam consigned to death, and death began its reign in him, until supervening grace should bring a remedy.[102]

Here Calvin takes as hermeneutical guide not the story of creation itself, nor the larger narrative of Adam and his family, nor the story of Genesis as a whole, but rather the story-line of the Christian faith. In other words, here we see an implicit use of the Rule of Faith.

Calvin's reading of Genesis as a whole narrative occasionally engages him in speculation regarding what the text fails to say, as was the case for Augustine.[103] For example, in the discussion at Gen 3:1 where he says that the serpent plays the part of Satan, Calvin remarks that Moses does not discuss the fall of Satan. After having conceded that we must conclude from our understanding of God that Satan's evil is a result not of nature but of defection, Calvin says that

Moses here passes over Satan's fall, because his object is briefly to narrate the corruption of human nature, to teach us that Adam was not created to those multiplied miseries under which all his posterity suffer, but that he fell into them by his own fault.[104]

After some discussion of this, Calvin notes that Moses does not treat every topic which any person might wish. This, according to Calvin, is because Moses has a specific goal in mind for his narrative. The goal is this:

to show in a few words how greatly our present condition differs from our first original in order that we may learn with humble confession of our fault to bewail our evils.[105]

Here we see an implicit use of the Rule of Charity interacting with a concern for literary features of the text to render literal meaning.[106]

Sometimes Calvin even fills in narrative details which are not present in the immediate text by appealing to narrative elements from elsewhere in Genesis. In commenting on the naming of all living creatures by Adam in Gen 2:19, Calvin says that God's bringing the creatures before Adam to be named endowed them with the disposition of obedience to him, which failed after the fall. Now, says Calvin, wild animals are a threat to us since our rebellion against God, even though some remains of their former subjection continue. This subjection is evident from the story of Noah in Gen 9:2 which shows God delivering the animals into the hand of Noah and saying that they will fear him. Calvin fills in these details into the text of 2:19 by referring to Gen 1:28 (obliquely) and Gen 9:1 (explicitly). These of course are parallels of a sort insofar as they both include the command to "be fruitful and multiply" and treat the theme of humanity's subduing of the animal kingdom.

Sometimes, however, it is intrigue which leads Calvin to fill in the details of the story, as he does in discussing the creation of Eve from Adam's rib. He says here that the reason that God caused a deep sleep to come over Adam (which itself is explicitly in the text of Gen 2:21) is so that Adam would feel no pain,

and further that neither had the rupture been violent, nor was any want perceived of the lost rib, because God so filled up the vacuity with flesh, that his strength remained unimpaired; only the hardness of the bone was removed.[107]

And in commenting on Gen 3:21, "And the Lord God made for Adam and for his wife garments of skins," Calvin wonders why the text seems to indicate that God made the clothing. Calvin argues that it is simply not believable, because all animals had been given to them earlier for their use. Why would God make them clothing? This, Calvin suggests, is answerable as follows:

> being now impelled by a new necessity, they put some to death, in order to cover themselves with their skins, having been divinely directed to adopt this counsel; therefore Moses calls God the Author of it.[108]

This is particularly remarkable for an exegete who insists upon the letter, for he seems to disregard completely the fact that the text quite "plainly" indicates that it is God who made the garments (*Fecitque jehova deus*). Clearly, then, as we saw was the case in his examination of verbal sense, his examination of narrative structure and context in literal reading does not rule out a certain degree of freedom with the story, as long as he remains within the constraints of Ruled reading. What is "believable" is allowable to guide the interpretation as long as the Rule of Faith is not violated.

Authorial Intention

One of the important features of Humanist reading, the concern to explicate the intention of the author, becomes more important for Calvin than it was for Augustine.[109] At many points in his commentary Calvin resorts to arguing on the basis of the author's intended meaning in an attempt to elucidate the literal sense of the text.[110] In fact, at points the literal sense seems to be equated with the meaning of Moses, which itself Calvin admits is not easy to determine.[111]

At Gen 1:1, Calvin disagrees with Augustine's interpretation of "the beginning" as referring to Christ. Calvin argues that Moses did not intend the words "the beginning" to refer to Christ.[112] Rather, Moses wanted simply to relate that the world was not perfected at the beginning but was created an empty chaos.[113] And at Gen 1:26, "Let us make man," he says that while it may be true that the image of God was only a shadow in man until he arrives at perfection, still this did not even enter Moses' mind.[114] In the opening Argument of the commentary, Calvin states that "the intention of Moses in beginning his book with the creation of the world is to render God, as it were, visible to us in his works."[115] Moses, as author, has a goal for his writing, and shapes the writing according to that goal. He begins the narrative with an account of creation to set before our eyes the works of God in which we can contemplate their creator.

But the question of the identity of the author whose intention Calvin seeks is not so easily answered as this would imply. Since he accepts the tradition of Mosaic authorship of the Pentateuch, Calvin sometimes portrays Moses as the author of Genesis, who crafts the story in order "deeply to impress upon our minds the origin of heaven and earth..." by means of thematic repetition and reiteration.[116] As human author, Moses apparently exercises the freedom to choose words,[117] and to present things in figures for pedagogical reasons.[118] At other times the characters seem to take on a life of their own which overtakes the authorship of Moses. Indeed, they even are understood to choose their own speech with their own intent: "in using the expression הפעם Adam indicates that something had been wanting him..."[119] And sometimes Calvin reads as though the Holy Spirit were peering around the human author to show its own agency in the composition: "I now return to the design of Moses, or rather of the Holy Spirit which has spoken by his mouth."[120] Sometimes the words of the text are not Moses' words but those of God: "for the words of God are to this effect... by these words God promises liberal abundance."[121] Even though the words of God can be argued to be simply the utterance of a character in the narrative (Gen 1:28), this character's words reach out to the contemporary reader (in this case, Calvin and his audience) such that they overlap with the words of Moses.

In commenting on Gen 1:31, God's declaration that creation is good, Calvin notes that

> God six times inculcates the same thing, that he may restrain, as with so many bridles, our restless audacity. But Moses expresses more than before; for he adds מאד, that is, very... that we may know that there is in the symmetry of God's works the highest perfection to which nothing can be added.[122]

According to Calvin, God repeats the affirmation of the goodness of creation for our benefit, rather than for the benefit of Adam nor Moses. And Moses adds the word מאד to the text. God "speaks"; Moses inscribes and crafts the narrative.

In turn, author intentionality itself is sometimes extended to include the intention of God. In discussing Gen 2:9 and the tree of life, Calvin says that "God therefore intended that man, as often as he tasted the fruit of that tree, should remember whence he received his life..."[123] In this instance, God, as a character in the story, has an intention for another character in the story, Adam. This in turn overlaps with Calvin's exposition elsewhere of God's intention for our lives: gratitude. Here again we see implicit use of the Rule of Charity. And later, this seems to be the case when he says, "Moses now explains the design of God in creating the woman; namely, that there should be human beings on the earth who might cultivate mutual society between themselves."[124]

Here Calvin seems to see Moses in the act of interpreting the work of creation much as Calvin himself interprets the text of Genesis, by inquiring into the intention of the Author.[125] According to Calvin, not only Moses but also God, as both character within and Author of the story, have a purpose in crafting the dialogue. The phrase in Gen 3:11, "of the tree of which I commanded you not to eat," is added according to Calvin in order to remove the possibility of Adam's feigning ignorance of God's command. God had already made it quite clear that Adam was not to eat of this tree, and reminds him of this here at the revealing of the act of disobedience. According to Calvin, there are to be no excuses: "For God intimates that Adam was admonished in time; and that he fell from no other cause than this, that he knowingly and voluntarily brought destruction upon himself."[126] "God" crafts the dialogue here. Again, at Gen 3:16, Calvin says "In order that the majesty of the Judge may shine the more brightly, God uses no long disputation."[127] In the midst of Moses' narration, God as character emerges as taking the creative reigns, not only with the telling of the story but in the interchange between the characters portrayed within the story.

We have seen here how the Humanist concern for author intentionality becomes a significant factor in Calvin's literal reading. However, for Calvin exploring author intentionality extends further than does the Humanist concern. In conjunction with Ruled reading and Calvin's understanding of the biblical text as inspired, searching for author intentionality means listening for the voice of the Divine Author speaking through the text.

"Ad Fontes": the Role of Tradition

Calvin also shares with the Humanists an interest in returning to the classical sources. He is he well-read in classical philosophy and literature, and often refers to such authors in support of an exegetical point he is trying to make. However, Calvin is not bound by those who came before him, but uses the classical sources freely in his exegesis where they are useful, "spoiling the Egyptians" as it were.

In his discussion of the identity and location of the rivers of paradise, Calvin refers to the works of Pliny, Pomponius Mela, Nearchus the commander of Alexander's fleet, Flavius Arrian, Strabo, and Quintus Curtius, all in his attempt to locate Eden.[128] He even quotes Horace as "handed down from the fathers" where he is understood to support the idea that whatever is disorderly in the world is a fruit of sin.[129] One wonders whose and which fathers Calvin means here! Yet, as willing as he is to bring in pagan literature in favor of his arguments, so is he equally willing to sweep the classical philosophers aside when they contradict a Ruled reading of scripture. At such times, he voices his disappointment in their wisdom.[130]

While Calvin may have the reputation of eschewing the role of the church's tradition in interpretation for the sake of the letter of the text, his actual relation to tradition, at least in his commentary on Genesis, is far more complex.[131] Calvin's humanist bent toward returning to the sources extends of course to the tradition of biblical interpretation and theology, and as with ancient philosophy, Calvin embraces the theological sources and uses them to his advantage in interpretation of scripture. His implicit use of "tradition" broadly defined in his interpretation of Genesis 1–3 can be seen to fall into two general categories. The first is the traditioning process as it comes to play in the "composition" of the text, and the second is the church's tradition in the history of interpretation of the biblical text.

Although Calvin would not explain it in these terms, he sees "tradition" at work even in the composition of the text. While he does not push this to the extent of cleaving the text along redactional fault plains, he clearly does not assume that the text appeared miraculously in its final form as is claimed, for example, of the *Book of Mormon* by the Latter Day Saints. The creation cycle itself is said to be handed down "through the ancient and perpetual tradition of the Fathers."[132] Even while still far from a modern critical understanding of textual "genesis", he understands a dynamic life behind the writing of the text. He implicitly discusses the "sources" used by Moses in knitting together Genesis from this "oral tradition":

> For Moses does not transmit to memory things before unheard
> of, but for the first time consigns to writing facts which the
> fathers had delivered as from hand to hand, through a long
> succession of years, to their children...No sane person doubts

that Adam was well-instructed respecting [his own origin and the origin of those things which he enjoyed].[133]

Calvin does not mention how Adam knows the origin of that which was created before him. Instead, Calvin simply says that "no sane person doubts" this idea. This tradition, according to Calvin, is then passed on in gratitude through Noah who was warned by such a memorable judgment as the Flood, down through Abraham who understood himself to be the teacher and master of his family (Calvin is thinking here of Gen 18:19), and down to Moses. The fixing in writing of this old, old story is according to Calvin itself not by chance, but crucial for its preservation and its authority:

> Yet, since nothing is more easy than that the truth of God
> should be so corrupted by men, that, in a long succession of
> time, it could as it were degenerate from itself, it pleased the
> Lord to commit the history to writing for the purpose of
> preserving its purity. Moses, therefore, has established the
> credibility of that doctrine which is contained in his writings,
> and which, by the carelessness of men, might otherwise have
> been lost.[134]

The inscription of this tradition establishes its textual credibility which over time would risk being corrupted in the process of being passed down. Thus it is the fixing of the "oral tradition" in written form which buttresses the text's authority. The written word holds greater authority than does the voice of "tradition."

The other more explicit understanding of tradition in Calvin's interpretation of Genesis 1–3 is the history of biblical interpretation, both Christian and Jewish. He refers to interpretations from the history of the tradition, sometimes citing the author to whom he refers and sometimes without naming the author at all.[135] Calvin's interest in referring to traditional interpretation sometimes involves the investigation of the understanding of verbal meaning, and yet sometimes the examination of the doctrinal conclusions which result from interpretation draws his attention.[136]

Calvin appreciated the rabbis with regard to their philological and lexical expertise. Interestingly enough, it seems that Calvin may not have had a first-hand knowledge of the rabbis himself, but rather it is likely that they were mediated to him through one of his colleagues. Calvin's positive appraisal of the rabbis has been, of course, used to impugn his exegesis. The best-known example of this is probably Hunnius' 1595 *Calvinus Judaizans*, in which the claim was made that Calvin's reading of the Old Testament was too literalist and allowed for "judaizing" and Arian interpretations. Calvin himself accused others, both Roman Catholics and Radical Reformers, of "Judaizing," a common polemical term in Reformation era writings.[137] Probably the two most significant figures from Jewish interpretation of scripture for Calvin's Genesis commentary are Rashi and Kimchi. Again, this is probably not an indicator that Calvin read Rashi and Kimchi. For example, his sometimes-unacknowledged reliance on Kimchi in his discussion of Hebrew vocabulary could have been mediated through the Hebrew Lexicon of Sebastian Münster which was based on David Kimchi's *Book of Roots*.[138] In his Genesis commentary, Calvin even refers to one of the Aramaic Targums, and approves of an interpretation which he draws from it. How he knew of it is not entirely certain, but it could easily have been through the Complutensian Polyglot Bible or through Bomberg's rabbinic Bible.[139]

However he knows of their writings, Calvin refers to the interpretation of "the Hebrews" and "the Rabbis" at several places in his Genesis commentary. Sometimes this is with positive reception, but more often with scorn. When the latter is the case, he includes a correction of their interpretation.[140] Sometimes he refers to a commentator by name, for example, "Kimchi takes it in this last sense..."[141] Often however the reference to rabbinic commentary is veiled with a reference to "the Rabbis."[142]

Rarely does Calvin offer much comment on the Jewish interpretation which he mentions. At Gen 1:15, the word for "seasons," מועדים, Calvin says that "the Rabbis commonly explain the passage as referring to their festivals. But I extend it further..."[143] This example shows Calvin's correction of Jewish interpretation on the basis of verbal sense alone. But at Gen 1:26, "Let us make man," Calvin remarks that "the Jews" commit sacrilege by claiming that God is speaking either with the earth or with angels.[144] And again at Gen 2:3, Calvin disparages a Jewish interpretation for its implicit understanding of God in anthropomorphic terms:

> Here the Jews, in their usual method, foolishly trifle, saying that God being anticipated in his work by the last evening, left certain animals imperfect, of which kind are fauns and satyrs, as though he had been one of the ordinary class of artificers who have need of time. Ravings so monstrous prove the authors of them to have been delivered over to a reprobate mind, as a dreadful example of the wrath of God...[145]

Of course, this interpretation may be Calvin's own fantasy of Jewish interpretation. However, when the Jewish "literal sense" violates Calvin's understanding of the nature of God, he offers a different "literal sense." For Calvin, the "literal sense" of an Old Testament passage cannot contradict the larger understanding of God which he draws from a Ruled reading of both Testaments. Therefore, some Jewish interpretations are disqualified.

Of course, Jewish interpreters are only a small part of the fund of theological tradition on which Calvin draws. One of the most important figures for Calvin from the history of Christian biblical interpretation is Augustine.[146] Calvin approves of Augustine's exegesis especially where he upholds the sovereignty and omnipotence of God, for example: "Augustine rightly affirms that injustice is done to God by the Manichaeans, because they demand a cause superior to his will..."[147] He concurs with Augustine regarding the sin of the first pair being pride, despite the lack of the text's direct statement in regard to this, and even expands on Augustine's view by saying that the root of their sin was unbelief (*infidelitatem*) which issues in pride.[148] Even where Augustine resorts to figural reading, Calvin can at times concur:

> Yet I am not dissatisfied with what has been handed down by some of the fathers, as Augustine and Eucherius, that the tree of life was a figure of Christ inasmuch as he is the Eternal Word of God: it could not indeed be otherwise a symbol of life, than by representing him in figure. For we must maintain what is declared in the first chapter of John, that the life of all things was included in the Word, but especially the life of men...[149]

Calvin's agreement with Augustine's figural reading is itself based on canonical prooftext. In order to link the tree of life with Christ, the Genesis 3 text is read in light of the prologue to the Gospel of John. This seems to be the reason why Calvin is "not dissatisfied" with it. Other times, however, Calvin rejects Augustine's interpretations when he "speculates with excessive refinement."[150] When Augustine removes himself from what Calvin deems to be direct confrontation and struggle with the words of the biblical texts, Calvin tends to part company with his interpretation.[151]

Another of Calvin's favorite authorities from the history of the tradition is, not surprisingly, Chrysostom, who has a reputation for upholding the letter of the text.[152] Even here, Calvin is a fiercely independent reader of scripture and can reject even what Chrysostom has to say, as he does for example under the topic of the image of God:

> The exposition of Chrysostom is not more correct, who refers
> to the dominion which was given to man in order that he
> might, in a certain sense, act as God's viceregent in the
> government of the world. This is truly some portion, though
> very small, of the image of God.[153]

Calvin clearly has read widely in the tradition of interpreters before him. He reads with care and uses with discretion even those with whom he disagrees on both exegetical and doctrinal grounds. At times he differs from the tradition's understanding of the verbal sense of a passage, while at other times he objects to the doctrinal implications of traditional readings. Even when doctrinally motivated, Calvin's arguments against the tradition engage exegetical and verbal matters to support his case.

We have seen how Calvin's search for the literal sense of Genesis 1–3 is shaped by the concerns of his Humanist training, such as verbal meaning, narrative structure, author intentionality and the importance of the traditional "sources." We have also seen how these aspects of Calvin's search for the literal sense are themselves implicitly pressed into the service of Ruled reading. While on the surface, Calvin seems much more committed to textual matters than was Augustine, he is still clearly bound doctrinally in his interpretation of the literal sense, even where he will not admit it. In the following section, we will examine the concrete, explicit ways in which Ruled reading constrains Calvin's interpretation of the literal sense of scripture.

Constraints of Ruled Reading on Literal Sense

Historical Referentiality

Historical referentiality, or the extent to which the interpreter understands the text to refer to or tell of events in time and space, is for Calvin an important element in the reading of the literal sense of scripture. While we considered this aspect of Augustine's literal reading under the broader category of textual matters, it will become apparent why we are considering this for Calvin under the category of doctrinal constraints. This will be seen to be in part a possible result of the changing scientific worldview. In other words, Calvin seems to want to guard the literal reading from the necessity of committing itself to any one worldview.

For Calvin, Genesis tells the "history of the creation of the world."[154]
This he says in the context of answering the charge that Moses is speaking

> fabulously at things unknown, because he was neither a spec-
> tator of the events he records, nor had learned the truth of
> them by reading...For if they can destroy the credit of this his-
> tory, because it is traced back through a long series of past
> ages, let them also prove those prophecies to be false in which
> the same history predicts occurrences which did not take place
> till many centuries afterwards.[155]

Even though Moses was not present to witness the events, this does not mean
he invented a story, says Calvin. Rather, Moses tells only what has been
proven true by the fulfillment of prophecy. One example which Calvin gives
of the fulfillment of prophecy which anchors the truthfulness of the narrative is
the biblical text's testifying to the inclusion of the Gentiles. Calvin pins the
truthfulness of the creation story and indeed of all of Genesis to a
prophecy/fulfillment schema here, which in turn is tied to his understanding of
the biblical text as inspired:

> Was not he, who by the Spirit foresaw an event remotely
> future, and hidden at the time from the perception of mankind,
> capable of understanding whether the world was created by
> God, especially seeing that he was taught by a Divine Master?
> For he does not here put forward divinations of his own, but is
> the instrument of the Holy Spirit for the publication of those
> things which it was of importance for all men to know.[156]

The reason that Calvin can read a prophecy/fulfillment schema here is because
he understands Moses to be an instrument of the Holy Spirit. In other words,
the logical requirement for reading prophecy and its fulfillment for Calvin is
the assumption that Moses is being guided by the providence of God. At this
point in his argument Calvin then turns to the notion of an primeval "oral
tradition" which Moses uses. Truthfulness of the account of Genesis is
anchored here in historical referentiality as it is tied to prophecy-fulfillment,
inspiration of the Holy Spirit, and antiquity of tradition. Genesis can thus
reliably recount the "history of the creation of the world." The text refers historically in part because it is directed to a people within history.

...it is to be observed that when he describes paradise as in the east, he speaks in reference to the Jews, for he directs his discourse to his own people.[157]

Calvin reads Genesis as a story which is intended for his present generation and time no less than for Moses' generation and time, and for Moses' no less than for his own. However, says Calvin, Eden is to be understood to be in a particular geographical region, not extended over all the earth or symbolically present in particular places, because Moses presents it as being to the east of his own audience. This observation is hermeneutically important: Eden is not to be read allegorically or symbolically, as though it represented anything other than a specific place in which the things narrated in Genesis 2 and 3 took place. What Moses describes of Eden is not to be transferred to the whole world, insists Calvin, for we must

infer that this garden was situated on the earth, not as some dream in the air; for unless it had been a region of our world, it would not have been placed opposite to Judea, towards the east.[158]

Likewise, when Calvin discusses the rivers of Paradise, he goes to great (and painful for the reader) lengths to identify them, and begins by pinning down the two which he says many interpreters agree refer to the Euphrates and the Tigris. He then extrapolates from there to search for clues which would indicate the identity of the other two rivers named in Genesis 2, and even includes a map of the region which offers his own proposed solution to the geographical problem.[159] This map, whether from the hand of Calvin's secretary, des Gallars, or from a later editor is not interpretively important here, for Calvin does in his comments attempt to situate geographically Eden from the witness of scripture. He even backs up his suggested location for the garden with prooftexts from Isaiah 37:12 and Ezekiel 27:23, both of which make mention of Eden.

Likewise, Calvin trusts the reliability of the historical referentiality of the depiction of Eve's creation from Adam's rib at Gen 2:21. And at the serpent's words to the woman in Gen 3:1, Calvin notes that "the impious sneer" at Moses' description of the serpent as talking and charge him again in dealing in fables. Calvin retorts

Now, if men decide that whatever is unwonted must be fabulous, God could work no miracle. Here God, by accomplish-

ing a work above the ordinary course of nature, constrains us
to admire his power.[160]

Charging Moses with dealing in fables is therefore to ridicule the power of
God whose Spirit uses Moses as an instrument. Especially important to note in
this example is the logical link between the biblical text's ability to refer historically and the sovereignty of God. The reason that the text can be trusted to
refer historically ultimately rests on the prior doctrinal basis of the sovereignty
of God over that history.

However, it must also be said that Calvin is no "creation scientist". He
does use ancient "scientific" worldview by way of illustration, but in such an
ad hoc way that no particular authority is granted it. Rather, it serves only a
descriptive capacity.[161] At Gen 3:17 when discussing the curse of Adam,
Calvin states that it indicates the inverse of the blessing of fertility, now
spreading the withdrawal of God's favor to all the earth. Calvin likens this
ruin of man driving likewise to ruin all the creatures formed for his sake to the
sphere of Aristotelian natural philosophy moved by God the Prime Mover, the
only sphere with which God has immediate relationship.[162] Calvin makes the
comparison here, however, without recommending the theory of the *primum
mobile* in any normative way. The implication in this *ad hoc* use is that this
illustration is useful only for heuristic purposes in his reading of Genesis.

At times, secular science can guide Calvin's reading of the text in a positive way.[163] At Gen 3:9, "Let the waters... be gathered together in one
place," Calvin remarks at the miracle of the waters receding to give room for
humanity:

> For even philosophers allow that the natural position of the
> waters was to cover the whole earth, as Moses declares they
> did in the beginning; first, because being an element, it must
> be circular, and because this element is heavier than the air,
> and lighter than the earth, it ought to cover the latter in its
> whole circumference.[164]

Here, "science" helps to make sense of the text and throws in relief, again, the
providence of God. However, in fact it is the doctrine of God which governs
the use of science in Calvin's reading of Genesis and not vice versa.[165]

Calvin, following Augustine and many others before him, generally
rejects astrology: "He who would learn astronomy and other recondite arts, let
him go elsewhere."[166] He argues against the interpretation which takes Gen
1:14, "let them be for signs," to allow the possibility of astrological divining.

> I call those men Chaldeans and fanatics who divine everything
> from the aspects of the stars... But confutation is easy: for they
> are called signs of certain things, not signs to denote whatever
> is according to our fancy. What indeed does Moses assert to
> be signified by them, except things belonging to the order of
> nature?[167]

It is interesting to note here that Calvin's objection to astrology is very similar
to his objection to allegory: both take "signs of certain things" as denoting
"whatever is according to fancy," whereas Moses (the author) writes about the
order of nature and that is what the signs are supposed to denote, things in the
order of nature. Astrology reads natural signs as referring "unnaturally," or to
another order; allegory reads the words of the text as referring a- or extra-
textually. However, the investigations of astronomers are not necessarily to be
despised or ignored, and rejected out of hand because they are secular (Calvin
uses the term "unknown"): "For astronomy is not only pleasant, but also very
useful to be known: it cannot be denied that this art unfolds the admirable wisdom of God."[168] Such knowledge is formally like the knowledge of God the
Creator gleaned from the "book" of creation: apart from the Word such
knowledge is (soteriologically) fruitless except in its ability to convict us of
our sin and hold us accountable to God.

> Let astronomers possess their more exalted knowledge; but in
> the meantime they who perceive by the moon the splendour of
> the night are convicted by its use of perverse ingratitude unless
> they acknowledge the beneficence of God.[169]

Calvin even allows the possibility that astronomers may have knowledge of the
physical world which would contradict the biblical stories. Calvin says that
whereas Moses makes the sun and the moon the two "great luminaries,"
astronomers know that Saturn is in fact larger than the moon although it
appears smaller to us. Calvin accounts for this seeming error on Moses' part
to his understanding of textual accommodation, which allows him to be able to
uphold biblical authority:

> Moses wrote in a popular style things which, without instruc-
> tion, all ordinary persons endued with common sense are able
> to understand; but astronomers investigate with great labour
> whatever the sagacity of the human mind can comprehend.[170]

Yet Calvin never uses in his material on Genesis 1–3 an argument from pagan science to refute a biblical text. This could arguably be because the soon-to-wane "science" of his day could not do so. However, Calvin's hermeneutical principles have in other respects not been willing to bend to extra-biblical authority where authority of the Bible would be compromised. It is therefore difficult to imagine his allowing the new science on the horizon to trump his reading of the biblical story even if he had adopted a Copernican worldview.

Calvin does not explicitly acknowledge in his Genesis commentary the incoming scientific worldview, although at times it does indeed seem that he is aware of the Copernican theories.[171] In the context of refuting objections as to why God would have created the world only so recently, immediately after referring to Augustine's warning not to push questions regarding the infinity of time, Calvin comments that

> We indeed are not ignorant that the circuit of heavens is finite,
> and that the earth, like a little globe, is placed in the cen-
> ter...[172]

Calvin uses this point to support his contention that we should not proceed in our investigation any further than the Lord "by the guidance and instruction of his own works invites us."[173] Thus he argues on the basis of what he apparently deemed to be the still-reigning worldview to constrain interpretation.

Yet, later he seems to waffle regarding his own opinion on the position of the planets and the sun. In commenting on Gen 1:3, he says that it is clear from the context of the account that light and darkness alternate one with the other, but he is not sure whether it is day everywhere at the same time and then night everywhere, or if the light alternates with darkness first here and then there. In the end, he says that he would "rather leave the matter undecided, nor is it very necessary to be known."[174] Here is a prime example of a comment which may indicate that Calvin may have heard of Copernicus' theories but refused to acknowledge them as hermeneutically useful. He may deem the whole discussion (conveniently) unnecessary, or possibly even theologically dangerous.[175]

In discussing Gen 1:15, "let them be for lights," Calvin claims that Moses knew that the moon "had not sufficient brightness to enlighten the earth unless it borrowed from the sun."[176] However, Calvin says, Moses wrote as do all theologians with respect to and for the edification of their audience, who see and perceive the moon as though it were a "dispenser of light" on its own accord.[177] Even if Copernicus is somehow in the background here, Calvin stops short of committing himself one way or the other. Thus he is able to use science in an adiaphoric way; where it is useful, he can appeal to it to make an interpretive argument, but he seems to shy away from discussing the text openly with regard to the Copernican worldview.[178] The sovereignty of God is the lynchpin of Calvin's ability to accept and reject in an *ad hoc* fashion the new theories of heliocentrism.[179] The explication of the plain sense of scripture for Calvin thus relies only loosely on scientific theories. Ultimately, it is not science which guides Calvin's reading. That is, Calvin is not constrained to square the creation accounts of Genesis with scientific theories, but with an "orthodox" doctrine of God, or what we have called a Ruled reading.[180]

Accommodation

The category of accommodation is clearly an important hermeneutical tool for Calvin and is linked theologically to his understanding of the historical referentiality of the text. Somewhat as for Irenaeus, accommodation functions for Calvin within a larger understanding of the developing relationship of God and Israel, to strip texts of their hermeneutical "offense" and to allow them to speak meaningfully within a Christian context.[181] Accommodation thus supports and elaborates the theological topic of the unfolding of revelation and with it the unfolding of the capacity of the people of God to grasp it.

At times, therefore, Calvin sees this accommodation to be the work of Moses himself. According to Calvin it is Moses who calls the sun and moon the "great lights" in Gen 1:16. As we have seen, Calvin says that astronomers have shown that Saturn is larger than the earth's moon, and Calvin "apologizes" for the Genesis account by saying that

> Moses wrote in a popular style...because he was ordained a
> teacher as well of the unlearned and rude as of the learned, he
> could not otherwise fulfill his office than by descending to this
> grosser method of instruction.[182]

Moses himself in his capacity as writer engages in accommodation, according to Calvin, because of the lack of the "capacity of the people" to understand.[183] In discussing the rivers of Paradise at Gen 2:10, Calvin comments on the difficulty of identifying the rivers called the Pison and Gihon in the Genesis account. After a short discussion he adds that "Moses, in my

judgment, accommodated his topography to the capacity of his age, yet
nothing is accomplished unless we find that place where the Tigris and
Euphrates proceed from one river."[184] And at Gen 2:8, "And the Lord God
planted," Calvin explains that

> Moses says that God had planted, accommodating himself by a
> simple and uncultivated style, to the capacity of the vulgar.
> For since the majesty of God as it really is (*qualis est*) cannot
> be expressed the scripture is wont to describe it according to
> the manner of men.[185]

Here, even if the people were not such a "puerile" and vulgar lot, Moses
would still be at a lack to describe the majesty of God because of the nature of
God "such as it is" (*qualis est*). Accommodation for Calvin, therefore, works
on the basis of three presuppositions: the greatness and inexpressibility of
God, the dullness of the people, and the "expressed-ness" of God in creation
and redemption, that is, providence. The first implies the difficulty of ever
speaking of God, the second of understanding any such talk at that stage, the
third of the necessity of such talk because of the datum of God's desire to be
known.

From Gen 1:5, "there was evening and there was morning, the first day,"
comes the Jewish custom of reckoning the day as beginning with sundown.
Interestingly enough here, Calvin does not say that this text is the source of
such a custom, but that the custom is itself the reason for Moses' construction
of the account in this fashion.

> Although Moses did not intend here to prescribe a rule which
> it would be criminal to violate, yet... he accommodated his
> discourse to the received custom.[186]

The interpretation of this verse which supports the reckoning of day beginning
with the evening is not invalid according to Calvin, nor is to be enforced as
law, for it is simply an accommodation to the custom of the people who
received and cherished this text. Here, through this understanding of accommodation, Calvin sees the text to function as a window on social practice or as
at least a partial result of social practices. This to some extent is not far from
modern etiological explanations.

While in these examples Calvin notes that Moses accommodates his
speech, at other points Calvin sees God as the one who accommodates. When
this is the case, God is understood to accommodate not through the narration

itself, but through the happenings or "events" narrated. At Gen 1:22 where God blesses the fish and birds, Calvin acknowledges that it may seem nonsensical for God to address such dumb creatures, but states that "this mode of speaking was no other than that which might be easily understood."[187] From the context of Calvin's exposition here, it seems that he means to say that the benediction might be easily "understood" *by the fish and reptiles* (!) and not only by the readers of the account. Calvin says that this blessing is "infused into their nature, has taken root, and constantly bears fruit," namely, in their reproducing.

Calvin objects to the reading of the creation account which would credit Moses with distributing the narrative of God's work over the course of six days. Rather, according to Calvin, it is God Himself who "took the space of six days for the purpose of accommodating his works to the capacity of men."[188] Accommodation itself is in this respect not only a literary phenomenon, but it is seen by Calvin to be itself a divine activity which impacts not only the text but the time-space continuum as well. It is not simply the creation account but the act of creation itself narrated in the account which was distributed over the course of six days so that "our minds might the more easily be retained in the meditation of God's works."[189]

An interesting instance of what could have potentially been interpreted as accommodation by Calvin but was not is in the discussion of the narrative at Gen 3:21 where God replaces the fig-leaf aprons with garments of skin. Calvin says that Moses describes this in a "homely style"; in other words, we are not to read this as though God were some sort of Divine Furrier. Calvin offers the explanation that, at God's direction, Adam and Eve made their own garments out of the skins of the animals which God had given for their use. Calvin says that skins were used because they are of a more degrading appearance than woven cloth, and that this is an example to "accustom us to a frugal and inexpensive mode of dress."[190] Here, if "accommodation" were used as a hermeneutical device, the moral of the story, frugality, would have been set aside. Thus, in order to preserve the moral lesson, Calvin cannot offer an interpretation which views the narrative alone as accommodated.

It is apparent from these examples that the hermeneutical device of accommodation which Calvin employs within the rubric of literal reading is not merely the file, so to speak, used to smooth the puzzle pieces that do not "want" to fit into place.[191] Instead, Calvin has to rely on accommodation not only because of the Augustinian principle which he accepts that scripture cannot contradict itself. More importantly are the three presuppositions at play with regard to the nature of God and creation. God's being is such that human language is not capable of articulating it; God's people are so dull that they could not understand it even if language were apt; because of who God is God attempts to articulate His will. Therefore, accommodation must enter to fill the breach.

Linked to the device of accommodation is Calvin's understanding of the role of the Holy Spirit. While in the *Institutes*, Calvin emphasizes the role of the Holy Spirit in the interpretation of scripture, here in his comments on Genesis 1-3 there is only one main function of the Holy Spirit, and this pertains to the "composition" of the narrative. The Holy Spirit speaks through the mouth of Moses. The Holy Spirit has an intention or goal in the narrating of the creation account.[192] The Holy Spirit also "designedly relates by Moses the greatness of Adam's happiness in order that his vile intemperance might the more clearly appear."[193] In other words, the Holy Spirit shapes the narrative and has a goal which the text is supposed to accomplish, which Calvin usually understands under the rubric of sanctification.

Also, Calvin understands the Holy Spirit to "build" figures into the narrative. In discussing Gen 3:1, Calvin asks why Moses did not mention the name of Satan but instead spoke of the serpent. Calvin answers this question by agreeing with received opinion that "the Holy Spirit then purposely used obscure figures because it was fitting that the full and clear light should be reserved for the kingdom of Christ."[194] The Holy Spirit builds into the text, and into the story which it depicts, figuration. This is not for literary effect, nor to confuse or obfuscate. The story itself is already obfuscated, and only becomes understandable in the "kingdom of Christ," which interprets everything behind it. However, it should be noted that nowhere in his commentary on Genesis 1-3 does Calvin offer what he believes to be a plain sense reading on the basis of his own personally inspired reading of the Old Testament. Nowhere in this material does he indicate that the figured aspect of the text is such that it requires personal illumination in the form of exclusive information to "decode" the text.

We have seen here how Calvin's understanding of the accommodation of the text, hinged to the understanding of its historical referentiality, entails assumptions about the Holy Spirit's building or writing "figures" into the text and into the history which it depicts. These assumptions are supported by and in turn support Ruled reading, and thus function to constrain literal reading in accord with Calvin's doctrine of God.

Prooftexting

Another matter of significance for Calvin's understanding of the literal sense of scripture as it is constrained by Ruled reading is his prooftexting, or the use of one passage to interpret and warrant arguments regarding another passage.[195] The immensity of this subject will unfortunately allow us only to skim the top here, but it is important in his reading of the literal sense.[196] Calvin engages in prooftexting sometimes on the basis of verbal meaning and word correspondence, and sometimes on the basis of a previously reached understanding of the subject matter of the biblical text. In the first case, verbal meaning governs the correspondence between the texts; in the second case, doctrine governs the linkage. The overall effect of Calvin's prooftexting, however, is the presentation and use of the Bible as though it were one overarching story with a complex but nevertheless unitary development of plot, theme, and characters.

An example where a text is chosen for prooftexting on the basis of a combination of verbal correspondence or "catchword" and thematic linkage can be found at Calvin's consideration of Gen 3:8, "And they heard the voice of the Lord God." After discussing the phrase לרואח היום, "the breeze of the day," Calvin points to Ps 104:3 where David calls the winds the messengers of God.

> Moses here in mentioning the wind, intimates (according to my judgment) that some unwonted and remarkable symbol of the Divine presence was put forth which should vehemently affect the minds of our first parents.[197]

Here Psalm 104 opens a window, so to speak, on the interpretation of Gen 3:8. Calvin takes "the breeze of the day" as an implicit indication of God's presence. Later in remarking how futile it was for the pair first to use fig leaves to try to hide from God and then resort to hiding amidst the trees, Calvin quotes the verse from Ps 139:7, "Whither shall I flee from thy presence?" Here the Psalm verse is quoted as though from the lips of Adam and Eve themselves in their predicament.

At Gen 1:2, at the phrase "and the spirit of God," Calvin quotes Ps 104:30, "Send forth thy Spirit and they shall be created, and thou shalt renew the face of the earth." The Psalm verse illustrates the dependence of creation on the sustaining power of the Spirit of God. Both the catchword "spirit" and the theme of creation bring these texts together. The second text is used to inform and expand the first hermeneutically, as though the Psalm verse itself were commentary on Gen 1:2.

Sometimes the catchword type of prooftexting makes use of other texts within Genesis. At Gen 1:26, "image and likeness," Calvin refers to Gen 5:1, where the word "likeness" is used without reference to "image."[198] At Gen 1:27, with regard to the words "male and female" Calvin reads this account in light of the second creation story in Genesis 2. He argues that "the woman was added (to the man) as a companion that they both might be one, as he more clearly expresses it in the second chapter."[199] Calvin then refers to Malachi 2:15 to support his contention that this verse in Genesis speaks of the oneness of the first pair. Later at Gen 2:21 where Adam is sent into a deep sleep for the removal of the rib from which the woman is fashioned, Calvin refers back to this verse in Gen 1:28 to say that both of these texts underscore the unity of the first pair. And at the curse of Eve in which she is subjected to Adam (Gen 3:16), Calvin prooftexts Gen 4:7. This verse echoes the curse of Eve: "unto thee shall be his desire and thou shallt rule over him," but, interestingly enough, comes from the scene of Cain's jealousy over the acceptance of his brother Abel's offering. Here the immediate narrative context of Gen 4 dissolves as this verse is used as commentary on Gen 3:16. These examples show how Calvin's prooftexting knits together the narrative of Genesis, picking up thematic threads dropped earlier and reincorporating them, while simultaneously assuming that the larger biblical narrative itself is internally coherent.

Sometimes Calvin counts on the text's thematic and doctrinal coherence to yield also propositional coherence and truth. In discussing the rivers of Eden and their location, Calvin points to Gen 25:18, in which we hear that Ishmaelites dwell from Havila to Shur. He uses this information about this region, as though garnered from a great encyclopedia, to further his quest for the location of the rivers. And at Gen 3:6 where the first pair eats of the forbidden fruit, Calvin sides with Augustine against Pelagius. In commenting on this verse, Calvin concludes that sin does not come from Adam by imitation as Pelagius taught, but that scripture teaches that we are born in sin. As evidence of this he refers to Ps 51:5 where David (so Calvin says) declares that he was conceived in sin.[200] Here again, via the use of prooftexting, the canon functions as a compendium of "factual" and doctrinal proofs for the buttressing of exegetical (broadly defined) arguments.

Sometimes passages which use similar wording but contradict the text at hand are called forth as prooftexts in which the doctrinal issues at hand are discussed. Calvin questions, at Gen 1:26, why Moses should speak of both man and woman as in the image of God when Paul denies that woman is in the image of God. Here Calvin apparently refers to the complex argument in 1 Corinthians 11. Calvin offers the solution that Paul is speaking of domestic relations, and the image of God there is restricted to the man who has superiority over the wife "in degree of honor." But in the Genesis text, argues Calvin, Moses is speaking of the image of God in human nature "where the mind, will, and all the senses, represent the Divine order."201 The idea here is that contradictory passages must in some way be shown to be ultimately congruent with each other. If they appear contradictory, the reader must look again and inquire if the passages are speaking of different subjects. Again, at Gen 3:6 "When the woman saw...," Calvin notes that "Paul" indicates in 1 Tim 2:14 that "Adam was not deceived but the woman" but that in Rom 5:12 Paul says that sin did not come by the woman but by Adam himself. This leads Calvin to point out that

> the reproof which soon afterward follows, 'Behold, Adam is as one of us,' clearly proves that he also foolishly coveted more than was lawful, and gave greater credit to the flatteries of the devil than to the sacred word of God.202

Of course, at stake here is Calvin's understanding of the coherence of the biblical canon, both thematically and doctrinally, such that there can be no internal contradictions.

At times the catchword approach to prooftexting is used to refute possible readings counter to his own. At Gen 1:14, "let them be for them signs," Calvin quotes Is 44:25 and Jer 10:2 in refuting an interpretation which would look kindly on astrology. He declares that "the same God who here ordains signs testifies by Isaiah that he 'will dissipate the signs of the diviners' (Is 44:25) and forbids us to be 'dismayed at the signs of heaven' (Jer 10:2)." The catchword "signs" enables Calvin to draw support from these texts against the reading he opposes.

While texts are often chosen as prooftexts on the basis of similarity of wording, at other times thematic or theological correspondence governs the choice of text. This thematic correspondence is often based on the doctrine of God. For example, out of concern to expand on the sovereign activity of God, Calvin reads Gen 2:2, "And he rested on the seventh day," in light of John 5:17 as does Augustine. Calvin also reads it in light of Ps 104:29 to which he had referred in his reading of Gen 1:2 in discussing the Spirit's activity in creation. Both Ps 104:29, "when thou takest away their breath they die and return to their dust," and John 5:17, "My Father is working still and I am working" seem to contradict Gen 2:2, which indicates that God rested after the completion of creation. At stake is the sovereignty of God who is seen by Calvin to be always active, ever giving life and holding at bay the otherwise encroaching chaos. It is thus his understanding of the doctrine of God rather than catchwords in the text which allows him to draw these texts together in a nexus.

At Gen 3:1, in the serpent's speech to Eve, Calvin notes the question of the "impious" who wonder how Moses can ascribe eloquence to an animal which usually only hisses. Here he says that the "Gospel" declares that disembodied voices proclaim the glory of Christ. If this is so, he says, then all the easier it is to imagine that "speech should be elicited from the mouth of an animal."[203] At issue here again is the sovereignty and power of God which is able even to make a dumb animal speak coherently. And at Gen 3:19 "You are dust and to dust you shall return," Calvin will not leave the story there on the subject of death, but quotes 1 Cor 15:22 "all die in Adam, as they shall rise again in Christ." This, according to Calvin, is proof that the wound of death was inflicted by sin. Here the New Testament passage is brought in to the discussion of the Fall to expand on sin and redemption.

These are just a few examples which illustrate the rich use of prooftexting in which Calvin engages. In spite of Calvin's insistence on the literal sense in interpretation, such prooftexting is not tied exclusively to "catchword" linkage. Rather, it extends beyond a purely flat-footed verbal correspondence into doctrinal and thematic linking of biblical texts. This is another example of the impact of Ruled reading on Calvin's attempt to interpret the literal sense of the biblical text. The understanding of the text as inspired allows and even necessitates prooftexting. The choice of texts which he brings together is itself governed both by verbal correspondence and by doctrinal commitments.

Interpreter's Common Sense

For Calvin, even the interpreter's reason or common sense must submit to the commitments of Ruled reading. This is not to say that the interpreter's reason plays no role in reading the literal sense. Indeed, one aspect of the hermeneutical payout of Calvin's understanding of the role of the interpreter's reason or common sense in interpretation is that it can guide the formation of questions to pose the text. However, reason cannot have free reign with the investigation of the text but must bend to the goals and expectations required of Ruled reading.

Calvin will often question a point or make an assertion regarding the text based on what he calls "common sense," *sensus communis*, or knowledge commonly available to the general reader.[204] At Gen 1:1 he says that Moses gives the name "heaven and earth" to the confused mass which he then calls "waters" not only because this is the "seed of all the world" but also because this is the "generally recognized division of the world."[205] It is generally recognized, and therefore a matter of common sense. He backs up his argument that Moses had received the story of creation through oral tradition with the statement that "no sane person will doubt" this.[206] No sane person doubts what is held true by common sense. At Gen 1:6, the firmament dividing the waters from the waters "appears opposed to common sense," and therefore some resort to allegory, but Calvin attempts to show how the text is not opposed to common sense.[207] And at Gen 1:28, "Be fruitful and multiply," Calvin argues that this command is not to give reign to lust but is to be carried out within the chastity and holiness of the marriage covenant which God ordained from the beginning. Calvin warrants his argument by saying that this is "that law of nature which common sense declares to be inviolable."[208] And at Gen 3:15, "I will put enmity," Calvin says that this phrase simply means that "there will always be hostile strife between the human race and serpents" for it is natural that humans should abhor serpents.[209] Common sense is a form of natural knowledge.

Calvin begins his exploration of Gen 3:8, "in the cool of the day," by noting that Jerome translates the phrase 'at the breeze after mid-day' (*ad auram post meridiem*). Calvin points out that his Hebrew text reads 'at the wind of the day' (לרוח היום), and the Septuagint translates it 'at the evening' (ὁ δειλινον). Thus, Calvin notes, the interpretation is held by many that Adam (!) sinned at noon and was called to judgment around sunset. Calvin points out that, besides the fact that the Hebrew text speaks clearly of the day (היום), "we know that at the rising of the sun the air is naturally excited; together, then, with this gentle breeze, God appeared."[210] This example shows how common sense serves to guide interpretation only insofar as it does not contradict verbal sense: "Moses would not have improperly called the evening air that of the day."[211]

An example of a reversal of this use of common sense is in his discussion of Gen 1:20, "Let the waters bring forth swarms of living creatures."[212] He notes that since it does not seem to make sense that birds would have come out of the waters, there are some who charge the text with absurdity. If the text is examined with the eyes of "common sense," it appears indeed to be non-sensical. To conclude that the text is non-sensical, however, would be a violation of Ruled reading. To this Calvin retorts

Why should it not be lawful for him who created the world out
of nothing to bring forth the birds out of water? And what
greater absurdity, I pray, has the origin of birds from the water
than that of the light from darkness? Therefore, let those who
so arrogantly assail their Creator look for the Judge who shall
reduce them to nothing.[213]

Common sense is therefore useful as long as it does not lead one to despise
either the text or its Divine Author. Calvin then goes on to engage in
"physical reasoning" as he calls it in the attempt to explain this text by saying
that "water has greater affinity with the air than the earth has."[214] Thus,
while common sense in this example initially threatened to reduce the text to
absurdity, an option which is hermeneutically unacceptable for Calvin, in the
end he takes another tack. He uses a conclusion derived from "common
sense" to his advantage to defend the text.

Again, at Gen 2:21, "And the Lord God caused a deep sleep to fall,"
Calvin says that "to profane persons this method of forming woman may seem
ridiculous... yet to us the wonderful providence of God here shines forth."[215]
He then asks why perverse people would object to this except that this is at
variance with custom. To this he retorts that the usual method of forming
people is also unbelievable![216] Common sense, therefore, is not to be the
ultimate arbiter of the text when it threatens its authority and internal logic.
Here, common sense can be seen to function positively in uncovering plain
sense as long as the resulting interpretation does not conflict with doctrine.
And where common sense or reason is to be trumped in interpretation, it is
trumped by a broad understanding of the character of God which is gleaned
from the larger narrative of the economy of God:

I hold it as a settled axiom that nothing is more unsuitable to
the character of God than for us to say that man was created by
Him for the purpose of being placed in a condition of suspense
and doubt; wherefore I conclude that as it became the Creator,
he had before determined with himself what should be man's
future condition.[217]

Common sense or reason can therefore serve to generate interpretive questions,
and to stake out a set of interpretive possibilities, but it cannot be allowed to
conclude with interpretations which would violate Ruled reading.

Apologetics, Doctrine and the Christian Life

The most significant aspect of Calvin's reading of the literal sense as it is constrained by Ruled reading is how apologetics, doctrine and sanctification engage and bear on interpretation. To speak of apologetics, doctrine and attention to the concrete shape of Christian lives as though they were discrete topics in the work of John Calvin would be nonsensical: these are woven throughout the whole. To try to untangle them would be exceedingly difficult and probably not very useful. But it will be helpful in sketching the final details of the constraints of Ruled reading to look briefly at the ways in which the concerns of apologetics, doctrine and the Christian Life are played out in his comments on the first three chapters of Genesis.

As regards apologetics and polemics, Calvin seeks to defend his own interpretation of the text over against that of an unidentified "some" who have vague complaints against certain parts of scripture.[218] Sometimes he finds their hermeneutical violations too obviously egregious even to bother arguing with.[219] In other cases, he mentions specifically those whose interpretations he finds problematic. The readings of Servetus, the Anthropomorphites and Pelagius are just some of the "heretical" interpretations which come under attack in Calvin's commentary.[220] He finds their interpretations problematic because of the picture they present of God and the world. They imply the eternity of the world, impugn the good of marriage, compromise the sovereignty of God, and deny the doctrines of original sin and the Trinity.[221] The interesting thing to note in these examples is that most frequently it is the doctrinal assumptions and arguments drawn from the opponents' interpretations which bother Calvin. Less frequently is it their interpretations' construal of verbal meaning alone to which he objects.[222] However, hermeneutical violations, or in Calvin's words, "violent glosses," are no less preposterous even though they may refute theological error, which in and of itself is certainly considered a worthy task.[223]

Sometimes Calvin engages in hermeneutical polemic against those within "orthodoxy" who "misread" the text. He rebuts Augustine's interpretation of Gen 1:1 which reads the word "beginning" as a reference to Christ, for this is "altogether frivolous."[224] He also argues over textual distortions of the Vulgate, which the "Papists" fail to recognize or correct, and which support their theological assumptions and practices. At Gen 3:15, the phrase which the RSV translates as "he shall bruise," the Vulgate reads "she shall bruise" (*ipsa*

conteret). Calvin himself translates it "it shall bruise" (*ipsum vulnerabit*).
Calvin states that

> This passage affords too clear a proof of the great ignorance,
> dullness, and carelessness which have prevailed among the
> learned men of the Papacy...There has been none among them
> who would consult the Hebrew or Greek codices, or who
> would even compare the Latin copies with each other.[225]

Calvin complains that what he sees as a textual corruption in the Vulgate
allows the reading of the pronoun as an implicit reference to the Mother of
Christ. This then strengthens the "Papists'" biblical basis for the practice of
the veneration of Mary. This is, of course, an example of polemic over textual
matters which bear on doctrine. There is conceivably no place where textual
matters would not bear on doctrine, because for Calvin doctrine is to be discussed only with reference to the text. Hence, polemic and apologetic runs
throughout his exegetical work.

Calvin's concern for apologetics and doctrine in his biblical interpretation
are hinged to his construal of the subject matter of Genesis in terms of the
storied portrayal of God's relationship with Israel. This comes out most
clearly in his Argument which prefaces his Genesis commentary. Calvin's
point there that the intention of Moses in beginning his book with the account
of creation is to "render God, as it were, visible to us in his works" reveals
several assumptions.[226] First, obviously, is that Genesis is a coherent whole
with a goal or function to accomplish which in part derives from the writer's
intention and construction of the work. Second, the text describes the activity,
presence, or self-disclosure of God. Third, this God is inaccessible apart from
and is made known only in God's "activity." As Calvin says, "We know God
who is himself invisible only through his works."[227] Genesis is itself more
than merely a portrait or "mirror" of God in his works. Indeed, it tells not
only of the fall of humanity but also even of the "history of restoration where
Christ shines forth with the benefit of redemption".[228] It recounts the preservation of the Church and the commendation of the true worship of God. In
other words, Calvin understands the first book of the Bible to tell the entire
"Christian story". Since Genesis tells the entire Christian story, Calvin's
literal interpretation of a given text is often tailored by Ruled reading to allow
him to speak of the entire range of doctrinal loci as well as the theological
virtues.

An example in which Calvin's understanding of sin can be seen to shape
the reading of a passage is in his discussion of Gen 3:11, "Who told thee that

thou wast naked?" Calvin says that Adam's fear in this episode is based "not his nakedness but the turpitude of the vice by which he had defiled himself."[229] There is no obvious evidence in the text for such a reading, but Calvin's grasp of the nature of the rebellion guides his reading here. Calvin's understanding of propriety and the restraint of lust also comes out in his exposition of Gen 1:28, "And God blessed them..." He understands the text to say that while God intends the human race to be multiplied via biological procreation, this does not mean

> as in brute animals by promiscuous intercourse, for God has joined the man to his wife that they might produce a divine, that is, a legitimate seed... Certainly he does not give reins to human passions, but beginning at holy and chaste marriage, he proceeds to speak of the production of offspring.[230]

There is of course no indication of this question at all on the verbal level of the text, but it is a question indicated by Calvin's prior understanding of sin.[231]

Calvin's understanding of the doctrine of the Trinity guides his interpretation at Gen 1:26, "Let us make man..." Here he argues that "since the Lord needs no other counselor there can be no doubt that he consulted himself."[232] Christians may therefore justifiably hold the interpretation that there is a plurality of persons in the Godhead. However, unlike this reading of Gen 1:26, Calvin states at Gen 3:22, "Behold, the man has become as one of us," that the argument in support of the doctrine of the Trinity from this passage is "not sufficiently firm." This, he reasons, is because here "Adam is included in the word 'us,' but in the other place a distinction in the essence of God is expressed."[233] In other words, the "us" of Gen 1:26 refers only to the persons of the Godhead, whereas the "us" of Gen 3:22 includes Adam. Since the Godhead cannot include a human, this "us" cannot be read as a reference to the plurality of persons in the Godhead. Even while the doctrine of the Trinity can be seen to guide Calvin's interpretation of Gen 1:26, such doctrinal shaping of exegesis is inadmissible where it is understood to violate the verbal sense.[234]

Calvin's understanding of the character of God guides his interpretation at Gen 2:24, "Therefore a man shall leave his father and his mother..." Here he says that this does not indicate that God willingly severs family ties, for God would thus be acting "contrary to himself." Calvin understands filial piety to be an important aspect of obedience to God as is commanded in the Decalogue. Yet he argues that "Moses" wants to show with the statement in Gen 2:24 how the bond of marriage supersedes even the demands of filial piety, the fifth commandment notwithstanding. To read Gen 2:24 apart from the fifth commandment could be a perfectly acceptable reading of the strict verbal sense of this phrase alone, but would be a misrepresentation of the character of God, according to Calvin.[235]

Calvin's concern to highlight the power, sovereignty and providence of God is apparent throughout his material on Genesis. At Gen 1:7 in discussing the firmament which separates the waters above from the waters below, Calvin states that this is an instance of the power and providence of God in restraining the "cataract of heaven."[236] At Gen 1:16, Calvin comments that while Moses says that the greater light rules the day and the lesser light rules the night, this in no way is to be taken as diminishing or threatening the power of God, for both the sun and moon are still servants of God.[237]

That Calvin's God is consistently "in control" comes to play again in the interpretation of the fall of Adam. In his opening discussion of Gen 3, Calvin wants to make clear that evil did not occur without the permission of God.

> I hold it as a settled axiom that nothing is more unsuitable to
> the character of God than for us to say man was created by him
> for the purpose of being placed in a condition of suspense and
> doubt; wherefore I conclude that, as it became the Creator, he
> had before determined with himself what should be man's
> future condition.[238]

He explicitly says that this does not mean that Adam did not sin by free choice, and that the discussion of whether or not he sinned by necessity or by contingency is a separate matter entirely. However, Calvin concludes that God foreknew of the fall. This conclusion is not based on any explicit verbal evidence in the text itself, but on Calvin's own understanding of God's sovereignty even over Adam's sin. Calvin's concern to uphold God's constant activity at the sustaining of creation shapes his interpretation at Gen 2:2, "And he rested on the seventh day." Here Calvin notes like Augustine before him that God is constantly at work,

> for it is certain that inasmuch as God sustains the world by his
> power, governs it by his providence, cherishes and even
> propagates all creatures, he is constantly at work.[239]

Of course, Calvin refers to the text from John 5:17, "My Father is working still and I am working" as does Augustine to back up his statement. Calvin also refers to a favorite prooftext in his comments on the first three chapters of

Genesis, Psalm 104:29, "When thou hidest thy face, they are dismayed; when thou takest away their breath, they die and return to their dust." But ultimately, God's rest on the seventh day could not possibly indicate God's passivity or aloofness from creation for Calvin because he cannot imagine a God who is not actively at work.[240] Not only does a broader understanding of the subject matter of the text guide interpretation, but interpretation also serves to promote an understanding of this subject matter.

The relationship between literal interpretation and the interpreter's prior understanding of the subject matter of the biblical text is thus two-directional. For example, Calvin reads the curse at Genesis 3 with a clear interest in promoting the appreciation of salvation. At Gen 3:14, "And the Lord said unto the serpent...," Calvin says that the reason God here examines Adam and Eve is because he cares about their salvation.[241] Since God already knows everything, his discussion of their disobedience with them is evidence that he cares to correct the fault and mend the breach.[242] Here the interpretation is not so much guided by the doctrine of God but is designed to promote a particular aspect of the character of God and in turn to promote Calvin's understanding of humanity's relationship and responsibility to God.

Likewise, many of Calvin's remarks on the literal sense of passages are made with the purpose of fostering particular dispositions in his readers. More precisely, Calvin understands the goal of interpretation to be the shaping of moral character and the theological virtues in his readers.[243] Here Calvin's interpretation of the plain sense engages the concrete shape of Christian lives. Like Augustine, Calvin sees that proper reading of scripture functions to inculcate love of God and neighbor. However, Calvin is often more explicit as to the concrete moral shaping which is to be demanded by the literal sense of a specific passage than is Augustine. Proper interpretation of scripture according to Calvin's material on Genesis 1–3 should impress upon us God's goodness and therefore form in us gratitude and humility, which are to issue in obedience and stewardship, and finally give us hope and comfort.

The function of the narrative of the creation of the world over the course of six days should be to cause us to contemplate God and his goodness, to "fix our attention and compel us, as if he had laid his hand upon us, to pause and to reflect."[244] Such contemplation allows us to see the providence of God at work.[245] Likewise, Calvin's interpretation of the tree of life in Gen 2:9 serves to inculcate in the reader an understanding of the providence of God, which in turn should foster gratitude. An acquaintance with the providence of God should call from us gratitude for all of God's gifts and guidance of our lives.[246] Calvin remarks that rather than gratitude, however, we are more likely to respond with ingratitude because of the weight of the sin of our first parents. In the discussion of the fall of Adam and Eve, Calvin states that it is "monstrous ingratitude" which is displayed in the eating of the fruit of the tree of the knowledge of good and evil, for "they had been made in the likeness of God, but this seems a small thing lest equality be added."[247]

Since we owe God nothing but gratitude and yet are more inclined to ingratitude, one of the chief virtues or dispositions which Calvin attempts to elicit from his readers in his interpretation is humility.[248] For Calvin, humility means depending "upon the sole will of God whom we acknowledge as the Author of all good" and "renouncing all self-confidence, offer[ing] ourselves empty to Christ that he may fill us with his riches."[249] Our own wickedness is displayed in the text, and our being confronted with this should inculcate in us a deep sense of humility.

Humility is again to be engendered by the reading of Gen 2:7, "And the Lord God formed man of the dust of the ground." Calvin balances the reading of the creation of Adam in the image and likeness of God at Gen 1:26, which was the "highest nobility," with the creation of Adam from the dust of the ground in the second chapter of Genesis.[250] While the animals were brought forth from the earth at Gen 1:24 *animam viventem*, as living creatures, Calvin says that Adam was created

> destitute of sense to the end that no one should exult beyond measure in his flesh. He must be excessively stupid who does not hence learn humility.[251]

Yet even this is balanced by the statement that while the animals were created from the earth in a moment, the creation of Adam is given a "peculiar dignity" for he was

> gradually formed...For why did not God command him immediately to spring alive out of the earth, unless that by a special privilege he might outshine all the creatures which the earth produced?[252]

Another very important disposition for Calvin which is enjoined throughout his interpretation of Genesis 1–3 is obedience. Of the prohibition of the eating of the fruit of the tree of the knowledge of good and evil in Gen 2:16–17, Calvin says that "it would have made no difference to God if [Adam] had eaten indiscriminately of any fruit he pleased." However, argues Calvin, the command was imposed as a test and token of obedience.[253] Abstinence from this one tree was, as Calvin says, a "first lesson in obedience" for this is the "only rule of living well and rationally, that men should exercise themselves in obeying God."[254] And so from the failure of this first lesson, we learn how great our own wickedness is, for neither the "kind commemoration of the gifts of God nor the dread of punishment was able to retain" Adam in his duty.[255]

The flip-side of obedience might be in Calvin's terms (borrowed from Augustine) *curiositas*.[256] Although he does not use this word here, curiosity is what Calvin says causes our suffering even today, as we follow in the footsteps of Eve who

> erred in not regulating the measure of her knowledge by the
> will of God. And we all daily suffer under the same disease
> because we desire to know more than is right, and more than
> God allows; whereas the principal point of wisdom is a well-
> regulated sobriety in obedience to God.[257]

This obedience entails a restraining of lust for purposeless knowledge, namely, that which does not result in the praise of God and upbuilding in virtue.

Stewardship, a form of obedience, is enjoined in the discussion of Gen 2:15, "And the Lord God took the man and put him into the Garden of Eden to till and keep it."[258] Indeed, Calvin's concern for stewardship and care for the earth would please even the more rigorous environmentalist:

> Let him who possesses a field so partake of its yearly fruits
> that he may not suffer the ground to be injured by his
> negligence; but let him endeavor to hand it down to posterity
> as he received it, or even better cultivated. Let him so feed on
> its fruits that he neither dissipates it by luxury, nor permits to
> be marred or ruined by neglect.[259]

Stewardship is the form of obedience which Calvin finds most fitting to be enjoined in the reading of this element in the story. In being granted such abundant blessings, we are called to take care of them as custodians.

Calvin offers an interpretation of Gen 3 which even though it tells of our ruin serves to console us and to give us hope in the promises of God.[260] The words of the curse addressed to the serpent are not really for the sake of the serpent but for humanity.[261] And where God curses the serpent, a foil here for Satan, this is done for a two-fold reason: to warn and to assure.[262] Further consolation is offered by the phrase "between thee and the seed of the woman" of Gen 3:15, traditionally known as the "protoevangelium," which reads the curse as a blessing in disguise, so to speak. Here, however, Calvin sees the consolation in different terms from the traditional interpretation, which reads "seed" as a figure for Christ. By focussing on the word "woman," not on the word "seed,"[263] the consolation which Calvin sees here is not immediately siphoned off to our generation, nor is it tied exclusively to Christ as the "seed." Rather, the consolation is firmly anchored in the narrative at hand and offered to the character of Eve in her distress, which was greater than Adam's because of her greater share of responsibility in the sin. While Calvin does read this as a word of blessing, it is not in purely christological-figurative terms as is the traditional reading. Rather, it is closer to what he regards to be the "letter" of the text.

We have seen how because of the constraints of Ruled reading, the letter of the text cannot be read without engaging doctrine and ethics. Calvin understands the text to speak of the doctrine of God and of human responsibility, and he interprets the text in order to foster love of God and neighbor. This is therefore Calvin's most explicit correlate to Augustine's Rule of Charity.

Conclusion

As we saw for Augustine, so also we see for Calvin that the matter of expounding the literal sense of scripture is not as straightforward as one might have thought. Calvin negotiates carefully between the two elements of his own implicit understanding of literal reading, verbal sense and the doctrine of God. Calvin places more emphasis than did Augustine on verbal and lexical matters, in part because he had greater knowledge of biblical languages than did Augustine but also because of the influence which Humanist scholarship played on his understanding of what it means to read a text. The element of authorial intentionality is therefore more important in Calvin's understanding of literal sense than it was for Augustine, but for both authorial intent is extended to include that of the Divine Author. While Augustine's interest in verbal meaning tended to be logically pinned to his appreciation of the text's inspiration, Calvin's interest in verbal meaning, while certainly not excluding this element, is more patently a sign of his cultural milieu marked by Humanism. And while Calvin tends to be more adept than Augustine at reading the text as a narrative unity, noting junctures in style and thematic breaks, he relies even more heavily than did Augustine on an understanding of the canon as a whole as interpretive context. Here one might observe that where Augustine's conception of the Christian narrative is more in Neo-Platonic terms of the ascent of the soul, Calvin's conception of the Christian narrative is more in terms of the narrative of Israel as people of God. Therefore the story told by the canon is and must be the greater interpretive context. While Calvin understands the text to be speaking primarily on the basis of the letter, Ruled reading implicitly permits and indeed necessitates the reading of the text figuratively and the use of the text to expound doctrine and ethics. For Calvin more than for Augustine, it seems that the letter is "spiritual" and that the spirit comes in the form of the letter.

Notes

1. Of the sermons in manuscript, 620 are on Old Testament texts and 189 are on New Testament texts. See T. H. L. Parker, *Calvin's Preaching* (Louisville, Ky.: Westminster/J. Knox Press, 1992), 179.

2. According to Colladon, "When lecturing, he always had only the bare text of Scripture... he never had any paper before him as an aide-mémoire. And it was not as if he had adequate time to prepare; for whatever he may have wished, he simply had not the opportunity. To say the truth, he usually had less than an hour to prepare." *CO* 21,198-9; T. H. L. Parker, *Calvin's Old Testament Commentaries* (Edinburgh: T. & T. Clark, 1986), 21.

3. *CO* 13, 536; T. H. L. Parker, *Calvin's Old Testament Commentaries*, 24.

4. T. H. L. Parker, *Calvin's Old Testament Commentaries*, 26. Cf. Richard Stauffer, "Les Sermons Inédits de Calvin sur le Livre de la Genèse," *Revue de Théologie et Philosophie* (1965): 29-30. Calvin also preached on our Genesis texts, chapters 1 through 3, from Monday September 4, 1559 through Wednesday October 18, 1559. To the best of my knowledge these sermons are still "inédits."

5. The English translation of Calvin's Genesis commentary which I am using is John King, trans., *Commentaries on the First Book of Moses Called Genesis by John Calvin*, reprint, 1847, Calvin Translation Society (Grand Rapids: Baker Book House, 1979). The French translation used will be André Malet, with Pierre Marcel and Michel Réveillaud, eds., *Le Livre de la Genèse*, by Jean Calvin, La Société Calviniste de France: Commentaires de Jean Calvin sur l'Ancien Testament (Genève: Labor et Fides, 1961). The Latin will be quoted from *Ioannis Calvini Opera Quae Supersunt Omnia* vol. 23, from the *Corpus Reformatorum* vol. 51. It is unfortunate that the newer English translation expected from Eerdmans is not yet complete, for the King translation leaves much to be desired. Of the Calvin Translation Society, T. H. L. Parker says "...the Old Testament volumes are generally very badly edited. In few instances

are the footnotes at all helpful; often they are downright silly... The editor of Genesis adds to the score against him that he omits anything that might bring a blush to the cheek of the young person—Genesis 19:31 and 38:10 are left out in toto. The translating in most volumes is unsatisfactory." T. H. L. Parker, *Calvin's Old Testament Commentaries*, 2. King excises far more than just these two passages mentioned by Parker.

6. Haroutunian emphasizes Calvin's discontinuity with Augustinian exegetical method, saying that "allegorizing was misunderstanding, and misunderstanding was the evil a scholar had to avoid by all means." Joseph Haroutunian and Louise Pettibone Smith, eds., *Calvin: Commentaries*, Library of Christian Classics (Philadelphia: Westminster, 1958), 28. However, others would emphasize Calvin's continuity with Augustinian and medieval exegesis, e.g. Robert H. Ayers, "The View of Medieval Biblical Exegesis in Calvin's Institutes," *Perspectives in Religious Studies* 7 (1980): 189, 193.

7. T. H. L. Parker, trans., *The Epistles of the Apostle Paul to the Galatians, Ephesians, Philippians, and Colossians*, by John Calvin (Grand Rapids: Eerdmans, 1965), 84-5.

8. It is true that [Calvin] will use the terminology—*sensus literalis, allegoria*, and *anagogé*—that he expresses occasionally a preference for the literal sense and that he frequently voices impatient criticism of allegory. But he is not using the words with their classic "four-fold sense" meaning. His attacks on "allegory" are not necessarily against the *sensus allegoricus*, but against an over-elaborated use of allegory in its general sense of extended metaphor as well as against an allegorical interpretation imposed arbitrarily on a passage. Calvin can define allegory calmly in literary terms: "This whole speech is metaphorical; in fact, properly speaking, it is an allegory, for allegory is nothing but extended metaphor *(continua metaphora)*." However, more often he treats it as a hermeneutical aberration and sets it in opposition to simple truth and edification. T. H. L. Parker, *Calvin's Old Testament Commentaries*, 70.

9. William J. Bouwsma, *John Calvin: A Sixteenth Century Portrait* (Oxford: Oxford University Press, 1988); Haroutunian, *Calvin: Commentaries*, 27-37.

10. This only occurs *in medias res*, in the process of his exegetical remarks. Cf. his comments on Gal 4:22 just mentioned above where he acknowledges the richness of scripture but rejects the possibility of its containing "various meanings." T. H. L. Parker, *The Epistles of the Apostle Paul to the Galatians, Ephesians, Philippians, and Colossians*, 84-5.

11. Indeed, Calvin has left us no systematic exposition on hermeneutical

method at all, apart from his considerations of the interpretation of scripture in the *Institutes* (e.g. 1.6-9; 2.9-11) as well as his prefatory letter to his commentary on Romans. We have nothing from Calvin analogous to Melanchthon's *Erotematum dialectices, de methodo*, Erasmus' *Ratio verae theologiae*, Bucer's *Quomodo S. Literae pro concionibus tractandae sint instructio*, or Bullinger's *Studiorum ratio, sic hominis addictis institutio*. Richard C. Gamble, "Brevitas et Facilitas: Toward an Understanding of Calvin's Hermeneutic," *Westminster Theological Journal* 47 (1985): 1.

12. E.g., see his comments on Gen 4:1, King, *Genesis*, 190. *CO* 23, 81.

13. See his comments on Gen 16:12, King, *Genesis*, 434. *CO* 23, 229-230.

14. Re: Gen 6:14, King, *Genesis*, 257. *CO* 23, 122-123. Note here how the "natural treatment" is distinguished from the allegories of Augustine and Origen, yet the resulting interpretation is such that the ark "was an image of the church." Of course, Calvin authorizes this figural interpretation on the basis of 1 Peter 3:21.

15. Cf. 49:1, King, *Genesis*, vol. 2, 439. *CO* 23, 590.

16. Cf. Gen 49:12, King, *Genesis*, vol. 2, 461. *CO* 23, 603.

17. For example, see Gordon Bates, "The Typology of Adam and Christ in John Calvin," *Hartford Quarterly* 5 (1965): 46. "Although he rejected allegorization as a hermeneutical method because it did not maintain the literal and historical meaning of the text, Calvin did make frequent use of typology, a method of interpretation which did do so, and which also had roots in the Bible (particularly in Paul) as well as in the Church Fathers." Bates appears to rely on a definition of typology such as that offered by G. W. H. Lampe and K. J. Woolcombe, *Essays on Typology*, Studies in Biblical Theology (Naperville, IL: Alec R. Allenson, 1957), 39. See also R. P. C. Hanson, *Allegory and Event: A Study of the Sources and Significance of Origen's Interpretation of Scripture* (Richmond, VA: John Knox Press, 1959), 7; Erich Auerbach, *Mimesis: The Representation of Reality in Western Literature*, trans. William Trask (Princeton, NJ: Princeton University Press, 1953), 53; Henri Crouzel, "La Distinction de la 'Typologie' et de 'l'Allegorie'," *Bulletin de Littérature Ecclésiastique* 65 (1964): 161-74. James Barr has questioned the "historicity" of typology and the "ahistoricity" of allegory assumed by Lampe and Woolcombe, et alii. James Barr, "Typology and Allegory," in *Old and New in Interpretation* (New York: Harper and Row, 1966), 103-48.

18. David Dawson describes typology is a subset of allegory: "...typology is simply a certain kind of allegorical reading promoted as non-allegorical for specific theological and rhetorical reasons." David Dawson,

Allegorical Readers and Cultural Revision in Ancient Alexandria (Berkeley: University of California Press, 1992), 16.

19. E.g. see his discussion of Gen 3:8, "And they heard the voice of the Lord God," King, *Genesis*, vol. 1, 160. *CO* 23, 65. Cf. *Institutes* 1.13.3-4; 2.11.7-8; and 4.17.20-25 for examples there of discussion of the way words function in scripture.

20. King, *Genesis*, 124. *CO* 23, 44.

21. Brevity is the first exegetical principle identified in H. J. Kraus, "Calvin's Exegetical Principles," *Interpretation* 31 (1977): 8-18, and is much emphasized in the work of Richard Gamble.

22. King, *Genesis*, 114. *CO* 23, 37.

23. Cf. Calvin's comments on Gal 4:22, where he calls allegorical interpretation which "twists Scripture" a "trick of Satan to impair the authority of Scripture and remove any true advantage out of the reading of it." T. H. L. Parker, *The Epistles of the Apostle Paul to the Galatians, Ephesians, Philippians, and Colossians*, 84.

24. King, *Genesis*, 114-15. *CO* 23, 37. Again, "What advantage is it to fly in the air, and to leave the earth, where God has given proof of his benevolence towards the human race?... since the eternal inheritance of man is in heaven, it is truly right that we should tend thither; yet must we fix our foot on earth long enough to enable us to consider the abode which God requires man to use for a time."

25. The question then presents itself how Calvin would read, say, Song of Songs. This, however, would be a topic for a different book.

26. King, *Genesis*, 79. *CO* 23, 18.

27. King, *Genesis*, 132. *CO* 23, 48. Again, he warns that allegorical interpretation is to be avoided at the episode of the flaming sword which guards Paradise at Gen 3:24. Calvin says that one should not read the word "turned" here (*versatilis*) as though this indicated that an opportunity to repent was allowed, for "allegory is unseasonable when it was the determination of God altogether to exclude man from the garden, that he might seek life elsewhere." King, 185. *CO* 23, 80.

28. For examples of his figurative readings in the rest of the Genesis commentary, see his comments re: 6:14, *CO* 23, 122-23; 7:17, *CO* 23, 133-34; 11:1, *CO* 23, 162-64; 14:18, *CO* 23, 200-203; 15:4, *CO* 23, 210-11; 15:10, *CO* 23, 216-17; 15:17, *CO* 23, 221; 17:8, *CO* 23, 238-39; 17:12, *CO* 23, 241-42; 19:1, *CO* 23, 267; 21:12, *CO* 23, 302-303; 25:23, *CO* 23, 349-52; 27:27, *CO* 23, 378; 28:12, *CO* 23, 390-92; 28:13, *CO* 23, 392; 48:16, *CO* 23, 585; 49:10, *CO* 23, 598; 49:24, *CO* 23, 607; 50:2, *CO* 23, 612-13; 50:24, *CO* 23, 621-22.

29. King, *Genesis*, 106. *CO* 23, 33.

30. "So far as the Sabbath was a figure of this rest, I say, it was but for a season; but inasmuch as it was commanded to men from the beginning that they might employ themselves in the worship of God, it is right that it should continue to the end of the world." King, *Genesis*, 106-7. *CO* 23, 33.

31. King, *Genesis*, 117. *CO* 23, 38.

32. King, *Genesis*, 117-18. *CO* 23, 39.

33. King, *Genesis*, 184. *CO* 23, 79.

34. King, *Genesis*, 141.*CO* 23, 53.

35. King, *Genesis*, 141. *CO* 23, 53.

36. Eric Kayayan, "Accommodation, Incarnation et Sacrement dans l'Institution de la Religion Chrétienne de Jean Calvin," *Revue d'Histoire et de Philosophie Religieuses* 75 (1995): 273-87; Ford Lewis Battles, "God Was Accommodating Himself to Human Capacity," *Interpretation* 31 (1977): 19-38; O. Millet, *Calvin et la Dynamique de la Parole: Etude de Rhétorique Réformée* (Paris: Librairie Honoré Champion, 1992), 247-56; D. F. Wright, "Accomodation and Barbarity in John Calvin's Old Testament Commentaries," in *Understanding Poets and Prophets: Essays in Honour of George Wishart Anderson*, ed. Grame Auld (Sheffield: Sheffield University Press, 1993), 413-27; Stephen D. Benin, *The Footprints of God: Divine Accommodation in Jewish and Christian Thought* (Albany: State University of New York, 1993).

37. King, *Genesis*, 141. *CO* 23, 53.

38. See King, *Genesis*, 186. *CO* 23, 79-80.

39. King, *Genesis*, 141. *CO* 23, 53.

40. King, *Genesis*, 142. *CO* 23, 54. See his comments on Ps 1:11, in which he claims that his christological reading ("[David], with his posterity, was created king, not so much for his own sake, as to be the image of the Redeemer") is not twisting the words but is the true sense, the primary referent.

41. King, *Genesis*, 165-66. *CO* 23, 68.

42. King, *Genesis*, 168. *CO* 23, 70.

43. King, *Genesis*, 168. *CO* 23, 70. Emphasis mine.

44. Cf. *CO* 24, 80 where Calvin comments on Ex 6:7: "We must hold that between us and the Israelites there is an anagogé or similarity." Cited in Parker, who defines Calvin's understanding of the term anagogé as "not merely a comparison that happens to arise in the expositor's mind but an application that is demanded by the letter of the text." T. H. L. Parker, *Calvin's Old Testament Commentaries*, 72. According to Calvin's description of the relationship between the two covenants, this anagogé between us and the Israelites indicates a similarity which goes further

than merely the descriptive or experiential. Cf. *Institutes* 2.10-11.

45. King, *Genesis*, 169. *CO* 23, 70.
46. King, *Genesis*, 170. *CO* 23, 71.
47. King, *Genesis*, 171. *CO* 23, 71.
48. This is not the usual reading of Calvin's interpretation of Genesis 3:15. See, for example, Wilhelm Heinrich Neuser, ed., *Calvinus Sacrae Scripturae Professor: Calvin as Confessor of Holy Scripture*, Die Referate des Congrès International des Recherches Calviniennes, 1990 (Grand Rapids: Eerdmans, 1994), 52.
49. C. T. R. Hayward, *Saint Jerome's Hebrew Questions on Genesis: Translated with an Introduction and Commentary* (Oxford: Clarendon Press, 1995), 33.
50. T. H. L. Parker is one of the few who comes close to pressing this question: "It will not be improper to ask, as a last word on *anagogé*, whether this is not the *sensus spiritualis, sensus mysticus*, under another name, so that what Calvin was doing was admitting the spiritual sense in such a way as to safeguard the historicity of the text—the historicity which was as good as dissolved by arbitrary spiritualising. In the following passages on Gen 15:11 it is hard to see much difference between his comments and 'allegory'..." T. H. L. Parker, *Calvin's Old Testament Commentaries*, 74.
51. This phrase is used much in the period of the Reformation, and can be traced back to Geiler of Kaisersberg in the fifteenth century. Basil Hall, "Biblical Scholarship: Editions and Commentaries," in *The Cambridge History of the Bible, Vol. 3*, ed. S. L. Greenslade (Cambridge: Cambridge University Press, 1963), 79. Calvin uses it elsewhere, for example: "What! So the Church's decrees are to be reduced to nothing, are they? The Scripture is a wax nose; it has nothing sure or consistent; it can be twisted into any direction, and hypocrites always abuse the Word of God." *CO* 38, 311; CTS Jer 2, 419.
52. On Calvin and Humanism, see Quirinius Breen, *John Calvin: A Study in French Humanism* (Grand Rapids: Eerdmans, 1931); Bouwsma, *John Calvin: A Sixteenth Century Portrait*; Millet, *Calvin et la Dynamique de la Parole: Etude de Rhétorique Réformée*. Also, see the chapter on "The impact of classical and biblical studies at the Collège Royale" in T. F. Torrance, *The Hermeneutics of John Calvin* (Edinburgh: Scottish Academic Press, 1988), 126-55.
53. Richard Simon greatly underestimated Calvin's knowledge of Hebrew according to A. J. Baumgartner, *Calvin Hébraïsant et Interprète de l'Ancien Testament* (Paris: Librairie Fischbacher, 1889) and William McKane, "Calvin as Old Testament Commentator," *Nederduitse*

Gereformeerde Teologiese Tydskrif 25 (1984): 250, the latter of whom believes that Calvin studied Hebrew under François Vatable in 1531 at the Collège de France, which had been founded as a trilingual college the previous year. For a more cautious view, see G. Lloyd Jones, *The Discovery of Hebrew in Tudor England: A Third Language* (Manchester: Manchester University Press, 1983), 71.

54. T. H. L. Parker, *Calvin's Old Testament Commentaries*, 6. Calvin may have had in his library, among other things, the Hebrew grammar of Conrad Pellican of 1503-4, and that of Johannes Reuchlin of 1506, Sebastian Münster's Hebrew and Aramaic lexicon of 1523, whose Hebrew grammar of 1556 which was based on the work of the Jewish scholar Elias Levita who himself was dependent upon David Kimchi. Pieter A. Verhoef, "Luther's and Calvin's Exegetical Library," *Calvin Theological Journal* 3 (1968): 17. Calvin may also have had the Hebrew grammars of Pagnini of Lucco of 1546 and W. F. Capito of 1518. The major editions of the Hebrew Bible text in existence at that time included the Complutensian Polyglot which contained the Hebrew text, the Septuagint with an interlineary Latin translation, the Vulgate, and the Targum Onkelos with a Latin translation beside it. Hall, "Biblical Scholarship: Editions and Commentaries," 51-52. The first and second Rabbinical Bibles of Daniel Bomberg (1516-17 and 1524-25), the latter of which provides the medieval *textus receptus*, were also available. Etienne's edition (1539-44) used the second Rabbinical Bible, and Münster's edition (1535) used the first. See H. F. van Rooy, "Calvin's Genesis Commentary: Which Bible Text Did He Use?" in *Our Reformational Tradition: A Rich Heritage and Lasting Vocation*, ed. H. F. van Rooy (Potchefstroom: Potchefstroom University, 1984), 204; Anthony N. S. Lane, "Did Calvin Use Lippoman's 'Catena in Genesim?'," *Calvin Theological Journal* 31 (1996): 404-19; and Baumgartner, *Calvin Hébraïsant et Inteprète de l'Ancien Testament*, ch. 1.

55. See the description of how Calvin lectured in T. H. L. Parker, *Calvin's Old Testament Commentaries*, ch. 1.

56. E.g., "I know not why the Greeks have chosen to render the word σ῀ερεωμα, which the Latins have imitated in the term *firmamentum*; for literally it means expanse." Re: Gen 1:6, King, *Genesis*, 79. *CO* 23, 18.

57. He also refers to Jerome, but never connects the name of Jerome with the Vulgate. R. J. Mooi, *Het Kerk- en Dogmahistorisch element in de werken van Johannes Calvijn*, (Wageningen ZJ, 1965) 136, cited in Verhoef, "Luther's and Calvin's Exegetical Library," 477.

58. King, *Genesis*, 113. *CO* 23, 36.

59. King, *Genesis*, 115. *CO* 23, 37, *falsus est vetus interpres*. This comment is also a product of Calvin's protracted attempt to locate the four rivers and the geographical area of Eden in order to insist upon its existence as a reality within the time-space continuum and not to allow it to be allegorized into an idea. See the discussion on this below.

60. King, *Genesis*, 103. *CO* 23, 50.

61. "Calvin first recited each verse in Hebrew and then turned it into Latin." T. H. L. Parker, *Calvin's Preaching*, 173. Most of Calvin's Old Testament commentaries, including most of the Genesis commentary, were originally composed in the form of extemporaneous lectures which were then transcribed. See the discussion above. Cf. T. H. L. Parker, *Calvin's Old Testament Commentaries*, 24–5; T. H. L. Parker, *Calvin's Preaching*, 65–69; Haroutunian, *Calvin: Commentaries*, 17, 24.

62. Even some of his forays into etymology have been supported, e.g.: "The word commonly rendered whales (*cetos vel cete*) might, in my judgment, be not improperly translated tynnus or tuna fish, as corresponding with the Hebrew word תנינם." Heinrich Lewy, *Die Semitischen Fremdwörter Im Griechischen* (Berlin: Gaertners, 1895), 15. Cf. Gen 1:21. King, *Genesis*, 89. *CO* 23, 24. The Hebrew word here in the Latin text is not in Hebrew characters but is transliterated: *thaninim*.

63. King, *Genesis*, 103. *CO* 23, 31. The Hebrew here in the Latin text is in Latin translation, not transliteration.

64. King, *Genesis*, 135. *CO* 23, 50. In the Latin text, the word הפעם is given in its Latin translation, but the word אשה is given in Hebrew.

65. King, *Genesis*, 150. *CO* 23, 53. The Latin text gives the Hebrew word.

66. He suggests that both significations of the participle מרחפת (moving; *agitabat se*) are applicable to its use in Gen 1:2, indicating both that the Spirit was in its activity putting forth vigor and brooding over the waters like a mother hen over her eggs. *CO* 23, 16. Latin text gives the Hebrew word here.

67. At the serpent's words in Gen 3:5, Calvin notes that some translate Elohim as angels while others as God. He states that he himself had no doubt that "Satan promises them divinity...moreover it is not without some show of reason that he makes the Divine glory, or equality with God, to consist in the perfect knowledge of good and evil..." King, *Genesis*, 151. *CO* 23, 59. In discussing Gen 1:14, he points out that מועדים (RSV: seasons) can mean time, season and assembly of persons. He goes on to say that while the Rabbis refer the term to the Jewish festivals, he would understand it to refer to seasons, fairs and forensic assemblies. *CO* 23, 21. The Latin text here gives the Hebrew word.

68. Malet, *La Genèse*, 83. This is from one of the many lacunae in the King

translation, where evidently prudishness has prevented King from translating Calvin's commentary in its entirety. *CO* 23, 71.

69. King, *Genesis*, 138; Malet, *La Genèse*, 63. *CO* 23, 72; cf. 23, 52.

70. A well-trained rhetorician, Calvin points out rhetorical devices in the text
of Genesis and uses these observations in coming to exegetical conclusions throughout his commentary. Cf. *Institutes* 4.17.21. See Millet,
Calvin et la Dynamique de la Parole: Etude de Rhétorique Réformée.

71. King, *Genesis*, 110. *CO* 23, 34, note 1: Ed. Gen. 1554.

72. King, *Genesis*, 168. *CO* 23, 70.

73. For example, in reading "let them have dominion" at Gen 1:26, Calvin
says that the use of the plural number of the verb is significant, for it
indicates that this authority is given not only to Adam but also to his
posterity. *CO* 23, 26. Again, in reading Gen 1:31, he says that now in
God's seeing that creation is good, the word "very" (מאד, transliterated
in the Latin text) is added, indicating that at this finishing touch of creation, the formation of humanity, God pronounces it perfectly good such
that nothing more needs to be added. *CO* 23, 30.

74. King, *Genesis*, 180. *CO* 23, 77.

75. King, *Genesis*, 181. *CO* 23, 77. The term *protoevangelium* refers to the
traditional christological reading of the curse of the serpent: "The first
announcement of the redemption to be effected in and through Christ
given figuratively to Adam and Eve in the words of God to the serpent, 'I
will put enmity between you and the woman, and between your seed and
her seed; he shall bruise your head and you shall bruise his heel' (Gen
3:15)." Richard Muller, *Dictionary of Latin and Greek Theological
Terms* (Grand Rapids: Eerdmans, 1985), 251.

76. King, *Genesis*, 181. *CO* 23, 77.

77. King, *Genesis*, 93-4. *CO* 23, 26.

78. He points out that in Gen 2:18, the preposition which he translates *coram
ipso*, "fit for him" (RSV) is in Hebrew כנגדו. *CO* 23, 47. Calvin says
that the prefix כ denotes similitude and is intended by Moses to denote
some equality between Adam and Eve. Therefore, on the basis of כ Calvin argues against the interpretation that would understand Eve to have
been formed only for the sake of procreation, and he argues that the כ
asserts that "marriage extends to all parts and usages of life."

79. Likewise, in discussing Gen 1:2, Calvin notes that the words תוהו and
בוהו ("without form and void") are used by the Hebrews to designate that
which is empty, confused, vain and worthless, and are used here in this
passage in contradistinction to the perfection of the created order. *CO*
23, 16.

80. King, *Genesis*, 95. *CO* 23, 27.

81. Another example of verbal sense trumping doctrinal reading is at Gen 1:1, where Calvin points out that the name of the divinity is a noun of plural number, אלהימ, Elohim. This is, however, no reason to insist that the three persons of the godhead are hereby noted. This argument is not based itself on purely grammatical grounds, but on doctrinal grounds: Calvin says that this "proof of so great a matter...has little solidity." To hang such an important doctrinal point on such a thin exegetical thread is therefore a "violent gloss". King, *Genesis*, 98. *CO* 23, 15.

82. King, *Genesis*, 91. *CO* 23, 25. *Faciamus* is also the present active subjunctive as well as the future active indicative. See also re: Gen 21:7. "I understand the future tense to be here put for the subjunctive mood." *CO* 23, 298. Reading the verb as subjunctive might have lent more weight to Calvin's statement that this is the language of one deliberating.

83. King, *Genesis*, 91. *CO* 23, 25.

84. King, *Genesis*, 92-3. *CO* 23, 25. King argues that since in the French translation the words translated "wisdom" and "power" are capitalized ("*Comme à la vérité, sa Sapience éternelle, et Vertu réside en lui*"), the second and third persons of the Trinity are hereby intended. He points to Calvin's comments on Gen 1:3 (p. 75, n. 2, 5) where similarly the French translation has capitalized the word translated wisdom ("*Sagesse*"), indicating Calvin's possible reference by Sagesse to the second person of the Trinity. Even though in this particular instance Calvin is clearly making a general reference to the Trinity, to hang such a doctrinal claim on such a narrow orthographical thread may be, as Calvin would say, a "violent glosse!"

85. Indeed, this is true of his reading of Genesis as a whole; in his opening Argument it is clear that it is the doctrine of God which generates narrative coherence and unity.

86. See his comments in the Argument which indicate that the story of Genesis becomes reiterated daily in the life of the Christian, King, *Genesis*, 57-66. *CO* 23, 6-12.

87. King points out that the printing of the word wisdom with a capital W (*Sagesse*, so Malet) "renders it probable that by it Calvin means the Son of God... he intends the whole of what he here says as an argument in favor of the deity of Christ." King, *Genesis*, 75, n. 3. The Latin text in the *Corpus Reformatorum* does not print *sapientia* with a capital. King may or may not have a point regarding the use of capital letters, but more apropos here would be Calvin's use of John 1:3 in conjunction with the interpretation of Genesis 1:3, for a "plain" reading of that text understands the Word in Christological terms.

88. King, *Genesis*, 76. *CO* 23, 17.

89. King, *Genesis*, 82. *CO* 23, 20.
90. King, *Genesis*, 100. *CO* 23, 30.
91. King, *Genesis*, 96. *CO* 23, 28.
92. King, *Genesis*, 97. *CO* 23, 28.
93. King, *Genesis*, 111. *CO* 23, 30.
94. King, *Genesis*, 180. *CO* 23, 77.
95. King, *Genesis*, 100. *CO* 23, 78.
96. King, *Genesis*, 145. *CO* 23, 52.
97. King, *Genesis*, 149. *CO* 23, 54.
98. King, *Genesis*, 150. *CO* 23, 58.
99. King, *Genesis*, 151. *CO* 23, 59.
100. King, *Genesis*, 155. *CO* 23, 62.
101. King, *Genesis*, 161. *CO* 23, 66.
102. King, *Genesis*, 127. *CO* 23, 45.
103. "Calvin wants the text to say more than it does. And when the text refuses to do so, Calvin provides the missing material. One reason Calvin does this may be that, if Auerbach is correct, there is a sense in which the text invites such a move. The hiddenness of the text may have something to do with its power to entice the reader into the world of the text. Precisely because the text is 'fraught with background' it invites the reader to engage in interpretation." George Stroup, "Narrative in Calvin's Hermeneutic," in *John Calvin and the Church: A Prism of Reform*, ed. Timothy George (Louisville: Westminster/John Knox Press, 1990), 164. "Fraught with background" is Auerbach's term. Auerbach, *Mimesis: The Representation of Reality in Western Literature*, 11–12.
104. King, *Genesis*, 142. *CO* 23, 54.
105. King, *Genesis*, 143. *CO* 23, 54.
106. Another example where Calvin comments on the story's silence is at the discussion of Gen 3:22, "behold the man is become as one of us": "There is a defect in the sentence which I think ought to be thus supplied: 'It now remains that in future he be debarred from the fruit of the tree of life,' for by these words Adam is admonished that the punishment to which he is consigned shall not be a moment..." King, *Genesis*, 183-4. *CO* 23, 79.
107. King, *Genesis*, 133. *CO* 23, 49.
108. King, *Genesis*, 181. *CO* 23, 78.
109. Breen, *John Calvin: A Study in French Humanism*; Millet, *Calvin et la Dynamique de la Parole: Etude de Rhétorique Réformée*, 299–310.
110. E.g., "the design of Moses," Gen 1:6, *CO* 23, 18 (*usum specialem exprimit Moses*); "the meaning of the words of Moses," Gen 2:2, *CO* 23, (*sonant Mosis verba*) ; "the design of Moses," Gen 2:4, *CO* 23, 34

(*consilium Mosis*); "Moses intended nothing more..." Gen 2:7, *CO* 23, (*referat Moses*); "Moses intended to note," Gen 2:18, *CO* 23, 48 (*exprimere voluit Moses*).

111. "Some take it thus...but this exposition is harsh", re: Gen 2:3, King, *Genesis*, 107. *CO* 23, 33.

112. Aurelius Augustine, *De Genesi Ad Litteram, Libri Duodecim*, ed. Joseph Zycha, Corpus Scriptorum Ecclesiasticorum Latinorum (Vindobonae, Pragae: F. Tempsky, 1894), 1.6.12.

113. Again, various interpretations of the participle מרחפת in Gen 1:2 arise because "all do not attain the meaning of Moses", and this is an important clue to plain sense. King, *Genesis*, 73. *CO* 23, 16.

114. King, *Genesis*, 95. *CO* 23, 27.

115. King, *Genesis*, 58. *CO* 23, 6.

116. King, *Genesis*, e.g., 108. *CO* 23, 32.

117. "Moses also designedly used the word 'built' to teach us that in the person of the woman the human race was at length complete which had before been like a building just begun." Gen 2:21, King, *Genesis*, 133. *CO* 23, 49.

118. King, *Genesis*, 141. *CO* 23, 56.

119. Gen 2:23, King, *Genesis*, 135. *CO* 23, 50. In like manner, in discussing the phrase from Gen 2:24, "they shall be one flesh," Calvin notes that this appears in the Gospel of Matthew: "Thus Christ cites the place in Matthew 19:5." *CO* 23, 51. The impression given by this turn of phrase is that Christ narrates and authors Matthew's own gospel.

120. King, *Genesis*, 59. *CO* 23, 7-8. Another example: "The Holy Spirit also designedly relates by Moses the greatness of Adam's happiness..." re: Gen 2:9, p. 115. *CO* 23, 38.

121. King, *Genesis*, 99. *CO* 23, 28.

122. King, *Genesis*, 100. *CO* 23, 30.

123. King, *Genesis*, 117. *CO* 23, 38.

124. King, *Genesis*, 128. *CO* 23, 46.

125. See also the discussion at Gen 2:11. "God designed that the whole human race should be accustomed from the beginning to reverence his Deity..." King, *Genesis*, 126. *CO* 23, 43.

126. King, *Genesis*, 163. *CO* 23, 67.

127. King, *Genesis*, 171. *CO* 23, 72.

128. Pliny, *Natural History*, 6.9, 27, 31; 5.26, 21; Pomponius Mela, *De Chorographia* 3.8, 77; 1.11, 63ff; Nearchus, *Fragmenta* 35, in Strabo, *Geography*, 15; Flavius Arrian, *Indica*, 40.8; *Anabasis of Alexander*, 7.21; Strabo, *Geography* 15. 3, 4; Quintus Curtius, *History of Alexander* 5.3. Malet, *La Genèse*, 51.

129. King, *Genesis*, 177. Horace, *Odes*, 1.3.29–34.

130. E.g., "We dismiss the reverie of Plato who ascribes reason and intelligence to the stars..." King, *Genesis*, 87. *CO* 23, 23. Also, "The corruption of our nature was unknown to the philosophers who, in other respects, were sufficiently and more than sufficiently acute. Surely this stupor itself was a signal proof of original sin. For all who are not utterly blind perceive that no part of us is sound..." King, *Genesis*, 154.

131. The work of Réveillaud, Besse, and Smits has done much to correct this faulty impression. See Michel Réveillaud, "L'authorité de la Tradition Chez Calvin," *La Revue Réformée* 9 (1958): 24–45; Georges Besse, "Saint Augustin dans les Oeuvres Exégétiques de Jean Calvin: Recherches sur l'Authorité Reconnue à Saint Augustin par Calvin en Matière d'Exégèse," *REAug* 6 (1960): 161–72; Luchesius Smits, *Saint Augustin dans l'Oeuvre de Jean Calvin*, 2 volumes (Assen: Van Gorcum, 1958) See also Johannes van Oort, "John Calvin and the Church Fathers," in *The Reception of the Church Fathers in the West: From the Carolingians to the Maurists*, ed. Irena Backus (Leiden: Brill, 1997), 661–700; Richard Gamble, *The Sources of Calvin's Genesis Commentary: A Preliminary Report*, Archiv Für Reformationsgeschichte 84 (1993): 206–21.

132. King, *Genesis*, 59. *CO* 23, 6.

133. King, *Genesis*, 58. *CO* 23, 6.

134. King, *Genesis*, 59. *CO* 23, 7–8.

135. E.g.: "I know that certain writers restrict the meaning of the expression here used to corporeal life. They suppose such a power of quickening of the body to have been in the tree...but I say they omit what is the chief thing in life, namely the grace of intelligence..." King, *Genesis*, 117–18. *CO* 23, 39. "It is sufficiently agreed among all..." 118; "Some conjecture...others refer...the opinion has been commonly received..." 151–152. *CO* 23, 60. For examples of his explicit citing of figures from the tradition, see his discussion regarding the time of the Fall in his material on Gen 3:6, 156–157. *CO* 23, 63.

136. E.g., Calvin argues with Jerome's translation where he feels that he takes too much liberty with the verbal sense in his choice of translation. "That Jerome improperly translates this ['in Eden', 2:8] 'from the beginning' is very obvious..."; King, *Genesis*, 113. *CO* 23, 36. Again, "...what Jerome translates 'at the breeze after mid-day'...I rather incline to a different conjecture", 160. *CO* 23, 65. "Jerome [in translating 3:15]...does it without reason" 168. *CO* 23, 70. In discussing Gen 2:18, "It is not good that man be alone", Calvin argues for the good of marriage over against the traditional interpretation which could appeal to

Jerome here (128). *CO* 23, 46.

137. See Calvin Augustine Pater, "Calvin, the Jews and the Judaic Legacy," in *In Honor of John Calvin, 1509-64: Papers from the 1986 International Calvin Symposium, McGill University*, ed. E. J. Furcha, ARC Supplement (1987), 256-96; Salo W. Baron, "John Calvin and the Jews," in *Essential Papers on Judaism and Christianity in Conflict From Late Antiquity to the Reformation*, ed. Jeremy Cohen (New York: New York University Press, 1991), 380-400; and Jerome Friedman, *The Most Ancient Testimony: Sixteenth Century Christian-Hebraica in the Age of Renaissance Nostalgia*, Ohio University Press (Athens, OH, 1983), 183-94.

138. McKane, "Calvin as Old Testament Commentator," 250; Baumgartner, *Calvin Hébraïsant et Inteprète de l'Ancien Testament*, 16; Friedman, *The Most Ancient Testimony: Sixteenth Century Christian-Hebraica in the Age of Renaissance Nostalgia*, 47.

139. Cf. King, *Genesis*, 147. *CO* 23, 57. The "Chaldee paraphrast" may refer to the Targum Onkelos. This is included in the *Complutensian Polyglot* of Alcalá (1514-1517, issued in 1522) below the Pentateuch in both an Aramaic and a Latin translation. See Hall, "Biblical Scholarship: Editions and Commentaries," 50-51. Calvin also refers implicitly to the Talmud and the works of the Rabbis, and he is also familiar with at least one detail from the Targum Jonathan, i.e. that Malachi was identified with Ezra. Cf. Verhoef, "Luther's and Calvin's Exegetical Library," 18-19. According to Baumgartner, it is most plausible that the Targumim and Rabbinical material are mediated to Calvin through his "cousin" Olivetan. Baumgartner, *Calvin Hébraïsant et Inteprète de l'Ancien Testament*, 16. Calvin may also have also known of the rabbis and the "Chaldee paraphrast" through Bomberg's Rabbinic Bible first published in 1517-18, which included the complete Targum as well as major and minor rabbinic commentary. Friedman, *The Most Ancient Testimony: Sixteenth Century Christian-Hebraica in the Age of Renaissance Nostalgia*, 36.

140. E.g., "Let Jewish fables be dismissed...", re: Gen 4:5, King, *Genesis*, 197. *CO* 23, 86. "Many Jews mutilate this sentence...", re: Gen 4:15, 213; *CO* 23, 97. Gen 4:23, 219; *CO* 23, 100. Gen 5:2, 228; *CO* 23, 105. Gen 6:3, 243; *CO* 23, 113. Gen 9:25, 306; *CO* 23, 146. Gen 11:7, 331; *CO* 23, 166-67. Gen 11:28, 337; *CO* 23, 170. Gen 12:3, 349; *CO* 23, 177-78. Gen 13:14, 375; *CO* 23, 193, etc.

141. King, *Genesis*, 145. *CO* 23, 56.

142. For example at Gen 2:18, "meet for him," Calvin says that "although some of the Rabbis think it is here put as an affirmative, yet I take it..."

At Gen 2:4, "These are the generations," Calvin notes that some Jewish interpreters think that at this point in the narrative "the essential name of God is here at length expressed by Moses, because his majesty shines forth more clearly in the completed world." King, *Genesis*, 130, 109. *CO* 23, 47–48; 34.

143. King, *Genesis*, 85. *CO* 23, 21.
144. King, *Genesis*, 92. *CO* 23, 25.
145. King, *Genesis*, 107. *CO* 23, 34.
146. See Smits, *Saint Augustin dans l'Oeuvre de Jean Calvin*. A.N.S. Lane has commented that Calvin's "almost unqualified respect for Augustine" does not extend to Augustine's exegesis. This is a misleading statement, for while it is true that Calvin can be critical of Augustine's exegesis, he does embrace at times both Augustine's method and the resulting commentary. Cf. A. N. S. Lane, "Calvin's Use of the Fathers and the Medievals," *Calvin Theological Journal* 16 (1981): 172.
147. King, *Genesis*, 61. *CO* 23, 9–10.
148. Re: Gen 3:6; King, *Genesis*, 152. *CO* 23, 60.
149. King, *Genesis*, 117. *CO* 23, 38. Calvin also approves of other "non-literal" interpreters in his Genesis commentary, e.g. Gregory and Bernard. Calvin adapts Gregory's statement that iconography is "the book of the unlearned" to the effect that creation itself is the book of the unlearned. King, *Genesis*, 80. *CO* 23, 18. Cf. Gregory the Great, *Epist.* 109, *Ad Lerenum*. Bernard also receives Calvin's approval when he exclaims of Genesis 3 that "since we read that a fall so dreadful took place in Paradise, what shall we do on the dunghill?" King, *Genesis*, 157. *CO* 23, 63.
150. "...for the purpose of fabricating a Trinity in man... but a definition of the image of God ought to rest on a firmer basis than such subtleties." King, *Genesis*, 93. *CO* 23, 26. Calvin here refers to Augustine's work in Books 10 and 14 of *de Trinitate* and Book 11 of *De civitate Dei*.
151. See his comments about differing in opinion (here he is speaking of his contemporaries, but Calvin could as easily have said this of the Fathers) in the Dedicatory Epistle to Grynaeus in his Commentary on Romans: "When, therefore, we depart from the views of our predecessors, we are not to be stimulated by any passion for innovation, impelled by any desire to slander others, aroused by any hatred, or prompted by any ambition. Necessity alone is to compel us, and we are to have no other object than that of doing good." Ross MacKenzie, trans., *The Epistles of Paul the Apostle to the Romans and Thessalonians*, by John Calvin (Grand Rapids: Eerdmans, 1973), 4.
152. John Robert Walchenbach, *John Calvin as Biblical Commentator: An*

Investigation Into Calvin's Use of John Chrysostom as an Exegetical Tutor (University of Pittsburgh: Unpublished dissertation, 1974).

153. King, *Genesis*, 94. *CO* 23, 26.
154. King, *Genesis*, 57. *CO* 23, 6.
155. King, *Genesis*, 58. *CO* 23, 6.
156. King, *Genesis*, 58. *CO* 23, 6.
157. King, *Genesis*, 113. *CO* 23, 36.
158. King, *Genesis*, 114. *CO* 23, 36.
159. King, *Genesis*, 120. *CO* 23, 41–42.
160. King, *Genesis*, 145. *CO* 23, 72.
161. The details of medieval cosmology and Calvin's appropriation and/or rejection of it are not within the scope of this book. For information regarding the natural philosophy of Calvin's day, see Christopher B. Kaiser, "Calvin's Understanding of Aristotelian Natural Philosophy: Its Extent and Possible Origins," in *Calviniana: Ideas and Influence of Jean Calvin*, ed. Robert V. Schnucker (Kirksville, MO: Sixteenth Century Journal Publisher, 1988), 77-92.
162. "Inner spheres were moved by virtue of their proximity to outer ones, thus forming a chain of influence extending to the innermost celestial sphere, that of the moon, and even to the cycles of generation and corruption on earth." Kaiser, "Calvin's Understanding of Aristotelian Natural Philosophy: Its Extent and Possible Origins," 82. Cf. Aristotle, *De Generatione* II.10.337a; II.11.338b; *Meteorologica* II.2.354b.26-31.
163. Here I am using the term "science" to refer to generally accepted theories of natural philosophy of Calvin's day. An important definition of science of the 16th century is "above all the firsthand acquaintance with ancient literature; and scientific method was the direct appeal to the sources instead of citing authorities." Brian A. Gerrish, "The Reformation and the Rise of Modern Science," in *The Impact of the Church Upon Its Culture: Reappraisals of the History of Christianity*, J. C. Brauer (Chicago: University of Chicago Press, 1968), 232, n. 5.
164. King, *Genesis*, 81. *CO* 23, 19.
165. While Aristotelian philosophy helps him elucidate the doctrine of providence in the above example, it can also detract from the sovereignty of God. Thus, Calvin's use of natural science is "ad hoc," always to be used in service of and subordination to the doctrine of God. G. B. Deason shows how Protestant formulations of the doctrine of God aided in the dismantling of Aristotelian worldview: "The radical sovereignty of God opposed (a) Aristotle's hierarchical cosmology and (b) his conception of nature as a being having intrinsic powers." G. B. Deason, "The Protestant Reformation and the Rise of Modern Science," *Scottish*

Journal of Theology 38 (1985): 235.

166. King, *Genesis*, 79, n. 2. This indicates that the word used here, "astrologia," meant for Calvin both astrology and astronomy. Thus, where Calvin rejects this he takes the word to refer to what we would call astrology, and where he approves he takes it to refer to what we would call astronomy. Cf. Pierre Marcel, "Calvin and Copernicus," *Philosophia Reformata* 46 (1981): 25; Christine McCall Probes, "Calvin on Astrology," *Westminster Theological Journal* 37 (1974): 27-28: "...the true astrology may be said to include the knowledge of the natural order and disposition God has made of the stars and planets, and additionally their effects such as rains, frosts, snows...[while the false astrology is] 'knowing [from the stars] not only the nature and disposition of men, but also all their adventures, and all that they must do or suffer in their life'...and the success or failure of their undertakings." Cf. Calvin's *Avertissement contre l'astrologie judicaire*, CO 7.516, 518-519, 530. For Calvin, "true" astrology becomes false when it compromises or impinges upon the doctrine of the sovereignty of God in practical matters.

167. King, *Genesis*, 84.

168. King, *Genesis*, 86. *CO* 23, 21.

169. King, *Genesis*, 87. *CO* 23, 22.

170. King, *Genesis*, 86. *CO* 23, 22. For the link between the idea of accommodation and cosmological reflection, cf. Gerrish, "The Reformation and the Rise of Modern Science" and Marcel, "Calvin and Copernicus".

171. There is great debate over whether or not Calvin read Copernicus or knew of his theories. Copernicus' *Revolutions of the Heavenly Bodies* was not published until a few hours before his death 1543. Calvin's Genesis commentary was begun in 1550 and was published in August 1554. T. H. L. Parker, *Calvin's Old Testament Commentaries*, 25, 225. Copernicus had written an earlier version of his theories in 1511-12 which was privately circulated, and Calvin may thus have known of his theories indirectly. Kaiser, "Calvin, Copernicus and Castelio," *Calvin Theological Journal* 21 (1986): 6. Luther had already rejected Copernicus as early as 1539 and Melanchthon denounced him in 1541. E. Rosen, "A Reply to Dr. Ratner," *Journal of the History of Ideas* 22 (1961): 386. Cf. Luther's *Tischreden* 1.419; Kaiser, "Calvin, Copernicus and Castelio." Stauffer points to a comment in Calvin's sermon on 1 Cor 10:19-24 which can be understood to indicate his rejection of heliocentrism, although Copernicus is not specifically mentioned there. R. Hooykaas, "Calvin and Copernicus," *Organon* 10 (1974): 140; CO 49:677. The famous "quotation" of Calvin spurning

Copernicus runs as follows: "Who will venture to place the authority of
Copernicus above that of the Holy Spirit?" This has yet to be docu-
mented in Calvin's writings, but has been traced to F. W. Farrar, *History
of Interpretation* (London, 1886), xviii and to A. D. White, *A History of
the Warfare of Science With Technology in Christendom* (1896), 127.
See the entertaining exchange between Rosen, Ratner and Hooykaas, all
reprinted for convenient reference in Richard C. Gamble, *Calvin and
Science*, Articles on Calvin and Calvinism (New York: Garland Publishing, 1992). For the purposes of the present study it will suffice to
note that Calvin seems to have chosen for whatever reason not to engage
in open polemic with Copernican theories. Cf. Gerrish, "The Reformation and the Rise of Modern Science," 247.

172. King, *Genesis*, 61. *CO* 23, 9–10.
173. King, *Genesis*, 62. *CO* 23, 9–10.
174. King, *Genesis*, 77. *CO* 23, 34.
175. "Calvin's varied comments on scientific issues might sound contradictory
at first reading. On the one hand, Calvin used Aristotelian ideas and
obviously appreciated their value as an antidote to Academic relativism
and Epicurean indeterminism. On the other, he repeatedly challenged
their self-evidence and pointed out gaps or contradictions in the purely
naturalistic account... Calvin stressed the natural order when he felt that
would strengthen faith in God; he qualified it when he felt it would
become self-contained and detract from faith." Kaiser, "Calvin and Natural Philosophy," 80.
176. It appears from this comment that Calvin thought that the moon reflects
the sun's light.
177. King, *Genesis*, 86. *CO* 23, 22.
178. Marcel, "Calvin and Copernicus," 34: "By his silence Calvin leaves
science to its own proper vocation; he embodies a model of impartiality;
he displays respect for its techniques and its legitimate hypotheses. He
keeps theology and the Church far from partisan squabbles and
demonstrates the peaceful relationships that science and the Christian
faith have in common if each remains on its own territory."
179. "For Calvin, God is free, he might have decided matters differently. We
know or think we know that he did not decide differently; but that is all."
A. LeCerf, quoted in Robert White, "Calvin and Copernicus: The Problem Reconsidered," *Calvin Theological Journal* 15 (1980): 243.
180. "The 'literalism' of Luther and Calvin was designed to rule out allegories
and other forms of fancy exegesis, but it still left room for maintaining
the autonomy of natural science. Where the reigning astronomical
opinions seemed to conflict with Scripture, they knew how to make the

Calvin 167

necessary adjustments. But this meant that they had to make the adjustments to Ptolemaic, not Copernican, science, precisely because the scientific revolution remained incomplete during their lifetime. Moreover, if Calvin himself did not apply the principle of accommodation to the problem posed by the new science, no others than Kepler and Galileo did so apply it, which raises intriguing historical questions about the origins and dissemination of the principle." Gerrish, "The Reformation and the Rise of Modern Science," 263-4. Regarding the statement about Kepler and Galileo Gerrish cites Dorothy Stimson, *The Gradual Acceptance of the Copernican Theory of the Universe*, (New York: Baker and Taylor) 1917, 41.

181. Gerrish treats the subject of accommodation and its use in matters of cosmology, and says that "Calvin's principle of accommodation...was used chiefly as a problem-solving device, to be rolled out only when needed." Gerrish, "The Reformation and the Rise of Modern Science," 263.

182. King, *Genesis*, 86-7. *CO* 23, 22.

183. "Moses, by a homely and uncultivated style, accommodates what he delivers to the capacity of the people, and for the best reason; for not only had he to instruct an untaught race of men, but the existing age of the Church was so puerile that it was unable to receive any higher instruction. There is therefore nothing absurd in the supposition that they whom for a time we know and confess to have been but as infants, were fed with milk." See also the example in the discussion of Gen 3:19, "Moses who according to his custom studies a brevity adapted to the capacity of the common people was content to touch upon what was most apparent..." King, *Genesis*, 141, 177. *CO* 23, 53; 75.

184. King, *Genesis*, 119. *CO* 23, 40.

185. King, *Genesis*, 113. *CO* 23, 36.

186. King, *Genesis*, 78. *CO* 23, 17.

187. King, *Genesis*, 90. *CO* 23, 24.

188. King, *Genesis*, 78. *CO* 23, 17. Calvin is here attempting to resolve a problem created by Eccl 28:1, which he ultimately resolves via an appeal to verbal meaning.

189. King, *Genesis*, 92. *CO* 23, 25.

190. King, *Genesis*, 182. *CO* 23, 78.

191. Hazlett regards the notion of accommodation in Calvin as a result of his understanding of the democratization of the gospel. W. Ian P. Hazlett, "Calvin's Latin Preface to His Proposed French Edition of Chrysostom's Homilies: Translation and Commentary," in *Humanism and Reform: The Church in Europe, England and Scotland, 1400-1643*, ed. James Kirk (Oxford: Basil Blackwell, 1991), 135. One could also link it with his

understanding of the Fall, as Peter Brown does Augustine's understanding of allegory. Peter Brown, *Augustine of Hippo* (Berkeley: University of California Press, 1969), 88-91, n. 117.

192. King, *Genesis*, 59. *CO* 23, 6.

193. King, *Genesis*, 115-16. *CO* 23, 38.

194. King, *Genesis*, 141. *CO* 23, 53.

195. An example of prooftexting can be found in his discussion of the phrase "in our image" at Gen 1:26. Calvin's question as to what is lost in the fall sends him to "Paul's" statements (Col 3:10 and Eph 4:23-24) about spiritual regeneration being a restoration of the image of God. While Calvin draws together texts from both Old and New Testaments alike in his comments on Genesis 1-3, most of the prooftexts here are drawn from the Psalms.

196. In fact, this subject has received no attention to the best of my knowledge in the secondary literature, but merits much further exploration than is possible here.

197. King, *Genesis*, 161. *CO* 23, 65. Cf. Ps 104:4.

198. King, *Genesis*, 94. *CO* 23, 26.

199. King, *Genesis*, 97. *CO* 23, 28.

200. The tradition of Davidic authorship of the Psalms was, of course, not disputed in Calvin's day.

201. King, *Genesis*, 96. *CO* 23, 27.

202. King, *Genesis*, 152. *CO* 23, 60.

203. King, *Genesis*, 145. *CO* 23, 56. Notice his use of the word "Gospel" here; he does not use the term in strictly literary terms, for a specific gospel is not mentioned and one can think of places in Acts where "disembodied voices" speak. "Gospel" here could almost refer to the New Testament stories in general.

204. The idea of "common sense" is logically related to natural knowledge for Calvin; see *Institutes* 1.1.

205. King, *Genesis*, 70. *CO* 23, 15.

206. King, *Genesis*, 58. *CO* 23, 6.

207. King, *Genesis*, 79. *CO* 23, 18.

208. King, *Genesis*, 98. *CO* 23, 27.

209. King, *Genesis*, 167. *CO* 23, 69.

210. King, *Genesis*, 160. *CO* 23, 65.

211. King, *Genesis*, 160. *CO* 23, 65.

212. King, *Genesis*, 88. *CO* 23, 23.

213. King, *Genesis*, 88. *CO* 23, 23.

214. King, *Genesis*, 88. *CO* 23, 23.

215. King, *Genesis*, 132. *CO* 23, 48.

216. "...en ce que les hommes sont journellement engendrés d'une semence pourrie et puante..." Malet, *La Genèse*, 58. Here is another unfortunate lacuna in King's translation on 133.

217 .King, *Genesis*, 144. *CO* 23, 55.

218. It is clear that Calvin engages in polemic even in commenting on scripture, although this might be seen as a violation of his "exegetical principle" of brevity. While it is true that Calvin does not engage in extended polemic in his commentaries, Richard Gamble defends an idealistic view of Calvin as commentator: "...it should be noted that as a general rule Calvin refuses to enter into debate with opponents in his commentaries and for that matter also deletes opinions that support him. The exception is when failure to mention contrary opinions may leave readers with further unanswered questions. The omission of detailed examinations of either friend or foe is a conscious part of Calvin's hermeneutical method." Richard C. Gamble, "Brevitas et Facilitas: Toward an Understanding of Calvin's Hermeneutic," 3 For other examples, see Calvin's discussion of 1:14, King, *Genesis*, 84, *CO* 23, 21. "Certain inquisitive persons abuse this passage...but confutation is easy..." And in his Argument on 58, (*CO* 23, 6) he defends the creation account against some who "suppose Moses to be speaking fabulously of things unknown," because he was not present to witness the events nor did he read about them in another source.

219. For example, cf. his comments on Gen 1:2 where he says that the reading of the word "spirit" as "wind" by some is "too frigid to require refutation." King, *Genesis*, 73. *CO* 23, 16. For other examples of the refutation of "violent" readings, see 78 (*CO* 23, 17-18) on the discussion of the first day of creation and the reading of Ecclus. 18:1.

220. Respectively, at Gen 1:3, King, *Genesis*, 75. *CO* 23, 16. Re: Gen 1:26 "in our image", and re: Gen 3:6, see 94, 154; *CO* 23, 26 and 61.

221. Respectively, see the discussion at Gen 2:4, "These are the generations," and at Gen 1:1, 109 and 70; re: Gen 2:18 "It is not good that man be alone," 128-131 and re: Gen 2:22, 134-35; re: Gen 3:1 about the sin of Adam, 143 ff. and re: Gen 3:6, 155; re: Gen 1:26, 92, and Gen 3:22, 183. *CO* 23, 34, 14–15, 46–48, 49–50, 52–56, 59–63, 25–27, 78–79.

222. This is true as well for his reference to the opinions of Jewish commentators, which, as has been noted, is generally negative in regards to their construal of theological content.

223. For example, at Gen 1:1 he recognizes that the word "God" is a noun of plural number (אלוהימ), and he notes that some infer the Trinity to be indicated in the plural noun. While he says that those who offer this reading think that they can thus refute the Arians and prove the divinity

of the Son and the Spirit, Calvin notes that in doing so they fall into doctrinal error, namely Sabellianism.

224. King, *Genesis*, 69. *CO* 23, 14.

225. King, *Genesis*, 170. *CO* 23, 71.

226. King, *Genesis*, 58. *CO* 23, 6.

227. King, *Genesis*, 59. *CO* 23, 6. Cf. *Institutes* 1.5.

228. King, *Genesis*, 65. *CO* 23, 11–12. The remarkable thing about this statement is that Calvin is speaking here of the argument of the book *of Genesis*.

229. King, *Genesis*, 163. *CO* 23, 67.

230. King, *Genesis*, 98. *CO* 23, 28.

231. Calvin's understanding of our "unbridled lust" and ingratitude at the gifts of God guide his reading at the words "let them have dominion" in Gen 1:26. Calvin notes that "in the very order of the creation the paternal solicitude of God for man is conspicuous, because he furnished the world with all things needful, and even with an immense profusion of wealth, before he formed man. Thus man was rich before he was born... Yet, that he often keeps his hand as if closed is to be imputed to our sins." King, *Genesis*, 96. *CO* 23, 27.

232. King, *Genesis*, 92. *CO* 23, 25.

233. King, *Genesis*, 183. *CO* 23, 79.

234. It must be stressed, however, that even a broad understanding of the subject matter of the text, be it an aspect of the character of God or human sin or salvation, cannot solely determine the reading of the plain sense for Calvin. Verbal sense must be allowed to trump any preconceived understanding of subject matter. For example, Calvin argues that it is true that Christ is the only image of the Father. Still, "the words of Moses do not bear the interpretation that 'in the image' means 'in Christ'." King, *Genesis*, 95. *CO* 23, 27. As important as is the larger subject matter of the text for the interpretation of the plain sense of scripture, Calvin's understanding of verbal sense cannot be violated by it but the two must be shown to "fit" logically in order to render a plain sense reading.

235. King, *Genesis*, 136. *CO* 23, 51. For another example of an interpretation concerned to promote "filial piety", see his comments on Gen 48:1, 421 ff., *CO* 23, 579.

236. King, *Genesis*, 80–1. *CO* 23, 19.

237. King, *Genesis*, 87. *CO* 23, 22–23. And at Gen 1:24, "Let the earth bring forth", Calvin remarks that this miraculous creation of living creatures, as though some sort of cosmic birthing from the substance of the earth itself, does not take place because God had need of the earth as

material from which to create the creatures. God had already created out of nothing at Gen 1:1. "He does not take his material from the earth because he needed it, but that he might the better combine the separate parts of the world with the universe itself." God's power again shines forth in Calvin's interpretation of God's blessing on the first pair that they be fruitful and multiply, for Calvin states that "we are fruitful or barren in respect of offspring, as God imparts his power to some and withholds it from others," 97. *CO* 23, 28.

238. King, *Genesis*, 144–45. *CO* 23, 55–56.

239. King, *Genesis*, 103. *CO* 23, 31–32.

240. "We must not infer that God so ceased from his works as to desert them, since they only flourish and subsist in him." King, *Genesis*, 104. *CO* 23, 32. Calvin's understanding of God's sovereignty governs his reading also of the words of the serpent to Eve. Calvin entertains the question of how the serpent could speak intelligible words, and concludes that at issue ultimately is the power of God. If one holds that God is ruler of the world, these details in the text are not problematic. And further on 158, Calvin says, "God created man flexible; and not only permitted but willed that he should be tempted. For he both adapted the tongue of the serpent beyond the ordinary use of nature to the devil's purpose just as if any one should furnish another with a sword and armour, and then, though the unhappy event was foreknown by him, he did not apply the remedy which he had the power to do." CO 23, 64. Here the doctrine of the sovereignty of God resolves a hermeneutical tangle.

241. "There would be no need of any trial of the cause, or of any solemn form of judgment, in order to condemn us; wherefore while God insists upon extorting a confession from us, he acts rather as a physician than as a judge." King, *Genesis*, 165. *CO* 23, 68.

242. "By this act of vengeance God would prove how highly he estimates the salvation of man, just as if a father should hold the sword in execration by which his son had been slain." King, *Genesis* 166. *CO* 23, 69.

243. Serene Jones, *Calvin and the Rhetoric of Piety*, Columbia Series in Reformed Theology (Louisville, Ky.: Westminster/John Knox Press, 1995).

244. King, *Genesis*, 77–8. *CO* 23, 17. At Gen 1:4, "And God saw that the light was good", Calvin states that "while God approves of the work, it remains for us to agree in that judgement." Such contemplation is the purpose of the rest of the seventh day. At Gen 2:3, where God blesses the seventh day, Calvin remarks that God did not need the rest of the seventh day any more than God needed the span of six days in order to create the world. Rather, since God used the span of six days for the

creation of the world in order that we might consider more fully his works, so God consecrated the seventh day in order that we might be exhorted to obedience in the imitation of him and apply ourselves to meditating on the goodness and providence of God. Calvin says that it is not as if God wants us to be indolent, but that in being released from the cares and occupations of our daily lives we might more easily devote our thoughts to God on that seventh day.

245. Regarding the first creation account (Calvin does not use this terminology, of course) Calvin says that God could have created humanity *en masse*, but did not do so in order that we should all come from the same source. This interpretation, Calvin points out, results in the fostering of "mutual concord...that each might the more freely embrace the other as his own flesh." King, *Genesis*, 97. *CO* 23, 28.

246. Gratitude is similarly stressed at the reading of Gen 1:29 where God gives to Adam all plants for food. Calvin's interpretation instructs us to look to God alone for all our needs and in enjoying his gifts we are to remember his goodness and care. Here when we read of God's promise of liberal abundance and Moses' description of the Lord's beneficence, we like the first pair have less excuse for ingratitude.

247. King, *Genesis*, 153. *CO* 23, 60.

248. For example, God's formulaic pronouncing the goodness of creation in Gen 1 is not random, but since "it would have been enough to have said once for all that God approved of his works," it functions to underscore our "wanton temerity." King, *Genesis*, 100. *CO* 23, 30. Moses' portrayal of the seduction by the serpent in Gen 3 is designed to "show succinctly how great our present condition differs from our first original in order that we may learn with humble confession of our fault to bewail our evils," 143. *CO* 23, 55.

249. King, *Genesis*, 157, re: Gen 3:6. *CO* 23, 63.

250. "...lest men should use it as an occasion of pride, their first origin is placed immediately before them... let foolish men now go and boast of the excellency of their nature."

251. King, *Genesis*, 111. *CO* 23, 35.

252. King, *Genesis*, 111. *CO* 23, 35. Likewise, on 116, the paternal benevolence of God which we are to infer from the planting of the Garden in Gen 2:8 which bestows upon Adam such abundance underscores Adam's "shameful ingratitude that he could not rest in a state so happy and desirable: truly that was more than brutal lust which bounty so great was not able to satisfy." *CO* 23, 38.

253. King, *Genesis*, 125. *CO* 23, 44.

254. King, *Genesis*, 126. *CO* 23, 44.

255. King, *Genesis*, 127. *CO* 23, 45.
256. Curiosity for Augustine is seeking and enjoying knowledge for its own sake instead of in its use to praise the creator. Cf. *De Vera Religione* 49, 94. Of the distinction between use and enjoyment, see *De Doctrina Christiana* 1.3-5.
257. King, *Genesis*, 151. *CO* 23, 59.
258. "Moses adds that the custody of the garden was given in charge to Adam, to show that we possess the things which God has committed to our hands on the condition that being content with a frugal and moderate use of them, we should take care of what shall remain." King, *Genesis*, 125. *CO* 23, 44.
259. King, *Genesis*, 125. *CO* 23, 44.
260. Consolation is also engendered in the reading of Gen 3:23 where God expels the pair from the garden, for God's mercy, says Calvin, provides Adam and Eve with a home elsewhere on the earth and a livelihood from an albeit laborious tilling of the soil. Thus "God mercifully softens the exile of Adam" from which Adam "thence infers that the Lord has some care for him which is proof of paternal love." King, *Genesis*, 184. *CO* 23, 79. Adam is therefore not punished without consolation, not expelled without comfort, not excommunicated so as to be without hope of pardon.
261. "...that they might be affected with a greater dread of sin, seeing how highly displeasing it is to God and hence they might take consolation for their misery because they would perceive that God is still propitious to them." King, *Genesis*, 169. *CO* 23, 70.
262. "...first, that men may learn to beware of Satan as of a most deadly enemy; then, that they may contend against him with the assured confidence of victory." King, *Genesis*, 169. *CO* 23, 70.
263. "[God] mentions the woman on this account, because as she had yielded to the subtlety of the devil and being first deceived, had drawn her husband into the participation of her ruin, so she had peculiar need of consolation." King, *Genesis*, 170. *CO* 23, 71.

Chapter Four:
Barth's Understanding of the Plain Sense
in the Church Dogmatics 3.1

Macroexegesis: Witness to the Word

Textual Polyvalence and Witness to the Word

Understanding the text as everywhere and throughout witness to Jesus Christ is the single most important assumption undergirding Barth's reading of the plain sense of scripture. It is this understanding of the text as witness to Jesus Christ which is Barth's theological rationale for the canon, and which justifies reading the Bible according to its "plain sense." This becomes apparent in the opening pages of his discussion of Creation and Covenant in volume 3 of his *Church Dogmatics*. In his discussion in paragraph 40 of this volume, after he states that the doctrine of creation is a doctrine of faith, he asks how we can make this confession side by side with the confession of Jesus Christ and of the Holy Spirit.

> How can [the Church] make it in such a way that if the confession of the work of creation is false and impotent and impossible, so too is that of the work of reconciliation and redemption? How can it make it in such a way that the whole necessarily stands or falls with the dogma of creation as with every other constituent element?[1]

In part his question is that of the earliest Christians who continued to read the Hebrew Bible as scripture while grappling with the given of the Risen Christ. One might even say that this is a question which Marcion answered by saying in effect that the doctrines of creation and redemption are *not* linked, and that if one confesses the truth of redemption, one must confess the falsehood of the doctrine of creation. Of course, the "orthodox" solution was to confess the truth of both, which necessitated a new reading of the Hebrew Bible, the "Old Testament." Barth's question itself is what generates his understanding of what we will call the polyvalence of the text, that is, the capacity of the text to unite or to cause to interact two or more biblical themes, motifs or stories.[2]

Barth says that the answer to the question of our certainty regarding the truth of the confession of the doctrine of creation is not only that the twofold creation narrative opens the Bible, but that the Bible gives us a reliable basis for our knowledge and confession because it tells the truth "by reason of the fact that [it] gives us God's own witness to Himself... the witness to Jesus Christ."[3] Because it gives us God's own witness to Himself, the Bible's testimony to creation also gives testimony to "the One in whom the Creator has reconciled the creature to Himself." Thus,

> The whole Bible speaks figuratively and prophetically of Him, of Jesus Christ, when it speaks of creation, the Creator and the creature. If, therefore, we are rightly to understand and estimate what it says about creation, we must first see that—like everything else it says—this refers and testifies first and last to Him. At this point, too, he is the primary and ultimate object of its witness.[4]

Not only the creation accounts themselves, but everything which the Bible says, refers and testifies to Christ. The whole Bible, not just certain parts of it, speaks figuratively and prophetically of Christ. The Bible's polyvalence therefore has a "center" into which it draws its various other themes, motifs, and stories. Reading according to the plain sense is to recognize this. In other words, Barth seems to be saying here that the Bible speaks plainly, or speaks "figuratively" according to the plain sense. Unlike Augustine, Barth is not advocating a reading of different senses of scripture. Rather, he is saying that within the plain sense reading lies the figurative and prophetic reference to Christ. This figurative and prophetic reference is not added on or read into, but ingredient in the verbal sense "by reason of the fact that the Bible gives us God's own witness to Himself" and "its word in all words is this Word."[5] It is the claim that the words of the text bear witness to the Word which is present at creation, at Sinai, at Calvary and Golgotha which logically necessitates figural reading of the Biblical text within the rubric of plain sense reading. Thus, Christ is the "primary and ultimate object" of the biblical text's witness, even in the creation narratives, and the "whole circumference of the content of Scripture, including the truth and reality of the creation of the world by God, can be understood only from this center."[6] The language here, besides being an apt description of Barth's hermeneutics, mirrors the theological structure of volume 3 of the *Church Dogmatics*. Here Creation is understood to be the "circumference" or "external basis of the covenant," and the covenant as the "center" or "internal basis of Creation."

The kind of figural reading which Barth is advocating here falls within the plain sense reading in part in its dependence on the narratival appropriation of the whole Bible. He insists that such reading, which he calls a "right and necessary and central Biblicism," reads the parts in light of the unity, "i.e., of the One of whom it everywhere speaks." Barth seems here to be saying that a proper or plain reading of scripture does not isolate one part of the narrative over against the whole or remove it from the context of the narrative flow. Since the "center" of the narrative is Christ the Word, the words must be read in light of that center. Proper reading allows "itself to be taught by Scripture, i.e., the whole of scripture, to know the Father through the Son, the Creator through the Redeemer." The content and center are inseparable from the story which bears it. At this point in the discussion, Barth warns against a reading of the letter which is not thus obedient to the Spirit:

> No insistence on the letter of Scripture can give the one intrinsically necessary and convincing answer to the question how we may know this truth [that God is the Creator].[7]

For Barth, the letter and the Spirit coinhere. Figural reading and "simple" reading are two aspects of plain sense reading because of the Bible's bearing of the Word as the primary and ultimate object of the witness of the words.[8]

There is also a fit between such a plain sense reading in which Spirit and letter coinhere and religious devotion, or as Barth says, "obedience" to the Spirit.[9] The reading which is not obedient to the Spirit Barth also classifies under the rubric of "biblicism" as he did of the "obedient" reading. However, it is clearly not the "right and necessary and central biblicism" as described above. This he calls a "scattered and peripheral" biblicism which slights the unity of the Bible in that it

> regards Jesus Christ merely as one object of its witness among others. It regards the Bible as a repository of all sorts and degrees of pious knowledge. It knows nothing of the triunity of the God whose revelation and work are attested. It may also confess a belief in the triunity of God in isolated connexions, but it does not take it seriously. It thinks it can talk about God the Father and Creator on the basis of Scripture, i.e. in light of

> this or that passage…but it cannot possibly be obedient to the
> Spirit of Scripture in this way because the Spirit of Scripture is
> the Spirit of God the Father and the Son.[10]

The disobedience to the Spirit of this peripheral biblicism is a direct result of
its scatteredness: it does not allow itself to be taught by the whole of scripture.
Reading scripture according to its plain sense thus defined requires an
obedience or submission to the triune God described by, portrayed in and
borne by the text. This in turn necessitates an obedience or faithful respect for
the whole of scripture, for the triune God, is according to Barth, the one object
of the text's witness.

An example of reading the biblical text where its figural or prophetic
mode comes clearly to the fore along with the plain sense is in Barth's discussion of the Christian Sabbath at the end of the second section of paragraph
41.[11] Here he says that his observation that the creation saga refers prophetically to Christ is supported by the early Christian practice of keeping the first
day of the week as its day of rest instead of the seventh.[12] This came to be the
practice, notes Barth, in commemoration of the day of the resurrection of
Jesus, the first day of the week and the day after the Jewish sabbath. Barth
then asks himself whether this "change" in Sabbath observation is in effect a
fair reading of the Genesis text:

> Was this an innovation, or was it a true understanding and
> application of Gen 2:3? If it is correct that the truth and faith-
> fulness of God in the blessing and sanctification of the seventh
> day are revealed in the resurrection of Jesus Christ…we have
> to admit that they were right; that this first day of this new
> time had to become literally as well as materially the day of
> rest which dominates life in this new time.[13]

Thus the prophetic application of Gen 2:3 is not a reading into the text, but a
"true understanding," and thus a plain sense reading, given the truthfulness of
the coherence between creation and redemption, of the Sabbath rest of the
Creator and the resurrection of Christ. Barth adds that there is also "direct
proof" of his assertion from the text of Gen 2:3 itself, apart from the canonical
proofs which he gives above. This direct proof is to be found in the narrative
element that while the Sabbath is the seventh day of creation, it is the first day
for humanity in the narrative:

While the Sabbath observed by God was the seventh day for
Him, it was undoubtedly the first for man...The 'Lord's Day'
was really his first day. Each week, instead of being a trying
ascent, ought to have been a glad descent from the highpoint of
the Sabbath...In Christian chronology the week has obviously
gained this meaning...[humanity's] first real day was really the
'Lord's Day.'[14]

This element from the narrative of Gen 2:3 itself lends proof to the prophetic
reading which understands the Sabbath christologically, and thus also lends
support to the Christian practice of celebrating the Sabbath on the first day of
the week, the Lord's day. This according to Barth is not a "reading into" the
text or an "innovation," but is a discovery of what lies within the letter of the
text itself, namely the witness to Christ. Thus it is a "true understanding and
application of Gen 2:3."

We have seen how Barth's understanding of the text as witness involves
understanding the text as polyvalent, and thus necessitates a figural reading
centered around Jesus Christ. We will now consider the second most significant element of what we are calling Barth's "macroexegesis," or the setting
of the controlling parameters for exegesis of the Genesis creation stories: his
construal of their genre. Then we will turn to an examination of other elements of Barth's "macroexegesis," including the narrative and literary structure of the text, and his assessment of the exegetical use of science and historical criticism. After considering these, we will turn in the second half of
this chapter to his "microexegesis," or his close examination of the text. This
will include an investigation of his reading of verbal sense, his assessment of
the authorship of the text, his use of the canonical setting of the text, his practice of prooftexting, and his exploitation of the narratival silences in his reading of the plain sense.

Historical Referentiality and Textual Genre

For Augustine, we saw that the inspiration of the Bible renders the text
trustworthy throughout to refer to time and space. For Calvin, we saw that it
was the doctrine of God, and particularly Calvin's understanding of God's
sovereignty, which entailed the assumption of a straightforward, transparent
referentiality to the time-space continuum. However, Barth's reading of the
plain sense displays a different controlling assumption: the text as witness to
Jesus Christ. Of course, Barth also assumes the inspiration of the text, but for-

mulates it differently from Augustine and Calvin.[15] He also accepts God's sovereignty, but these assumptions do not come to the fore as controlling factors in his reading of the plain sense of Genesis. For Barth, the Biblical text serves as witness to Jesus Christ, and since what is witnessed to is an event in history, indeed the event of the whole of history, the text speaks "historically." This "historical" speaking becomes more subtle and nuanced in Barth's assessment than in either Calvin's or Augustine's, for the degree to which the Bible refers "historically" for Barth depends on its genre, which will differ from text to text within the Bible.

One does not have to hunt in order to piece together Barth's understanding of the relationship between the text's ability to refer "historically" and the reading of the plain sense when it comes to interpreting Genesis 1-3. A full consideration of this hermeneutical problem appears in his discussion of Creation and Covenant in the *Church Dogmatics* 3.1, paragraph 41. Barth here proposes understanding the opening chapters of Genesis under the generic rubric of "saga," instead of the usually accepted genre of "myth." According to Barth, saga is "an intuitive and poetic picture of a pre-historical reality of history which is enacted once and for all within the confines of time and space."[16] While Gunkel opposes saga and history (*Geschichte*), Barth opposes saga and myth. Saga for Gunkel is "non-historical," but for Barth it is "historical" (*geschichtlich*). Viewing the Genesis creation accounts in this way is based on a close reading of the text at hand, which has the side-effect of reformulating the issues of the "creation science" approach which assumed a direct historical referentiality of the creation stories:[17]

> It will perhaps be asked in criticism why I have not tackled the obvious scientific question posed in this context. It was my original belief that this would be necessary, but I later saw that there can be no scientific problems, objections or aids in relation to what Holy Scripture and the Christian Church understand by the divine work of creation. Hence in the central portion of this book a good deal will be said about 'naive' Hebrew 'saga,' but nothing at all about apologetics and polemics, as might have been expected. The relevant task of dogmatics at this point has been found exclusively in repeating the 'saga,' and I have found this task far finer and far more rewarding than all the dilettante entanglements in which I might otherwise have found myself.[18]

This understanding of "saga" should not be understood as a reticence to use the term "history," for Barth willingly and liberally speaks of history, even speaking of scripture as "historical narrative" (*"die geschichtliche Erzählung"*).[19] Barth is not interested, however, in academic historiography, but in the history of the covenant of grace, which is "from the theological standpoint *the* history." Indeed, for Barth it is the aim of creation itself.[20] Even though the genre of the first chapters of Genesis is saga, Barth can affirm with Calvin that they hold the history of creation. We can and should be grateful that "the biblical witness begins neither with silence about creation nor with a philosophy of creation but with the history of creation."[21] Barth goes to lengths to emphasize that the "whole relationship between God and man... is a historical relationship... [not] incidental, external or merely apparent, but genuinely historical."[22] He wants to stress that the covenant of grace takes place in these histories and not merely in the ideas represented by the histories, alongside, beside or above these histories. He says that if we reverse the relationship and read these histories as mere illustrations of general truths about God and humanity, we rob them of their character and authority as the Word of God.[23] He does not want to be understood as claiming that the biblical witness is "non-historical" (*"geschichtslose"*):

> Not even the pure, eternal being of God as such is non-historical pre-truth, for being triune it is not non-historical but historical even in its eternity. How, then, can creation be a non-historical pre-truth? If it were, how could the continuation harmonize with this beginning? In that case, the continuation of this beginning would undoubtedly have to consist in the depiction of a non-historical truth, basis and regulation of the relationship between God and man. This is contradicted by the continuation as it actually worked out according to the witness of the Bible.[24]

In other words, the incarnation confirms the "historicity" of the biblical witness, not only of the gospel narratives, not only of the New Testament, but also of the Old Testament and therefore of the creation saga as well. The "historicity" of the biblical text, or the biblical witness in Barth's terms, is dependent upon and logically tied to the doctrine of God. God enters the time-space continuum in Jesus of Nazareth. The biblical witness everywhere points to this God. Therefore, the "historicity" of which Barth speaks, while certainly not that of the academic historian, at some level does engage a referentiality to the time-space continuum and cannot be described in purely non-referential terms. Thus Barth says that if God's creation is a history, it takes place in time and is the ground and basis of time, the form of existence of the creature.

> Is it not inevitable, then, that creation should itself be a history, the supremely distinctive pre-history, clearly distinguished from all that follows, but bearing throughout the character of a history? Is it not inevitable that we should find it attested and presented as such on the first pages of the Bible?[25]

This non-historical and pre-historical view of history is depicted in the form of "saga."[26] Yet it is at the same time not to be understood as history in the sense of academic historiography.[27] History in the sense of academic historiography is in Barth's terms "the history which is accessible to man because it is visible and perceptible to him ...[that is] creaturely history in the content of other creaturely history."[28] For this reason, the history of creation cannot be said to be historical, and in these terms can only be said to be "non-historical" ("*unhistorisch*") in that "it cannot be deduced and compared and therefore perceived and comprehended."[29] Since the only content of the history of creation is God the Creator, it is a "'non-historical' history."

> The rest of history is mediate to God as well as immediate, and therefore historical as well as non-historical. The rest of history subsequent to creation has a creaturely element, i.e., a similarity and relationship with other creaturely occurrences.[30]

In one sense, Barth is dealing here with the same problem which bothered Calvin. For Barth, to say that the creation account is non-historical is

> to take seriously the fact that the Bible tells the story of creation as one which (apart altogether from its content) had no human witnesses...If there is no historian, even for this reason (accepting his ability to perceive and understand what took place) there can obviously be no 'history.'[31]

Calvin assumes that the pre-Mosaic history is passed on to Moses via "oral tradition." However, since Adam was (according to the storyline) not present at creation, the question arises as to how Adam could have known the story of creation to pass on to his descendants. Of course, Calvin could have solved the problem by declaring that Moses was divinely illuminated with the story, but instead says that God revealed the history of creation to Adam. The point at issue here is that Calvin, too, noticed the special problem of the historical referentiality of the first chapters of Genesis, the "events" of which "had no human witness." Calvin "solved" this problem, however, by reference to an extra-textually derived explanation (God's immediate revelation to Adam). Barth's proposal of non-historical history, saga, is closer to the text itself: it depends on no extra-textual explanatory theory but on the genre and narration of the texts themselves.

Barth adds that the history of the covenant of grace is more than mere history, for indeed all history is important only to the extent that it is non-historical, as Barth says, not only mediate to God but also immediate.[32] He holds up two instantiations of this mix between history and non-history in the Bible: the external basis (creation) and the center (the resurrection of Jesus Christ) of the history of the covenant of grace. In the case of the accounts of the resurrection appearances, Barth says that the historical element seems almost entirely to have disappeared and that the non-historical takes over, for the accounts break through the framework of historical categories.[33] Even still, while there is a "deep historical twilight" in the accounts of the resurrection appearances, to some extent one can speak of visible history insofar as there is a certain congruence between these accounts and other creaturely occurrences. Barth points out that this is clearly not the case, however, with the creation stories which depict events that neither had human witnesses nor which correspond to other creaturely occurrences.

> If the history of the covenant of grace with its miracles and especially its great central miracle, is not only undoubtedly historical [*historisch*] but also (to the extent to which it is itself a continuation of the history of creation) highly 'non-historical' [*unhistorisch*], we can only say of the history of creation [*Schöpfungsgeschichte*] in itself and as such that it is by nature wholly 'non-historical' [*unhistorisch*], and that the biblical accounts of it are also by nature wholly 'non-historical' and can only be read and understood as such.[34]

Thus Barth sets up his proposal for understanding the creation stories as non-historical: the history of creation in itself is non-historical. Therefore, so are the biblical accounts of it, and they must be read accordingly. He notes that this is not a judgment of historical criticism, as though one were to conclude that the accounts are unhistorical or factually false and thus void of their own historical reality. Rather, it is a theological proposition which is based on an analysis of the form and content of the narratives themselves. The content of the narratives tells us that there could be no human witness, therefore there could be no historian and likewise no history. Instead, the narratives are of a pre-historical character in that they are prior to natural history. The form of the narrative of the first two chapters of Genesis shows us that there are two different accounts of creation which expand and contradict each other, indicating derivation from different sources and different intellectual and social backgrounds. Thus the accounts (plural) cannot be read as history without doing injustice to the text (singular). Such injustice to the text is to Barth's mind exactly what Calvin and Augustine's understanding of direct historical referentiality in effect would allow.

> Even if it were intrinsically possible to construct a 'historical' picture from the narratives we cannot actually do so without doing violence to one or the other or both. The older expositors who attempted a 'historical' harmonization of the two accounts did not adhere too closely to what is actually written. What is written—and this may be said independently of all source-hypotheses—is ill-adapted in its juxtaposition of two different accounts to mediate a 'historical' substratum. We can only do violence to it if we read and interpret it in this way.[35]

While the text must be read as non-historical, or pre-historical, Barth claims that he does not mean to say that the text is not genuine history. In stinging vituperation, he rejects what he calls a "ridiculous and middle-class habit of the modern Western mind which is supremely phantastic in its chronic lack of imaginative phantasy" which would dismiss as inferior or untrustworthy such non-historical narration of history.[36] One must not assume that only "historical" history were true and that the "non-historical" were therefore false. Indeed, Barth says that every history in its immediacy to God is non-historical, and that "in genuine history the historical and the non-historical accompany each other and belong together."[37]

In the Bible, says Barth, we usually have a mixture of both history and saga. The failure to appreciate this mixture in biblical narrative plagues both Liberalism and Orthodoxy. In both alike the failure to note this leads to a crisis of faith when it is assumed that the Bible declares the Word of God only when it speaks historically, understood in a narrow sense.

...the presumed equation of the Word of God with a 'historical' record is an inadmissible postulate which does not itself
originate in the Bible at all but in the unfortunate habit of
Western thought which assumes that the reality of a history
stands or falls by whether it is 'history'... We have to recognize that as holy and inspired Scripture, the Bible is forced to
speak also in the form of saga precisely because its object and
origin are what they are, i.e., not just 'historical' but frankly
also 'non-historical.'[38]

Notice here how Barth insists that the interpretive strategy used for reading the
Bible must "itself originate in the Bible." This is his version of the
Reformer's maxim *scriptura sui interpres*. This is also the basis of his objection to both the Liberal and Orthodox hermeneutics, which allow themselves to
be governed and constrained by extra-Biblical categories and criteria. Barth
insists that non-historical saga is an integral part of biblical narrative because
its "object and origin" are both historical and non-historical, that is, mediate
and immediate to God. Thus one's set of interpretive strategies when it comes
to reading the Bible is fundamentally tied both to the text and to the reality
depicted in and mediated through the text.[39]

Barth has pointed out that most of the Bible is a mixture of saga and history. However, he also notes that the creation narratives are pure saga, just as
other portions of the Bible may be pure history. This means that Barth rejects
the reigning scholarship of his day in its assignment of the creation narratives
to the literary genre of "myth." Barth argues against the conventional defini-
tions of myth as a story of the gods in which both the gods and the story are
not the real point at issue, or myth as the expression of the other-worldly in
terms of this world.[40] Rather, the crucial element in myth is that it clothes
"the essential principles of the general realities and relationships of the natural
and spiritual cosmos, which in distinction from concrete history, are not confined to definite times and places."[41] For Barth, the biblical creation narratives are not myths because they are not clothing for general realities and relationships of the material and spiritual world. They are not myths because on
the surface they tell of concrete history and not general phenomena or riddles
of existence.

It is at this point in his discussion of saga and the capacity of the Genesis
creation narratives to refer to the time-space continuum that he speaks openly
about the relation of this to the reading of the plain sense. He says that while
both of the creation accounts in Genesis are pre-historical pure saga, one must
not read them as though they were historical clothing for non-historical

speculation. That is, the accounts are still to be read according to their plain sense:

All their utterances should be taken literally: not in a shallow but a deep sense; not in a narrow but an inclusive sense; yet in such a way that the obvious meaning of the direct narration should always be given its proper weight; in such a way too that the account as such does not give rise to a picture of all kinds of timeless connexions and relationships which cannot be recounted; but in such a way that the narrative has also and primarily to be taken in all seriousness; in such a way that even the deeper and more inclusive literal sense is sought only on the plane of the historical and therefore of that which can be recounted and is in fact recounted in what follows.[42]

The creation sagas can and must be read therefore according to this deeper literal sense. Here, then, is the significance of Barth's classifying the biblical creation narratives as saga and not myth. Myth does not lend itself to be read according to the literal sense thus defined. On the contrary, myth

chooses and uses the form of a story, but in the case of all intelligent persons it makes the demand that they should look through this story, that they should not cling to it as such, but that in all the enjoyment of its events and forms, spurred on by its cheerful play, they should press on to its true non-historical, timeless and abstract sense, to a perception of the eternal truth presented in the play... It can and will be genuinely understood... only when the web of its narrative is again thoughtfully and yet imaginatively and feelingly analyzed and reduced to its non-historical and timeless and abstract sense.[43]

Myth is monistic, says Barth, knowing only the reality of "man and his cosmos as self-moved and self-resting." According to Barth this means that the very phrase "creation myth" is an oxymoron: real myth excludes the possibility of the reality of a Creator and Master. However, the biblical creation narratives as saga do not exclude this possibility. As saga, they do not

leave the hearer and reader to guess and interpret what lies behind or stands above the historical picture as such: a truth in face of which the historical picture is only a covering which can and must be abandoned. Its truth is identical with the historical picture which is presented by it.[44]

The genre of narrative is therefore an essential ingredient in saga in its ability to bear literal meaning and to be read according to its literal meaning, and it is in part the use of the narrative genre which again is a distinguishing mark between saga and myth:

> [Saga] does not merely use narrative as an accepted form. It is itself a narrative through and through. It has no philosophical system as an accompanying alter ego whose language can express abstractly what it says concretely. What it says can be said only in the form of its own narrative and what follows.[45]

Here the genre of the biblical creation stories as saga, their narrative form, and their ability to bear "literal meaning" and the interpreter's attendant responsibility to read the text according to its "literal sense" converge in a nest of hermeneutical observations. These elements are inseparable from one another. It may help therefore to set the opposing elements in their own categories as in the chart on the following page.[46]

One very interesting observation which comes to the fore here is the fact that for Barth the biblical creation sagas call for reading a "deep" literal sense, one which "points beyond itself." This of course is exactly how figural reading is often seen. However, instead of pointing beyond the text, beyond the narrative, the creation sagas point to the reality of the Creator by pointing the reader to the narrative itself. Creation myth, however, (if such could in fact exist) would call for reading which in a sense falls within the rubric of allegorical. "Creation myth" as such would use the narrative as clothing for timeless truths, but would not be able to refer to anything beyond the created realm, and therefore could not speak of a "creator" at all. Myth is therefore categorically a-theological.

The importance of "taking the narrative seriously on the historical plane" in interpreting the creation sagas is apparent in Barth's mention of two possible exegetical errors which restrain the text's freedom "to speak as a true and time-fulfilling history of the acts of God the Creator."[47] The first error is to read the texts as though they dealt with "timeless, metaphysical or physical explanations of the world" and not with "genuine events."[48] While the narratives are clearly "pre-historical," one is not to read them as though they contained timeless truths, as did Augustine in his *Confessions*.[49] Barth notes that Augustine was led ultimately from this erroneous reading to assume that the

SAGA (Saga)	MYTH (Mythus)
deep, inclusive literal sense	timeless connexions, relationships not recounted
in einem teifen, umfassenden Wortsinn	*zeitlose und unerzählbare Beziehungen und Verhältnisse*
takes narrative seriously on the historical plane	narrative as embodiment of what happens everywhere, ergo not anywhere at any time
die Erzählung als solche gelten und ernst auf der Ebene der geschichtlichen Dinge genommen sein will	*Einkleidungen für das, was sich immer und überall insofern auch nie und nirgends begeben hat*
speaks properly	timeless and abstract; historical covering for non-historical speculation
redet eigentlich	*geschichts-, zeit- und bildlosen Sinn; geschichtlichen Verkleidungen ungeschichtlicher Spekulation*
truth identical with historical picture	perception of eternal truth
ihre Wahrheit identisch mit dem Geschichtsbild	*Erkentniss ewigen Wahrheit*
points beyond itself only to historical saga and history, and not to non-historical meaning	monistic
Weist auch sie über sich selbst hinaus, dann auf die ihr folgende Geschichtssage und Historie, aber gerade nicht auf einen geschichtslosen Sinngehalt	*monistisch*
does not accommodate, wink or nod	accommodates, winks and nods
nicht augenzwinkernd, akkomodierend	*augenzwinkernd, akkomodierend*

creation narratives had many different senses, one of which dovetailed neatly
with Neo-Platonic metaphysics. Neither is one to read the narratives as clothing for an interest in physics, harmonizing them with one's own natural
science as did Basil, Ambrose, and as do many modern apologists. Instead,
one must read them as "once-for-all words and acts."

The other mistake, according to Barth, is not to recognize the connection
between the creation sagas and the rest of the Old Testament, for "the decisive
commentary on the biblical histories of creation is the rest of the Old Testament."[50] In other words, the creation sagas do not tell of just any creator of
the world, but of the One who later makes himself known as Yahweh-Elohim
to his covenant people. The texts have to be read, therefore, within their
larger narrative context, which is biblical and not general religio-historical.

> It should be plain enough that even under this aspect the pas-
> sages cannot clearly convey what they intend to convey; that in
> a new form a timeless meaning is foisted upon them in exactly
> the same way as with Augustine, and at the very point where
> the real context demands that regard should be had to their
> temporal meaning.[51]

The creation sagas, placed as they are at the head of the covenant history, have
an "intention" to convey which cannot be appreciated apart from the literal
reading which takes seriously their "temporal meaning." Again, reading the
creation sagas according to their literal sense is bound inextricably to an
understanding of and respect for their genre as saga and their placement within
the larger narrative of covenant history. Yet, as Barth says, the truth of the
narrative is identical with its historical picture, and if it points beyond itself it
points to the historical saga itself. Even still it would not be proper to say that
for Barth the creation narratives do not refer extra-textually. This very statement itself is tied to his understanding of reading the letter of the text:

> A thoughtful interpretation will be all the more careful and
> reverent with the biblical witness when its humanity is most
> clearly recognized: not for its own sake; not out of any magical
> respect for the letter, which as such is a letter like others; but
> out of respect for the object which has not been ashamed to
> raise up these human witnesses with their limitations and to
> make use of this letter, and which we can know, if at all, only
> through this witness, and through the letter of this witness.[52]

An example of how this concern to restrain interpretation to intra-textual explanation and avoid the concerns of defending the text's supposed ability to refer to the time-space continuum is in Barth's discussion of the rivers of Paradise and the location of the Garden in the second creation saga. Barth says that in addressing the question of the location of the Garden of Eden one must avoid two possible errors, "both of which are equally excluded by what the passage really says." One is to assume that the Garden is not depicted by the saga as being a definite place on earth, and the other is to assume that given the description one can determine where the Garden was, or is. It is clear, says Barth, that the saga presents the Garden as a specific place on earth and not merely a representation of an ideal utopia. The Garden is described, Barth points out, as being "toward the East" in Gen 2:8. Two of the rivers which border it are identifiably geographical realities, the Tigris and the Euphrates. The other two rivers are linked with identifiable regions, Havilah and Ethiopia.

> The whole description of the Garden excludes any suspicion that we do not have here a concrete terrestrial region. But it is also clear, of course, that a geographical localization of this region with the help of the indications of the passage is quite impossible and is obviously not intended by the saga.[53]

Not only is Calvin's attempt to draw a map a logical impossibility, it actually goes against the intent of the text itself. Barth then raises a series of questions which are unanswerable and which indicate, he believes, that the saga does not intend to pinpoint the geographical locale of Eden. The Euphrates and Tigris do not spring from the same source, and there is no identifiable original river that divides into four. Also, there is nothing to prohibit reading "in the East" as referring simply either to the inaccessible desert or to the rising sun.

> It is of the very essence of such passages that while they are concrete in their mention of such places they are only semi-concrete... because as sagas they do not aim to present 'history' but 'pre-historical' history. Necessarily, therefore, we have to accept both the fact that Paradise was planted and existed somewhere and not just everywhere or nowhere but also the fact that there can be no actual investigation of this 'somewhere.' It is palpable that in these passages we have to do with a genuine consideration of real events, persons and things, but only with a consideration and therefore not with a

historical review but with constructions which do not have their origin in observation but in imagination.[54]

Since the saga presents "real events, persons and things," one is impelled and entitled to ask the question of where the Garden of Eden is situated geographically. However, since the saga is not historical review but imaginative prehistorical history, Barth urges that "to be true to the passage, we must drop the question as soon as it is raised." Thus, in his classification of the biblical creation stories as saga and in his definition of saga itself as distinguished from myth, Barth is not bound to apologize for the text's problematic referentiality. Rather, he redescribes the whole problem. This enables him to limit interpretation of the Genesis creation sagas to intra-textual explanation, which he believes is closer to the letter of the text than are the traditional orthodox and modern liberal readings of the first two chapters of Genesis.

Narrative Structure

The most significant factors for Barth's reading of the plain sense of Genesis 1–3 after his classifying the first two chapters under the genre "saga" is his attention to the literary and narrative structure of the text. His keen eye for the literary features in the text allows him to read the stories of Genesis 1 and 2 in particular as a coherent witness, even while he acknowledges and uses to his favor redaction critical conclusions regarding the distinct units. While Calvin tends to rely on the doctrine of God to unify the narratives logically, Barth reads the text as a whole on the basis of what he understands to be literary clues in the text itself. These clues allow fresh plain sense readings which open the text in ways not available either to Augustine or to Calvin. This allows Barth's theological exposition to claim a basis integrally grounded in the biblical text.

The first such clue which he notes is the "indisputable literary connection" between Gen 1:1 and Gen 2:4a. The phrase which opens the first saga, "In the beginning God created the heavens and the earth," and that which closes it, "These are the generations of the heavens and the earth when they were created," form a thematic inclusio which brackets the first saga. Barth notes that the final phrase is a summary which is subjected to a refinement by Gen 1:1 such that "the works of the divine ברא ...are the תולדות, the 'generations' of the heaven and of the earth, as the word is rightly ascribed in the rest of Genesis to all kinds of people, but wrongly ascribed in myths to the reality of the world as such."[55] Thus, by reading Gen 1:1 and Gen 2:4a as commentaries on each other and on what they include, the word תולדות is modified from its meaning within a mythic linguistic field. The effect is such that the word cannot indicate the "eternal self-generation of the world-reality... [but rather] God's free positing of this world-reality." Barth approvingly quotes Gunkel's comment:

> Simply but effectively the author at once establishes the dogma that God has created the world. There is no word in the cosmogonies of other nations that can compare with this first word of the Bible.[56]

Barth's reading relies on this thematic link and at the same time incorporates while disarming any possible mythic connotations brought to the saga by Gen 2:4a.

The next point he makes regarding the narrative structure of the first saga is that the work of the third day is two-fold. He remarks that the words "And God saw that it was good," in his interpretation "God saw how good it was," which is consistently used with the works of the other days, is absent at the work of the second day in Gen 1:8, but appears after the description of the first work of the third day in Gen 1:10.[57] He then notes that in both the work of the second day and the first work of the third day the saga deals with the delimitation of water. That is, in the second day the firmament separates the waters below and above, and in the first work of the third day the dry land divides the seas. The former Barth calls metaphysical and the latter physical. But both, according to Barth, are so clearly related in the author's mind that the concluding statement "God saw that it was good" is added after the conclusion of the first work of the third day. This internal literary link between the work of the second day and the first work of the third day would have been obscured if the work of the second day had included the repetition of the formula "And God saw that it was good."

Barth then turns to the matter of the twofold nature of the work of the third day. He notes that the work of the sixth day is itself twofold as well. There is thus a textual parallel between the work of the third and sixth days, for both include a dual creation. Barth then cites Gunkel's conjecture that the P narrative arranges into six days what in a hypothetical "source" may have been arranged into eight or possibly ten days. The theory posits that this is done in order to establish the sanctity of the Sabbath, and Gunkel complains that the other material has been "completely destroyed" in the process. Barth responds that while Gunkel's theory is "not intrinsically impossible," it itself completely destroys literary and thematic elements of the biblical text. Barth intends to show that one can read the text according to "what the text really says," in other words according to its plain sense, and at the same time make sense of the evidence the text presents without resorting to extra-textual theories of origin or background of the saga.

The first of the elements which Gunkel's theory would distort according to Barth is this correspondence between the two-fold work of the third and the sixth days. In each of these, the second work indicates a transition to a new stage of divine creation. This observation neatly divides the first part of the first saga into two parallel series: days one through three, and days four through six. The first series of days one through three culminates with the creation of vegetation and the second series of days four through six with the creation of humanity.

The second element which would, according to Barth, be destroyed by Gunkel's extra-textual explanation of the origin of the saga is the inner connection between each of the two works of these days. That is, on the third day the dry land separating the seas forms the *sine qua non* of the survival of the vegetation. Likewise, the destiny of the animals and humanity, the works of the sixth day, are inextricably interrelated as Barth later shows through canonical "linguistic usage" of these terms. To suggest that the six-day cycle is a misshapen eight- or ten-day cycle would effectively prohibit this observation.

The third element is the relationship between the concept of creation presented in the first saga and that of time. The final element which Gunkel's theory would destroy is the nuance presented by the saga that "although the author counts the days he does not count the works of God because they are innumerable."[58] The first two observations, of course, are more directly tied to the narrative structure of the saga, and the second two are more thematic. The first two observations add to our list of textual correspondences between the third and sixth days and to the inner correspondences between the works of each day respectively.

Barth then notes that, having divided the days of creation into two series of three, there are correspondences between the work of the first and the fourth days, between the work of the second and fifth days, and between the work of the third and sixth days.[59] The creation of light on the first day is the "indispensable presupposition" of the lights of the firmament created on the fourth day which "are not themselves light but participate in the light."[60] The correspondence between the stages of the two series points to "a new order of creation." The divinely created light of the first day does not need the luminaries of the fourth day, and neither does the vegetation of the fifth day, but the beasts and humanity of the sixth day do. The heavenly luminaries are portrayed by the saga as belonging to the "sphere of human knowledge and

power." Barth notes that unlike the works of the first three days which God
expressly names in the saga, the luminaries of the fourth day are not named.
They are merely described, for it is up to humanity to give them their names,
says Barth.[61] In other words, Barth here implicitly notes a parallel between
the two creation sagas: the lack of divine naming in the second series of days
of the first saga corresponds to the divine instruction for Adam's naming the
creatures in the second saga at Gen 2:19-20, 23. Barth shows via the canon's
usage of the words "sun" and "moon" how they are ascribed personality,
which itself reinforces their place within the second series which culminates
with the creation of humanity. He also distinguishes this biblical understanding of the luminaries as personalities from the Ancient Near Eastern tradition
which tends to assign them divine identity. In addition, Barth shows how the
work of the fourth day points to work of the sixth day by the appearance of the
phrase "let them be for signs and seasons and days and years." It is humanity
which will benefit from the luminaries' function as signs of the times:

> The service which they render is to make it possible for man—
> assuming that he for his part can and does realize this—to live
> a life which is not merely dreamy and vegetative, but which is
> marked by a wakeful consciousness of time and of history.[62]

Thus, while the work of the fourth day corresponds to the work of the first
day, in and of itself it belongs properly within the rubric of the second series
culminating with the creation of humanity. Just as the work of the fourth day
corresponds with the work of the first day, so the work of the second day corresponds with that of the fifth day.

Gunkel, of course, has pointed out that, since normally fish and birds
have no existential correspondence with each other, his theory that the "six-
day schema does not fit the material" here is strengthened. Barth, however,
responds by observing the correspondence of the second and fifth days, and
points out that the correspondence between the fish and fowls has "nothing
whatever to do with zoological questions."[63] The correspondence here again
hinges on literary matters. The fish and birds, created on day five, occupy the
spheres of the firmament and the waters, created on day two. However, one
might have expected that the birds would be mentioned first in day five since
the firmament was mentioned first in day two. Barth puzzles over this and
points out that mentioning fish first in a series of living creatures is consistent
with the linguistic practice of the Old Testament, except where humanity is
mentioned. Barth points out how the fifth day increases the crescendo which
will climax with the creation of humanity on the sixth day, for here we see the

creation of the first autonomous living creatures. This is reinforced by what he understands to be the purposeful use of the verb ברא to depict the creation of the sea monsters at Gen 1:21, for it is the same verb which was used at Gen 1:1 and which will be used again at the creation of humanity at Gen 1:27.

Barth also points out that the internal correspondence between the two works of the third day itself parallels the internal correspondence of the two works of the sixth day. The protection of the land against the sea is the *sine qua non* for the second work of the third day, the creation of vegetation. Likewise, the creation of land animals which inhabit this protected dwelling place is itself the corresponding prerequisite for the creation of humanity, the second work of the sixth day. The second work of the third day likewise corresponds to the second work of the sixth day: the creation of vegetation is the climax of the first series of days and the creation of humanity is the climax of the second series of days, as well as of all that precedes it.

Barth then points to the internal correspondences between the two works of the sixth day, for the land animals are "at every point... inferior to man and yet his companion and even forerunner." Barth relates the description of humanity's dominion over these creatures in Genesis 1 with the "linguistic usage" of the Old Testament which depicts humanity to be as dependent upon the animal world as the creatures are upon humanity.[64] Barth even goes so far as to speak of the "prefigurative character" of the internal correspondence of the works of the sixth day. In other words, he thus bases a "figurative" reading on the plain sense of the text, which is itself reached via attention to the narrative structure and literary coherence of the text itself.

> Precisely in its lowest humiliation, as the animal slain and sacrificed, it will bring before him the final mystery of his own history, i.e., that of his own fatherhood and sonship; the indispensable but saving offering of the promised Son of Man as the proper content of the permission and promise given to him. For in all its animal limitation and impotence, the beast could hardly have been a more important precursor of man than by giving him this picture which he has good reason to try to escape and which he himself is quite unable to fulfill. Significantly, the creation of man and of these living beings is the work of one and the same day.[65]

The fruit of Barth's parsing of the literary structure of the first saga here is thus a figurative linking of the two works of the sixth day of creation in proclamation of the "theme of human history" as he understands it. All of this he draws from a close reading of the Genesis creation sagas.

Barth also parses the second saga and indicates correspondences between the first and second sagas.[66] In other words, his attention to literary structure does not leave each creation narrative in isolation, but seeks to find the links which bind the one to the other. Thus they are read, even while discrete units, as forming a whole. The first sequence is Gen 2:4b-7, which itself abbreviates the material presented in the first saga. Gen 2:6-7 forms a parenthesis in which man is formed from the dust of the ground, but the force of the sequence is on the description of "the earth and the heavens" (Gen 2:4b) with emphasis on "the earth." Barth notes the parallel between the second saga's phrase, "and there was no man to till the ground" (Gen 2:5), which describes the earth as a uncultivated place, and the first saga's "darkness was on the face of the deep" (Gen 1:2). Both represent "the state which God in creation has negated and rejected".[67]

The second "passage" of the second creation saga Barth marks off as Gen 2:8-17. In this second unit, humanity is now the focus. While the first passage had the earth in view, there is in this second passage no reference to the earth as such. The focus is now on a specific place on earth: the Garden of Eden. Barth argues that, while Gen 2:15 says that God placed man in Eden to till the ground, the description of the garden in Gen 2:9-14 is significant. Eden is a lush, well-watered garden where there grows "every tree that is pleasant to the sight and good for food" (Gen 2:9). According to the saga, Eden is a sanctuary. Barth uses this observation to ground his argument that man is given rest there: Eden itself is a kind of spatial Sabbath which corresponds to the "temporal sanctuary in the first saga" which introduces the Sabbath.[68] Here is another link between the two sagas, according to Barth: Sabbath and Eden. Both are sanctuaries, the first temporal and the second spatial. It is then only a short skip to the next link. The Garden of Eden is seen to be a prototype for the promised land with which there is an "inner connection", for both are a definite place on earth, a sanctuary watered by the miraculous providence of God where the will of God may be known. Barth notes that humanity is not created in Eden but placed there graciously. After all, Gen 2:8 does follow Gen 2:7! Likewise, Israel is not created in the promised land but graciously led there by the providence of God.

> The creation story tells us that the particularity of God's revelation and salvation, as it emerged in the promise granted to Israel and in the gift of this land and its determination as the 'holy' land, was not a mere coincidence but was deeply

embedded in the nature of all things; that this 'holy' land
already had its prototype in God's creative act establishing all
things; indeed that the divine creative act had its meaning in
the fact that it constituted this prefiguration.[69]

Barth furthers his argument based upon what he sees to be a literary connection
between the Garden of Eden and the promised land. Creation is the external
basis of the covenant according to the "plain sense" of the text. Not only is
there a link to be drawn between the Garden of the second saga and the Sabbath of the first, but also between the Garden and its literary counterpart later
in the Pentateuch, the Promised Land. In fact, the biblical-theological themes
of creation and providence, law and promise are integrally linked according to
a reading of the plain sense of the first two chapters of Genesis.

When discussing the literary unity of Gen 2:8-17, Barth refers to the
theory which posits an earlier form of the saga according to which there was
only one tree, namely the tree of the knowledge of good and evil. He says that
this theory is not without some merit, for saga by nature composes its picture
out of different elements. It is not inconceivable, then, that such an element
would be a precursor saga with only one tree. However,

> It may be asked whether we are not demanding too great preci-
> sion from a passage of this kind if we allow ourselves to be so
> concerned about such obscurities that we are incited to break
> up the sources...there are as good grounds for affirming that
> (originally or later) the text must have had a good coherent
> meaning in its present and not merely in certain underlying
> forms, so that it is legitimate and even obligatory to ask con-
> cerning it.[70]

In other words, while Barth is quite willing to entertain the possibility of an
earlier source which speaks only of the tree of the knowledge of good and evil,
he is not willing to explore that possibility at any great length. To do so
would distract him from the task at hand, which is to make sense out of the
text before him. He does not react to the theory in this way on the basis alone
of a pre-conceived notion of what he understands the text to say, but rather on
the basis of observations of literary features of the text itself. He acknowledges that in Gen 2:9 the geographical relationship between the two trees is not
clear, and that in Gen 3:3 the tree of knowledge does indeed seem to be the
"tree in the midst of the garden." But he asks whether the "silence by which
the tree of life is surrounded" in Gen 3, until the tree is emphasized in Gen

3:22, may have been originally important. Barth argues that if the tree of life had not been present even in this absence, it would have been impossible for the discussion with the serpent to have taken place. This presence is introduced in Gen 2:9 with the phrase "the tree of life also in the midst of the garden" which precedes the mention of the tree of the knowledge of good and evil. If the tree of life were indeed a later addition, the "completed whole owes its present wealth and depth decisively to this addition."

Barth later picks up this discussion of the two trees of the Garden of Eden and says that if one is to read the saga in its existing form, one must acknowledge that the story (*das Bild*) is "as much dominated in the foreground by the tree of knowledge as it is in the background by the tree of life."[71] Here he begins to sound as though he were discussing a painting rather than a text, and the analogy may be fitting. That is, one sees a painting as it were all at once, the left in light of the right and vice versa, the top in light of the bottom and vice versa, the foreground in light of the background and vice versa. It is thus that Barth reads the Biblical text, the parts in light of the whole and the whole in light of the parts, unrestricted even though guided by the linear movement of the text. That is, Barth's attention to literary features of the text and its narrative structure does not restrict his reading to linear movement through the text, as though he were reading a novel for the first time. The text of the Bible is for Barth more like a "painting" and reading this painting is more like entering a three-dimensional world than following a two-dimensional narrative line. Foreground, background, left, right, top and bottom confront the observer of the biblical text/world simultaneously. Barth would say that it is the nature of the Biblical text *per se* to confront the reader from all directions at once, and that is why he can and does read in this canonical fashion.

Thus he reads the two trees in light of the entire canon, and argues that while the tree of knowledge is the reason for the expulsion from the Garden, the tree of life is "the more distinctive of Paradise and man's existence in it and the act of creation as such." Bringing together pictures of the tree of life in Rev 2:7, Rev 22:2, and Ezekiel 47:12, he concludes of the tree of life in Gen 2 the following:

> The fact that it stands in the midst of God's garden surely indicates that it stands in a special relation to the Lord of this Garden...by the planting of the tree of life in its midst God declares that His primary, central and decisive will is to give [humanity] Himself.[72]

By holding the picture of the tree of life in Gen 2 against other representations of it elsewhere in the canon, Barth argues that it indicates God's very presence. From here he then makes the move of comparing it with other representations of God's presence in the canon such that the tree of life in Gen 2 "prefigures" (*vorbildet*) the tabernacle in the camp of Israel, the temple in Jerusalem, and the Holy of Holies in the tabernacle and temple. Barth also points to the provisions God makes in Gen 3:22-23 to ensure that the couple is mercifully prevented from access to the tree of life and thus from God's presence, now that the tree of life has been turned into a threat. This Barth reads in light of God's protection of Israel from His immediate presence at Sinai (Ex 19:24), and God's shielding of Moses in the cleft of the Rock (Ex 33:18). Likewise, Barth points out that the ark of the covenant brings to the Philistines nothing but destruction (1 Sam 5-6) and the High Priest is permitted into the Holy of Holies only once a year (Lev 16:2). All this, and the observation that the tree of the knowledge of good and evil has no parallels elsewhere in the Old Testament, leads Barth to argue that the tree of life is distinctive of the Garden of Eden, and of man's existence, and thus of the act of creation itself.

The third section of the second creation saga, Gen 2:18-25, is according to Barth its climax and conclusion. The theme of this section is the creation of humanity in the duality of male and female, "the basic form of all association and fellowship which is the essence of humanity." This section Barth thus considers to be an expansion of or commentary on Gen 1:27, "So God created man in his own image, in the image of God he created him; male and female he created them." Even while these verses also contain stories about the creation of animals and the origin of language, says Barth, these are not the central thrust of the unit. He argues this by appealing to the placement of this section immediately before Gen 3, that is,

> immediately before the transition from the 'pre-historical' history of creation to the 'historical' history of the covenant, i.e., to the account of the event in which man will perform his first responsible action, and will do so at once in the twofold form, both the man and the woman being conjoined as the doubtful heroes of this event.[73]

Thus he determines the theme of this particular unit in part from its placement within the larger narrative context of the second creation saga.

Barth also notes other literary connections between the first and second sagas. One such correspondence is Gen 1:26, "Let us make man in our image," and Gen 2:18, "It is not good that man should be alone." Both of these, says Barth, serve as a "divine pause" which clue the reader in to the fact that what follows is the climax, the "decisive moment in the whole creative act."[74] The emphasis in both is on the creation of the dual form of humanity. Thus, the final goal and climax of this section is the cry of Adam in Gen 2:23, "This is now bone of my bones, and flesh of my flesh." Barth notes that this is, significantly, the first human speech expressly recorded by the saga. This cry turns the story of Adam's naming of the animals into part of the thematic crescendo. Adam had previously been unable to find any among the animals whom he could "address as Thou." It is only with the creation of Eve that Adam has found his "Thou" and can exclaim, "This is now bone of my bones and flesh of my flesh!"

Internal connections between the two sagas, according to Barth's reading, also appear at Gen 2:19, Gen 1:24, and Gen 2:7. In Gen 2:19 as in 1:24, the animals are called "living creatures," as also humanity is called in Gen 2:7. Again, Adam's naming of the animals in the second saga (Gen 2:20) is a formal parallel to man's dominion over the creatures in the first saga (Gen 1:26, 28). Also, the phrase in the second saga, "The man and his wife were both naked, and were not ashamed" (Gen 2:25), is parallel to the statement in the first saga where God saw all that He had made, including man, "and behold, it was very good" (Gen 1:31). However, Barth says that the most exact parallel to Gen 2:25 is the divine sabbath observance in Gen 2:2-3 for there, says Barth, humanity is given a share in the sabbath rest. The word "both" ("the man and his wife were both naked") here underscores the central theme of the twofold creation of humanity. No longer here is man the only spokesman as he was in Gen 2:23.[75] Here the two human creatures, male and female, are spoken of as one, and both know themselves as they are created and are not ashamed.

After noting the internal formal and literary parallels between the two sagas, Barth says that if we read them in isolation from the rest of the Bible, we might conclude that the sagas tell of the "divine basis of love and marriage as the fulfillment of the relationship between man and wife."[76] But even this would not make sense of Gen 1:27, the creation of man both male and female in the image of God. Neither would it make sense of the second saga's presentation of the creation of humanity male and female as the climax of creation. Instead, says Barth, one must ask the question of the relationship between these themes and the problem of human existence and God's dealings with Israel in the rest of the Old Testament. In answering these questions, one will find that the creation sagas place one "before the mystery of the divine covenant of grace as the inner basis of the divine creation."[77] Barth then reads texts from the Song of Songs, Ezekiel, Hosea and Jeremiah, and finally

Ephesians 5 to explore and defend this thesis that the covenant of grace is the inner basis of creation. This, then, is also the thesis of his *Church Dogmatics*, paragraph 41, section 3. Thus Barth's exegetical observations regarding the literary structure and unity of Gen 1-2 support his dogmatic framework and his dogmatic framework supports his observations regarding the literary structure and internal coherence of Gen 1-2. Ultimately, however, his theological observations are based on literary features of the biblical text itself.

Secular Science

For Barth's reading of the plain sense of Gen 1-3, it has been shown that the text is to be read according to the central assumption that it witnesses everywhere and throughout to Jesus Christ. Because of this, the text is not to be read according to the rules and assumptions of modern science when they "decenter" this assumption. That would be to apply an interpretive element which is foreign to and stands outside the text, which would result in the distortion of the plain sense of the text. This does not require an a-historical or un-scientific worldview. Instead, one must indeed read with the eyes and ears of the ancients, those who "wrote" the text and those who first treasured the text. For example, Barth comments on the creation of light before the creation of the luminaries, a problem which has disturbed many an interpreter before Barth's time. Barth says that

> the offense which modern science is the first to take is very obvious. Indeed, it is almost too obvious to be taken too seriously, although whether it has the same weight for more recent physics as that previously ascribed to it is another matter. We certainly cannot attribute this circumstance to the naiveté of ancient science which regarded light as an independent thing...[78]

One must not take the offense which Barth considers "modern science" to have taken, which is presumably to have thought that since the sun is the generator of light it must be part of the creation of the first day. Instead, one is to read "with the ears of an ancient Egyptian," who would notice the difference between this description of the origin of creation and that of his or her own culture's understanding of the origin of creation. Since in the biblical creation saga light precedes the creation of the sun, there is no possibility allowed by the text for sun-worship.

Again, at the creation of the firmament on the second day, one is neither to resist the biblical portrayal nor to force it into harmony with a modern scientific worldview. Instead, Barth points out that Gen 1:14, Gen 1:17 and Gen 1:20 refer to this celestial firmament. This element may in fact be important enough to the saga that we should try to understand what the biblical account means by it. Barth then looks at some other biblical uses of the word רקיע and concludes that the biblical witness expressly accepts the view of a celestial ocean, the "metaphysical danger of the upper sea held back" by the firmament. Therefore, we cannot accept the explanation of some moderns such as Delitzsch and Calvin and some of the ancients that the waters above the firmament are simply the clouds. Barth points out that Calvin's explanation of the "waters above" as clouds rests on rationalistic argumentation, for Calvin says that such waters are *alienum sensu communi*, contrary to common sense. Barth argues that this type of reasoning is "quite out of place in the exposition of Gen 1:6." Barth then cites Luther as treating this verse with exemplary closeness to the text, for Luther willingly admits that we cannot know what this water above the firmament is, "but that we must accept the fact that heaven is placed between the waters."[79] After a rather lengthy treatment of the topic of the firmament's representation by the canon, Barth shows that what interests the saga is not the firmament itself or the metaphysical danger which it holds back, but the fact that its repulsion is accomplished by the Word of God. He also notes that the biblical view of the transformation expected at the end-time will render the firmament unnecessary and will "thus be removed without involving the end of all things for the lower cosmos." Here, again, intra-textual explanation is to be preferred over against the extra-textual categories of modern science.

Indeed, at one point Barth proposes that the creation sagas can best be understood as being discordant with not only the modern worldview but the ancient worldview as well.[80] According to Barth, the end-result of the "worldview" of the first creation saga, in particular up to the point where the creation of man is introduced, is to overturn both worldviews. To expect to be able to read it in accord with one's worldview is to make a hermeneutical error which prevents one from reading the plain meaning of the text. Barth claims that both the ancient worldview which finds in the planets powerful ruling deities and the modern worldview which posits millions of solar systems and thousands of light years are offended by the first creation saga which insists on the purposiveness of the cosmic system in its relationship to earth and humanity. Barth claims that Gen 1 cannot conceive of the cosmic system apart from its service to the earth and most importantly its inhabitants.

In this way the heavenly bodies are no longer deities and lords
to whom man owes and shows respect, worship and service,
nor, according to modern interpretation, representatives of the
infinite universe which absolutely determines man.   On the
contrary, they are helps given by God to man.[81]

Both worldviews will distort the reading of the plain sense, therefore, if they
are allowed to form the hermeneutical framework against which the text is
read.   Here we have yet another instance of Barth's "intratextuality," where
the text itself and the world which it depicts are to govern interpretation
instead of allowing the importing of textually foreign categories for interpretation.

    But the implication here is greater than simply the prohibition of extra-
textual frameworks for interpretation of the biblical text.   One could
understand Barth to be arguing also that the modern interpreter is not in any
"new" hermeneutical situation vis-à-vis the biblical text, as Bultmann would
argue.   Since the dependence on worldview is to be excluded for both the
ancient and the modern interpreter for the explication of the biblical texts, the
modern worldview is no more of an impediment to the reading of the plain
sense of the creation sagas than was the ancient.

Gunkel is right: 'Faith in Yahweh has triumphed over the worship of the heavenly bodies.'   But do we realize what this
means?   A more radical volte-face cannot be imagined.   The
author accomplished this in the framework of a pre-Copernican
conception of the world.   But even the Copernican discovery
only means a readjustment within the view which is here questioned not only in its pre-Copernican but also in its Copernican
form.[82]

The creation sagas turn upside-down any assumptions of the purposelessness of
the cosmos or the insignificance of humanity against the powers and laws of
the cosmos.   Thus, both ancient and modern interpreters misread the sagas if
they do not at least read this element in them.   The chance may be that the
modern, with modernity's clear difficulty with reading the direct historical
referentiality of the sagas, may in fact be in a privileged position over against
the ancients with regard to the reading of the plain sense of the biblical text.
The opportunity is ours then to reach for what the text does affirm according
to its plain sense, instead of to assume that its plain sense is "false" according
to the judgments of modern science.   If the text is read with the assumption

that it is not affirming science at all but rather the theological relationship of the cosmos and humanity, it will still have something to say to moderns as it did to ancients.

This is in effect what Barth says at a later juncture in his discussion. In treating the creation of the sea and air creatures of the fifth day, Barth points out that the

> Church Fathers can only obscure what the passage is really trying to say when in their commentaries and sermons they try on the one hand to make use of all the natural science of their day, and on the other to attach to its constituent parts the most diverse edifying and naturalistic allegorisings... (e.g. Ambrose)... If we are to understand the passage we must turn our backs resolutely on all scientific or pious considerations and look only in the two directions which it indicates, namely, the depth of the ocean and the height of the atmosphere...[83]

Thus, Barth's exegesis is not recommending a return to all patristic methods as has been suggested from some quarters. The Fathers were just as susceptible as modern interpreters are to falling into the hermeneutical error of letting scientific and other extra-textual concerns govern the explication of the plain sense. Instead, Barth urges us to look only in the directions which the text indicates. Here, according to Barth, both ancients and moderns trip over their own questions and expectations instead of letting the text guide them.

Modern Commentators and Historical Criticism

Barth's assumption that the text functions to witness to Jesus Christ is, of course, an assumption that historical-critical scholarship would prohibit from guiding exegesis insofar as it is understood to admit theological eisogesis. One might therefore think that Barth would reject historical criticism in its various forms. While this is clearly not the case, Barth's relationship with historical critical scholarship is, to be sure, complex.[84]

Barth refers his readers in 3.1 to commentators both ancient and modern, Christian and Jewish. Of the modern commentators, among the most frequently cited here are the Jewish scholar Benno Jacob, with whom Barth often agrees, and the Christian scholar Gunkel, with whom Barth often disagrees.[85] He also refers often to the work of Delitzsch, Zimmerli, and Jeremias among others.[86] All of these use historical-critical methods, and while Barth generally finds their methods and conclusions useful for his own reading, he usually finds them at best incomplete. He often finds it necessary to correct and build on their comments.[87]

For example, Barth notes that scholarly opinion concludes that there is no direct dependent relationship between the creation myth of the Babylonian epic *Enuma Elish* and the cosmogony of Berosus and the biblical creation stories of Genesis 1 and 2, but only of a common relationship to older traditions still from which all may derive.[88] Barth includes this observation within his comments as though to indicate that he accepts the scholarly opinion. He then goes on to say that it is also generally accepted that there is material agreement between the stories of Genesis 1 and 2 only

> 'in certain parts' (Gunkel, p. 129) or 'isolated relics' (p. 128); and that the mythical tradition in Gen. 1-2 has been 'very much deflated' (p. 122), or 'muffled,' or even 'reduced to a mere fragment' (p. 130), having been 'amalgamated' (p. 129) with the religion of Israel... it has been said that in Israel myth has been 'historicised' and rendered 'impotent' as myth...[89]

This, however, Barth proceeds to counter in his entire reading of the biblical creation stories. He begins by arguing that historicised myth is not myth at all but "saga," which, as we have seen above, is a different genre which demands different rules of reading. One must not approach Genesis 1 and 2 expecting myth such as one finds in the Ancient Near East, for one will only read the texts "against the grain," so to speak. By reading the biblical creation stories as saga Barth is freed to read the texts at face value, according to their "plain sense." Furthermore, throughout his reading of Genesis 1 and 2 he goes to lengths to note the material coherence of the accounts, even while acknowledging literary seams and disjunctures.[90] His refusal to judge the texts by external standards (such as those of the Ancient Near Eastern creation myths) allows him to read the biblical texts according to their plain sense as he sees it. This allows him to acknowledge and appreciate the internal thematic and literary unity of the text. Thus his use of historical critical research in the reading of the plain sense is as follows: such research functions as a negative foil against which Barth sets up his own categories which he argues account more adequately for the evidence of the biblical creation narratives themselves. Thus, while he acknowledges the possibility that an "alien and non-theological historical criticism" can potentially distort the reading of the plain sense of scripture, here he clearly takes full advantage of historical criticism (even if negatively) to highlight the reading of the plain sense.[91]

Again, Barth can use the observations of historical critical inquiry to open his own literary examination of the text. In one such example of this he picks up on what would be deemed in more conventional historical criticism to be a conclusion or solution of a textual problem. Instead of settling for its use as a conclusion, however, Barth uses it as the grain of sand which in his interpretive oyster produces the pearl of exegesis, to use a rabbinic image. In discussing Gen 1:5b, "and there was evening and there was morning," Barth notes that

> The curious order, evening-morning, obviously corresponds to the Jewish way of calculating a day and especially the Sabbath. But this does not explain it, because for its part the Jewish calculation (as it may be seen in Neh 13:19 and Dan 8:14 in the Old Testament and in 2 Cor 11:25 in the New) may be traced back to our text or to the tradition which lies behind or runs parallel with it.[92]

This etiological explanation often given for this verse (even Calvin gives it) does not really explain anything according to Barth. The question still remains as to what "the calculation of our passage and tradition" is, and what the text is indicating by such a word order.

Barth uses this brief note as a springboard for literary inquiry. First he points out that there are two clearly distinguished yet parallel clauses, a "parallelism which rightly and even necessarily reminds us of the two-fold covenant of Jer 33." He also points out that evening indicates the idea of fulfillment and morning of beginning, and that the ordering of the terms thus encloses and hems in the night. Thus night is "always in the sphere of God's power and glory." The enclosing of night between evening and morning forces even this fleeting triumph of darkness "into the order of creation... compelling it in its own involuntary way to join in creation's praise." Because of these observations, which began with an historical critical conclusion and moved to literary and theological inquiry, Barth says that one must therefore be willing to accept Luther's translation, "the first day was made of evening and morning." While this is not a "literal" word-for-word translation, it is true to the substance of the phrase. Here Barth's examination of the text is much closer to the words than is the broader historical critical reading, or either the reading of Augustine or Calvin for that matter. Yet even while Barth's interpretation is much closer to the words of the text, he can opt for a translation which itself is not word-for-word. In his closeness to the words, he is not bound by the words but is true to what he regards to be the substance of the text.

Microexegesis: Words

Verbal Meaning

The examination of grammar, syntax and verbal meaning in the reading of the literal sense of scripture deepens significantly in Barth's interpretation of Genesis in comparison with that of Augustine and of Calvin. Barth's knowledge of Greek, Latin and Hebrew is excellent, and he compares the Hebrew text with the Septuagint and the Vulgate as though they were commentaries on the Hebrew. This he does just as freely as he compares the Hebrew text with the translations of Luther, Calvin and the prominent vernacular translations.[93] He freely corrects the translations, as is evident from warnings against the Septuagint translation of the Garden of Eden at Gen 2:8 as "Paradise" and against its translation at Gen 2:2 of the seventh day as the sixth day.[94] Of course, Barth has the advantages of modern scholarship to which our pre-critical readers did not have access, such as concordances and lexica of both classical and biblical literature. But Barth's reading is close to the text and results in such observations as noting functional synonyms,[95] the importance of voice,[96] verbal repetition,[97] person and number of verbs,[98] prepositions,[99] word order,[100] introduction of new terminology,[101] and plays on words,[102] just to mention a few examples.

Working closely with the Hebrew text, he explores verbal meaning to help uncover the plain sense.[103] At Gen 1:1, he notes that the meaning of the verb ברא "points to the creative act whose subject can only be this Elohim." Here he is able to conclude from this observation of verbal sense the traditional doctrinal reading of *creatio ex nihilo*, for the creative act of God indicated by this particular verb can exclude any idea of cooperation of or conflict from a pre-existent reality.[104] Thus we have an example of his examination of verbal sense which confirms a traditional reading according to the letter of the text.

His investigation of verbal sense itself is not limited to the use of lexica, but also draws on the use of intra-canonical word study. For example, when he attempts to explain the meaning of the words of Gen 1:2, תהו ובהו, Barth notes that according to A. Jeremias, the term תהו is related to the Babylonian mythological arch-mother *Tiamat*. He also points out that this term is used in the Old Testament to signify either desert places, whether city or wilderness, or even an empty assertion. Barth points out that in 1 Sam 12:21 it is used to describe the idols of the heathen nations and in Is 41:29 and Is 44:9 it describes those who make and worship such idols. He then notes that the word בֹּהוּ occurs only in conjunction with תֹּהוּ and means simply "vacuum." He suggests that it may possibly be verbally related to the Phoenician and Babylonian goddess "Bau," the personification of night as arch-mother of humankind.

> The two terms thus bring us to the heart of the mythical world
> whose figures did not and could not have any precise or posi-
> tive meaning for the thought and language of Israel-Judah but
> were simply personifications of that which is abhorrent.[105]

Barth thus analyzes these two terms against the background of their "linguistic usage"[106] within the linguistic fields of both (secondarily) Ancient Near Eastern myth and (primarily) the Old Testament. In other words, Barth does not disregard the fruits of historical critical research and does not shy away from this phrase's connotations within the world of myth, but uses these conclusions in order to understand how the Old Testament appropriates material from the surrounding cultures within its own religious understanding. Finally, he looks at two passages, Jer 4:23 and Is 34:11, in which both terms are mentioned together as they are in Gen 1:2, and which depict visions of the horrors of the final judgment. Barth concludes these observations by saying that

> The earth as תֹּהוּ ובֹהוּ is the earth which is nothing as such,
> which mocks its Creator and which can only be an offense to
> the heaven above it, threatening it with the same
> nothingness.[107]

By this exploration which embraces lexical investigation, history-of-religions research, and the canon's usage of the terms, Barth offers an understanding of the phrase תֹּהוּ ובֹהוּ which is deeper and more nuanced than was Calvin's on account of his exploration of verbal meaning within Ancient Near Eastern myth and the Old Testament.

Text and Author

Certainly Barth does not follow Schleiermacher's interest in the inner life of the author in his attempt to understand a text, nor does he equate the plain sense of the biblical material with what the author was trying to convey.[108]

However, he does notice in the course of textual interpretation the "author's" use of words,[109] distinctive stylistic or thematic features of a particular author,[110] sources on which the author draws,[111] particular interests of the author[112] or what the author may have had in mind.[113] While "harmonization" can sometimes be a proper interpretive device according to Barth, when applied improperly it can distort the intention of the author which distorts in turn the plain reading of the text.[114] Sometimes instead of referring to the "author," Barth will speak of the text itself or the "saga" or sometimes the "witness" or even the "editor."[115] Thus he is ultimately interested more in the text itself than any postulated author behind the text. The text itself can even be said to have an "intention."[116] But the text is recognized to be of composite nature, and even the intentions and interests of the composite parts of the text can be discerned and are of help to the interpreter.[117]

One of the reasons why Barth cannot limit his understanding of plain sense to authorial meaning is that "there are questions not answered by the Old Testament." In fact, there are very important questions indeed which are not answered by the Old Testament, especially with regard to the "objective christological meaning" of the text.[118] To limit one's inquiry into the literal meaning of a biblical passage to investigation of the author's intention would be to limit oneself to the "subjective meaning" of the passage. This subjective meaning itself could possibly have been unfolded simply by reference to "the history of Israel and the general anthropology secondarily and implicitly revealed in it." This limitation would ignore questions which the Old Testament does not answer, to be sure, but which according to Barth it clearly asks.

As earlier noted, Barth recognizes and accepts the modern theory of authorship of the creation stories. He freely speaks of the "juxtaposition of the P passage Gen 1 and the J passage Gen 2."[119] He argues that Gen 2 is neither a supplement to nor commentary on Gen 1, but that both are independent sagas, both of which deal with the same God, the same pre-historical event, and the same world. They are different histories of creation and can be harmonized only by doing violence to the text. Each of the accounts must first be read as if it were the only one, and only subsequently are they to be read in conjunction:

> Our best course is to accept that each has its own harmony, and
> then to be content with the higher harmony which is achieved
> when we allow the one to speak after the other.[120]

Doing so, Barth finds internal links, as we noted above, between the two accounts which he finds theologically fruitful. He arguably might not have found these internal links if he had been willing to settle either for the more traditional approach which reads the second saga as a commentary on or supplement to the first saga, or for the modern approach which assigns one account to P and the other to J. Likewise, there are elements distinct to each saga which Barth may not have been able to recognize had he not read them each as their own internally independent story.[121]

Exegetical clues and grist for the theological mill can be gleaned not only from the authorial meaning and the redaction of sources, but even from the later rabbinic scribals addition of chapter and verse demarcations. In commenting on Gen 2:1–3, Barth points out that

> It was not for nothing, but as a commentary worth noting, that a later age opened a new chapter with the depiction of what took place on the seventh day. Nor was it for nothing that in this way what took place on the seventh day was brought into the vicinity of the second creation saga which is so very different in orientation.[122]

Barth's reading of the connection between the divine Sabbath rest in the first saga and the story of the Garden of Eden in the second is buttressed by this observation, which respects the final form of the text as a whole.[123] Thus to say that man was placed in the Garden of Eden for rest and not for labor is not to force the text or to read into the text according to Barth. This is the "intention," he might say, of the text which was followed by those who later took the biblical text and divided it into chapter and verse. In a sense, he is saying that the scribes agree with him! The important thing to note here is the degree to which Barth stays close to the text, even in this case noting the interpretive significance of scribal additions.

We have seen how Barth accepts modern theories of biblical authorship as would assign the creation accounts to different authors. Yet there is clearly at work the underlying assumption of Divine Authorship as well. This must be the case or Barth could not claim that the text witnesses to Jesus Christ throughout; if the Bible were merely a collection of texts authored by different groups in the Ancient Near East (for it is certainly this in part for Barth), it could have no coherent voice with which to witness.

Canonical Setting and Prooftext

Barth's prior commitment to the notion of the Bible as witness allows him to read the text very closely while at the same time "jumping" from location to location within the canon. His exegetical method places great value on investigating the use of words, motifs, and themes in the canon for understanding how such an element is to be read in the passage at issue. This is part of the way his appropriation of the Reformers' *scriptura sui interpres* plays itself out in his exegesis.

For example, in his discussion of the relationship between the first Genesis creation saga and Ancient Near Eastern creation myth, Barth points out that the distinctive element in the biblical sagas is the emphasis on the "divine utterance as the unique instrument of creation."[124] He then shows how this has been "keenly noted and adopted in the rest of the Biblical tradition," citing texts from the Psalms, Isaiah, Amos, 2 Corinthians, Romans, the Gospel of John, Hebrews, and Job. He concludes by returning to the Genesis saga, saying

> What counts is that we are actually told by the saga—whatever may have been the circle and shape of its vision at the time when it was written down or in the underlying form—that God's utterance is for everything and all things distinct from God the absolutely first thing, the whence, behind and above which there is nothing else...not saying this in a vacuum but in the context and at the head of the whole witness of the Old and New Testament...[125]

Thus the distinction between the Genesis saga and its Ancient Near Eastern "counterparts" is made not only on the basis of the saga itself, but on the basis of the saga within the context of the entire canon, and indeed on the basis of the placement of that saga in opening the rest of the canon. This is just one such example, of which one could cite many, in which Barth reads the passage at hand in light of the canonical context in order to uncover its own plain sense.

Another example of a canonical reading is in his discussion of Gen 1:3-5, in which he uses the canonical representation of light to read Gen 1:3-5 in what he might claim is a justifiably plain sense reading. He observes by exploring other biblical passages that light in Gen 1:3 is the sign of all the rest of creation. Indeed, says Barth, like the apostolic office, it is "the sign and witness of God Himself at the heart of the cosmos." He says of the biblical texts which he cites in support of this statement that they are "not just pictorial utterances or analogies but highly exact representations of the meaning already given to the creation, existence and function of light in Genesis 1:3." That is, these other biblical passages interpret light such that they read Gen 1:3 according to its plain sense. Not only are these texts which he cites "exact representations" of the meaning given to light in the Genesis passage, but Barth insists that he himself is reading both the other biblical texts and Gen 1:3-5 according to what he might say is the plain sense, although he does not use the term here. Notice the terms which he does use:

> What is constituted once and for all with the creation of light is the law of the history willed by God. Where this law is proclaimed and recognized by the creature; where there is revelation in an objective and subjective sense of the concept, there we have the ministry of the light created by God according to Gen 1:3, so that we may speak of light and its work *not pictorially and hyperbolically but with supreme strictness and realism.*[126]

Here he is commenting on Gen 1:3 by a broad canonical reading such that what he observes about Gen 1:3 could not be observed apart from the rest of the canon. At the same time, he maintains that it is an "exact representation of the meaning" of Gen 1:3 itself. Reading the light of Gen 1:3 as the "law of the history willed by God" and "revelation in the objective and subjective sense of the concept" is to read with "supreme strictness and realism."

His understanding of canonical reading leads him not only to read thus in word-study fashion, but also to note parallels within the canon, just as he noted parallels between the two creation sagas themselves. One such observation is that the living space for the creature marked by the creation of the first day, and therefore time and the promise of time to come, in Gen 1:3-5 is paralleled in Gen 8:22: "While the earth remains, seedtime and harvest, cold and heat, summer and winter, day and night shall not cease."[127] By noticing that this promise is given after the destruction of the Flood, Barth points to the

> necessary connection between creation and the new creation, between created time and the last time to which it moves. God has not created time without this reference to its own eschaton. In creating it He has made it a time of hope. It is for this reason that morning...emerges as a second and absolutely indispensable constitutive element in the first day.[128]

By linking these two texts thematically with regard to the promise of time, he is able to make exegetical sense out of the order of the words "evening and morning" in the Gen 1:3-5 text: the placement of morning after evening in Gen 1:5 indicates the same promise of Gen 8:22 of the continuation of time and also "living space."

Likewise, he uses texts from elsewhere in the canon as "commentary" on the Genesis sagas, and suggests that one cannot fully understand the Genesis sagas apart from these biblical commentaries. Ezekiel 37, in which the prophet is instructed to prophesy to the valley of the dry bones, gives us clues by which to understand the anthropology of Genesis 2, says Barth. It gives us a commentary from salvation history in which we see

> That this God-given breath as the vital principle of the soul and body of man can and will be withdrawn; that in respect of both soul and body man is subject to death and has no immortality; but that even when this breath is taken from him it does not vanish, or cease to be the living and quickening Spirit; that by God's free disposal He can and will return and genuinely requicken man from the death to which he has fallen victim and in which he has actually perished...[129]

Thus we cannot truly understand what Gen 2:7 means by God breathing into man the "breath of life" if we read it apart from the description of the breath of life being prophesied into the dry bones in Ezekiel 37. Barth then questions regarding the relationship between the נשמת חיים of the Old Testament and the πνευμα ἅγιον of the New Testament. He considers briefly Jn 20:22, 1 Thess 5:23, Acts 5:5-10, Acts 12:23, Luke 23:46 and Acts 7:59, and concludes that the "spirit continues beyond death, not as something belonging to man but as the divine address and gift to man." It is therefore reasonable to equate the spirit which Paul calls the "first fruits" (ἡ απαρχη) in Rom 8:23 or the "downpayment" (ὅ αρραβων) in 2 Cor 1:22, 2 Cor 5:5, and Eph 1:14 with this "breath of life." These terms are usually understood to refer in these instances to the Holy Spirit. From a canonical reading, however, Barth offers a lower-flying interpretation. Thus these texts, too, comment on and are commented on by Gen 2.

Again, he claims that Ezekiel 47 is the "most exact parallel" to Gen 2:10ff. It is in this prophetic passage, says Barth, that we "must seek the meaning of the hydrographically impossible and geographically indefinite river system" described in Gen 2.[130] He notes that Ezekiel 47 speaks of the river of life which nourishes and renews all creation. Both texts turn what Barth calls the universally chaos-element of water from the "suppressed enemy of man" into "his most intimate friend." Thus water is no longer the principle of death but now the principle of life, for "a change of meaning in respect of the sign of water" has taken place. Barth sees a link between this and the second creation saga's understanding of the inner basis of creation being in the history of the covenant "whose purpose is not only the preservation but the transformation of man and the cosmos." Thus Ezekiel 47 makes sense out of the otherwise almost non-sensical river system of Eden in Gen 2, and lends weight to Barth's theological link between the presentation of creation in Gen 2 and the history of the covenant of grace. This is another example of how his practice of prooftexting brings to the fore the assumption of textual polyvalence while also opening up and exploring the text at hand in deeper and more fruitful ways than either Augustine or Calvin were able to do.

Barth vs. Traditional Interpretation

From the previous discussion of Barth's use of canonical setting to read the plain sense of a biblical text and his corresponding practice of prooftexting, one might conclude that he should be classified as *nouveau* pre-critical. However, his assessment of the contribution of the church's tradition of biblical interpretation is not so easily classified as this might suggest. In this section, we will examine his use of traditional exegetes and his assessment of their interpretations in comparison with his own plain sense reading to help us further clarify his "microexegesis."

Of the ancient and Reformation commentators Barth refers to, Augustine and Calvin are the two most oft-mentioned in his *Church Dogmatics* 3.1. Barth also makes reference to the opinions, both positively and negatively, of Luther, Cocceius, Basil, Anselm, Ambrose, the Didache and the Heidelberg Catechism, Origen and Philo, and even the twelfth century rabbi and champion of *peshat* Rashi, just to name a few. While Barth clearly has read extensively in the history of interpretation, his use of the history of the tradition is neither slavish nor iconoclastic.[131] Like Calvin, he will agree or disagree with the tradition freely as he sees fit. Unlike Calvin, however, when Barth disagrees with the interpreters from the history of the tradition, he does so on the basis of literary features of the biblical text, either of the text at hand or of the whole biblical treatment of the theme in the text at hand.[132]

When commenting on the words of Gen 1:1, "heaven and earth", Barth remarks that the opinion of Augustine in *De Genesi contra Manichaos* 1.7.11 of the "*informis materia*," an opinion which is shared by Aquinas, Luther,

Calvin, Protestant and Catholic Orthodoxy ("and even by Wellhausen"!) must be rejected.

> The view that God first created chaos, that He accomplished a 'positing of the formless and unordered universe' (so also B. Jacob), and only then called out of this *rudis indigestaque moles* the reality of heaven and earth potentially existing in it, is not only entirely foreign to the rest of the Bible but also to these first verses of Genesis.[133]

He then cites (in agreement!) Gunkel's statement that "the thought of a creation of chaos is in itself contradictory and amazing; chaos is the world prior to creation." Barth then says that it is proper to understand Gen 1:1 ("In the beginning God created the heavens and the earth") not as standing in a "positive relationship" with Gen 1:2 ("the earth was without form and void"), but referring in advance to what is developed from Gen 1:3 onwards ("And God said, 'Let there be light'"). Following his usual method, Barth then examines the biblical witness, both Old and New Testaments, for the understanding of the words "heaven and earth" throughout and argues that by these terms the earthly totality is generally meant. He then concludes that

> The point of Gen 1:1 is that God has created the totality of everything above and below, of the invisible and the visible universe, and that there is nothing either in the one or the other that does not stand under the sign of the בְּרָא אֱלֹהִים. It may be said then that too much has not been read into it in the creed, which also refers to this inclusive twofold reality of the world-order, but that the interpretation there given is essentially correct.[134]

Thus his insistence on reading Gen 1:1 in light of the appearance and use of its terms in the rest of the canon allows the verse to have a "point." If the text is read according to the plain sense of the words, this "point" agrees with the credal formulation but disagrees with the traditional interpretation. Barth's reading claims to be closer both to the text of Genesis 1 and its reverberations elsewhere in the canon and to the doctrinal formulation of creation in the creeds than is the *opinio communis*!

Because of his understanding of the polyvalence of the biblical text, Barth can accept the readings of precritical interpretation even when they are what one might think of as figural, if they are judged to be sufficiently close to the text. Here, "close to the text" can include canonical reading which draws on and brings together elements from disparate biblical texts. For example, Barth argues that the traditional interpretation offered by the Fathers which understands the Trinity to be represented in the "And God said" of Gen 1:3 is justifiable.

> The Fathers were right when they saw glimpses of the whole mystery of the Trinity in the ויאמר אלהים of Gen 1:3f. Describing God's utterance as His creation, the biblical author—whatever he may have thought of it in detail—has equated the utterance of God, which is as such His 'expression,' with God Himself... To describe His Word as 'creating' is to say that His Word is God Himself—the One God.[135]

Barth approvingly refers to Anselm and Luther's exposition of John 1:3, which he says need to be considered in order to understand fully the "inner scope of Gen 1:3." Thus, "All things were made through Him" and "In the beginning was the Word" are indispensable commentaries on Gen 1:3. Because of this the reading of the Genesis saga's presentation of God as creating through the Word which sees here "glimpses of the whole mystery of the Trinity" is valid and justifiable. Notice from the above quote that this is in part because "the biblical author has equated the utterance of God...with God Himself." The interpretation is in part grounded on the biblical author's intention.

Of course, one of the places where Barth differs most substantially from the history of interpretation is in his consideration of Gen 1:26–28, in identifying the image of God with the relatedness of the male-female unity in difference.[136] Because of this identification of the image of God, Barth sweeps aside the debate over whether or not the image is obliterated in the Fall, for Barth contends that the image "remains a total contradiction" of the Fall. He gives a neat summary of traditional and modern opinions on these verses, from which he concludes that

> if we are to agree that we must keep close to the wording and context of the passage...we shall have to reject a good deal of that has been said in supposed exposition, and decide for a path which is more direct.[137]

He points to Vischer and Bonhoeffer as coming "closest to the actual text of the narrative," for they both focus on the idea of a "counterpart realized in free differentiation and relationship," the *analogia relationis*.[138] Bonhoeffer, however, unlike Vischer, delves further into the text, noting the threefold application of the verb ברא in Gen 1:27 and, according to Barth, also the content of Gen 1:27 itself. Barth's discussion of the pitfalls of the traditional exposition of this passage is telling:

> Is it not astonishing that again and again expositors have ignored the *definitive explanation given by the text itself*, and instead of reflecting on it pursued all kinds of arbitrarily invented interpretations of the imago Dei?—the more so when we remember that there is a *detailed repetition of the biblical explanation* in Gen 5:1... Could anything be more obvious than to conclude from this *clear indication* that the image and likeness of the being created by God signifies existence in confrontation....*the text itself says* that it consists in a differentiation and relationship between man and man, and they *ought to have kept to this point*...But when it is twice there in *almost definitive form*, why did they not let themselves be constrained to consider it instead of speculating at large... Why did they not *allow such passages as Hos 1:2f., 2:2f., 16, 3:1f.; Is 54:5f., 62:5; Jer 3:1, 6, 4:30, etc; Ezek 16:1, 23:1; 2 Cor 11:2; Eph 5:23f., Rev 12:1, 21:2 to put to them the question* whether this differentiation and relationship...might not actually have the constitutive meaning for the being of biblical man... There is indeed no good reason why we should continue to neglect this aspect of the matter, loitering at the distance where one explanation may indeed be more attractive but is also more arbitrary than another.[139]

This example shows not only Barth's rhetorical passion and flourish, but underscores the extent to which he believes and defends his interpretation to be based on the "the explanation given by the text itself." And the reason he can say this is because he is not only reading the Genesis creation sagas extremely carefully in isolation. He does indeed do this, but also reads them in canonical context such that the cited passages from both the Old and New Testaments force themselves on the reader and bring with them questions which illuminate Gen 1:26-28. These questions also throw into relief the inadequacies of the interpretations from the history of exegesis to address the letter of the text. Thus it is his intricately careful reading of the text at hand, which we have been calling "microexegesis," coupled with his reading of these words and themes against the backdrop of the canon, or what we have been calling "macroexegesis," which allow him to accept in appreciation or to reject with equal passion and scorn both the interpretations of centuries of Christian writers before him as well as that of his contemporaries.[140]

Thus, while traditional interpretation is held in high esteem by Barth,[141] and he adopts some traditional hermeneutical practices, he never forfeits attention to the letter of the text for the sake of following the methods and/or interpretive conclusions of the tradition. Where the traditional exegetes' commitments to extra-textual explanatory "narratives" or theories lead them away from the plain sense, Barth's microexegesis points this out and leads him back.

Silences: What the Text Fails to Say

While we have noted James Barr's insistence that a concern for "literality" will limit reading to what the words say, and disallow reading between the lines, Barth offers us another option. At times Barth will read the silences or narrative absences according to what could arguably be called their plain sense. This is an element which he shares more with Augustine than with Calvin. However, whereas Augustine often reads such narrative absences with the result that his exegesis takes extra-textual or extra-narrative flight, Barth stays closer to the narrative at hand. For him, even the silences can comment on the surrounding narrative.

Barth notes in commenting on Gen 1:3–5, the work of the first day, that God says that the light is good, which is followed by a reference to the existence of darkness. Barth then points out that since the text does not say that God created darkness, it therefore does not say that the darkness is good. Barth uses to his theological advantage the detail in the text that the divine *fiat* creates only light and separates out the darkness:

> The fact that the divine *fiat* is: 'Let there be light,' and not: 'Let there be darkness,' means that the possibility of the latter creation and creature is rejected by God.[142]

Thus darkness is not properly speaking a creature of God but the possibility which God rejects. Sin likewise is that possibility which is properly speaking an "ontological impossibility" because it is that which God has rejected and indeed cancelled at Golgotha. It is in part this theological move that averts the consideration of Gen 3 and the story of the Fall at any length along with Genesis 1 and 2. There is in fact no extended exegetical treatment of Genesis 3 anywhere in the *Church Dogmatics*.[143] Genesis 1 and 2 are considered together as a unit apart from Genesis 3 even though they are, Barth admits, integrally related narratives. Sin itself is considered further on in the *Church Dogmatics* in volume 4 in the context of the discussion of Reconciliation,[144] a move which is supported exegetically by Barth's observation of this narrative absence in Gen 1:3-4.[145]

He also observes that the formulaic "And God saw that it was good" is missing from the work of the second day, as we have pointed out above. This leads him to link this unit thematically with the work of the third day which includes a two-fold work and a two-fold refrain, "And God saw that it was good." The work of the second day and the first work of the third day both deal with the holding back and separating of the waters of chaos from the living space being prepared for the vegetation. The vegetation is created as the second of the two works of the third day and the climax of the series of the first three days. Barth will not let his comment rest with the remark that the phrase is missing, for "an accidental omission of these words is almost inexplicable in a passage where every word counts."[146] Since every word counts, even the silences need to be interpreted.

Another significant use of noting narrative silences in interpretation comes in his comments on the institution of the Sabbath in Gen 2:3, where Barth says that while humanity is invited to share in the Sabbath rest,

> It is to be noted that, to the tacit annoyance of many readers
> and expositors, there is no corresponding invitation to action
> as participation in God's creative work. It is not in the latter
> but in the former that God calls man to follow and accompany
> Him...Finally it is to be noted how unmerited is this freedom
> offered to man. So far he has not done any work.[147]

Thus his noticing an element absent in the narrative here opens the possibility to link both the doctrines of creation and eschatology (as represented in the Sabbath) with the doctrine of grace. While there are to be sure many dualisms in Barth's theology, there is no sharp division at this point in the text between "nature" and "grace," for creation is understood to be the "external basis" of the covenant of grace, and the covenant is the "internal basis" for creation. This is in part both supported by and supports his exegetical observation regarding this narrative absence.

One of the most significant instances of Barth's noting the narrative silences comes in his comments on the dual work of the sixth day on which the beasts and then humanity are created. Barth notes that the text says nothing "about groups and species (i.e. races, nations, etc.) in the account of man's creation, but an eloquent silence is maintained."[148] Barth uses this "eloquent silence" as a springboard to launch his discussion of a narrative element which he sees as highly important. Instead of remarking on the divisions of humanity into races, Barth points out, the text mentions one differentiation or division which is, according to the text, the only division which is significant for humanity.

> According to Gen 1 it is the fact that in the case of man the differentiation of sex is the only differentiation. Man is not said to be created or to exist in groups and species, in races and peoples, etc. The only real differentiation and relationship is that of man to man, and in its original and most concrete form of man to woman and woman to man. Man is no more solitary than God.[149]

Thus from an observation about a narrative silence Barth is able to move to a conclusion regarding the phrase "in the image of God," turning the entire history of interpretation of this issue on its head. After noting the silence, Barth points to the parallelism between the clauses "in the image of God" and "male and female," and concludes that the image of God must be in this relationship of unity in differentiation.

On occasion Barth will ask of the text a question which the text does not directly address. For example, he says that a question which cannot be evaded in the reading of Gen 2:17 is why man must die the moment he eats of the fruit of the tree of the knowledge of good and evil. He says

> The connexion is clear. The knowledge of good and evil is not a human but the supreme attribute and function which basically and radically distinguishes the Creator from the creature.[150]

The connection is clear to Barth; however, it is clear not from a strict reading of Gen 1-2 alone, but rather from a broad reading of the Bible as a whole. That is, he cannot conclude from reading the creation sagas alone that the knowledge of good and evil is a divine attribute and function alone, for the text here does not explicitly address this. Again, he asks why the divinely-given prohibition not to eat of the fruit of the tree was not more effective. He answers

> If we keep to the teaching of the passage...the teaching of the passage is that we have to do at this point too with a well-

planned arrangement of the divine wisdom and justice...the
freedom to obey is obviously the true *tertium comparationis*
and therefore the sign of the fellowship already established
between God and man at his creation.[151]

Again, his attempt to read "between the lines" of the narrative here requires a
reliance on his dogmatic constructs for the answer. He asks questions of the
text which the text neither explicitly addresses nor directly answers. Even so
he claims to be keeping to the "teaching of the passage."

Indeed, at times Barth will even acknowledge that the questions which he
poses the text are not always "answered directly by the Old Testament" but are
indeed questions which the text actually "imposes."[152] Barth says that these
questions are worth asking, in part because the text imposes them and in part
because the Old Testament does not directly answer them. The reason that the
Old Testament does not directly answer these types of questions, which are
nonetheless important, is that they deal with the "objective christological
meaning" of the passage.

Barth's elucidation of the "objective christological meaning" of the passage benefits from his exploring a narratival silence toward the end of paragraph 41. Speaking of the relationship between man and woman expressed in
Genesis 2, he points to a "surprising gap in the text":

The missing feature is what the rest of the Old Testament
regards as the heart of the matter...namely, the problem of
posterity, human fatherhood and motherhood, the family, the
child and above all the son.[153]

Barth notes that while the rest of the Old Testament considers human sexuality
almost exclusively in connection with procreation, the promise and hope of
Israel "and therefore its determination and Messianic expectation," the Genesis
2 saga considers the fulfillment of that relationship in the "eros of both sexes,"
in their "encounter and relation" for its own sake. Barth points to one other
place within the Old Testament which shares this view, and that is the Song of
Songs. Thus, Gen 2 does not offer an "isolated riddle," and since the existence of these texts can be "no accident,"

the only explanation is that the authors of the creation saga and
these love songs had in mind another covenant... almost
unrecognizable in historical reality and yet concluded, sealed,
persisting and valid...[154]

This observation leads Barth to ask and answer a series of questions all pertaining to this issue. Why could the human creature not be alone? Because Jesus could not be alone but had his counterpart in the Church. Why could the human creature not be satisfied with the partnership of the animals? Because like had to come from like, and thus the Church draws her nature from Christ. Why did the first man have to fall into a deep sleep when the woman was created? Because the Church of Jesus Christ comes to life only in His mortal sleep and stands before Him in His resurrection. Barth continues in this vein, linking the relation between man and woman expressed in Genesis 2 and later in the Song of Songs with the Christological relation between Christ and the Church. Here Barth explores what he sees to be the "objective christological meaning"[155] of the Genesis 2 saga by noting a thematic absence there (that is, the problem of posterity) in comparison with most of the rest of the Old Testament. This is an instance where noting the silence in the narrative lends to his figural reading of the Genesis text. However, it is a figural reading which takes seriously a close reading of the letter of the text.

We thus see how far Barth's understanding of "plain sense" is from James Barr's understanding of "literality." Whereas Barr would understand literal sense to reject the reading of the silences of the narrative, Barth includes this as a significant element of plain sense reading. Yet even this element of Barth's reading of the plain sense keeps his attention focussed on the narrative at hand and within the rubric of microexegesis.

Literal vs. Non-Literal

An examination of a few key places where Barth makes a self-conscious attempt to distinguish between plain sense readings and violations of this in his biblical exegesis of Gen 1–3 may illuminate our own understanding of Barth's construal of reading the plain sense of scripture. First, it is helpful to note some of the terms which Barth uses to distinguish between plain sense readings and violations of it in his exegetical material in his *Church Dogmatics* 3.1.[156] The columns on the following page may be useful here:

Plain sense	**Violations**
literal	metaphorical
wörtlich	*nicht bildlich*
reality	ideal
real	*ideal*
what is written	ideal reality
was dasteht	*ideale Wirklichkeit*
says exactly what it says	allegory
sagt genau, was sie sagt	*Allegorie*

After examining some concrete instances of these distinctions in Barth's exegesis, we will return to these oppositions.

At his discussion of the meaning of the word "day" in the first creation saga, Barth wants to remain close to the "plain and simple meaning" (*diesem schlichten Sinn*) of the word day which he argues denotes "that which is limited and designated by evening and morning."[157] He points out that while Ps 90:4 speaks of one thousand years being as a day in God's sight, it is clear from the narrative of Gen 1 that here the biblical authors understand the days of creation to be of twenty-four hours. He argues that introducing an apologetic reading which takes the day here to refer to geological periods or astronomical light years can only confuse and "cloud the picture." He says that he even finds unconvincing Delitzsch's (and Augustine's!) argument that since the sun, the measure of time, is not created until day four the prior days cannot be real "days" at all.[158] He says that one must read the text as it is, that God creates day here regardless of what we think we know to be the cause of light and darkness. He asks a question which implicitly underscores the relationship between the plain sense and the authority of scripture:

> What authority have we to retranslate this concept into that of the divine reality? It is thus unfortunate that Delitzsch too— laughing after the manner of Sarah—thinks it is necessary to discredit and possible to reject a literal understanding of this concept as 'childish and wholly absurd.' Why cannot we allow the saga quietly to finish what it has to say on this point before we consider what we are going to make of it?[159]

What the saga does say on this point, argues Barth, is that God created time as a sequence of days in a week by giving to light the name "day." This is the simple sense of the passage according to Barth. He then goes on to note that this means formally that the day as a unit of time is a divine gift and not merely a human convention. Materially it means that it is light by which God sets our unit of time such that we are allowed to exist under the divine Yes, for light is the creation of the first day and thus the beginning of time.

> This is the teaching we evade if we do not take the saga literally...If we filch from Gen 1 the relationship of light to a real day, the relationship of light to our time is destroyed, and Gen 1:3 ceases to be a proclamation of the meaning of history and becomes a more or less interesting, credible and binding scientific or philosophical theory.[160]

Thus Barth opts for what is in effect the "fundamentalist" interpretation of the word "day" in Gen 1, and yet he refuses to push the fundamentalist line which insists that the world was created in six days! This is in part because of his classification of the Genesis creation stories under the genre of saga and the implications of this for the historical referentiality of the text, and in part also because such a reading would fail to appreciate the "formal" and "material" meanings to be gleaned from such a literal reading.

Here we see that the relationship between literal and figurative meaning for Barth is one of intimate closeness yet distinction. Scripture is read "plainly" in the inextricable conjunction of simple and figurative reading. In Barth's discussion of Gen 1:9–13 and the twofold work of creation of the third day, this coinherence or inextricability between simple and figurative meaning is apparent. Simple meaning as such is much more, as Barth would say:

> The sea of which [the passage] speaks is, of course, *literally and concretely* the fluid element in all its earthly fullness, gathered and maintained in its place in relation to the earth, forming the natural western boundary of Palestine. But *as such it is much more... it is a sign which points beyond itself...* Similarly, the 'earth' is *literally and concretely* the terra firma on which, protected from the onslaught of the sea, man may and will have his being. But while it is this, *it is much more.* The miracle of its existence *as such is also a sign... visibly and palpably* it is a presentation of the grace in virtue of which God sustains and protects man for Himself and His purposes...[161]

Thus the simple meaning of the words in this passage does not exhaust plain meaning. Indeed, the simple meaning is not even the "primary" meaning in this case, according to Barth.

> The primary things which they really have in view are not the billows of the Mediterranean Sea, nor the frequently mentioned sand of the Palestinian shore which forms its boundary, but the miraculous passage of Israel through the Red Sea... and its repetition at Israel's entrance into the land promised to their forefathers. What the account of the creation of land and sea has in view (beyond the general processes and natural events portrayed) is the fact that at the Red Sea the Israelites passed through...[162]

Thus the plain meaning of the Genesis passage involves an allusion to other canonical presentations of sea and water. After examining these other canonical instances of the appearance of sea and water, Barth asks

> What is really meant by water and sea and their submission and limitation in all these passages? Are they a mere image: for as an image and representation of this reality—the real course of the divine history of salvation—they fully participate as an image in the actuality of a higher order which is the theme of the history of Israel...But in light of this participation of the image in the reality itself, how can we overlook the thing itself, this actuality of a higher order...[163]

This quasi-sacramental quality of scripture and its implications for the reading of the plain sense are also apparent shortly after this discussion when Barth reviews the canonical understandings of earth, and in particular the word "mountain":

> These mountains of God are not only on the earth; they are themselves, and particularly mount Zion, the earth in its assured stability as envisaged in Gen 1:9f., the place where God's honour dwells, and where man can and will therefore dwell. And as mount Zion is for its part the Abrahamic promise given to Israel, *we can differentiate here too between the sign and the reality, but we must not separate them.*[164]

Even in the reading of the plain sense, the sign and reality, the simple sense and the figurative sense, or the letter and the spirit, cannot be separated. One may differentiate but not separate. Therefore, one may speak of the simple sense of the text and figural or prophetic sense, but ultimately they are not opposed readings. Neither is the latter an obfuscation or overlayering of the former. Letter and spirit, simple sense and prophetic sense, coinhere within the rubric of plain sense reading.

Likewise, at his discussion of the words "light" and "sun" in the work of the fourth day of creation, as his usual methodology prescribes, Barth considers the biblical uses of these words. He then concludes by saying that while these instances all make use of the image of light to represent the revelation and will and righteousness of God, it is not accidental that the image of light is thus used in these passages. It is no accident because the sun and stars serve as signs to indicate seasons and time for the recognition of God's revelation and will and righteousness.

> Thus if they are used as images of the righteousness of God
> and the life of the righteous, Israel's Messiah, Jesus, and the
> Christian Church, it is because on the biblical view they are
> *originally and properly*, by reason of their creation, the image
> of these very things, i.e., the imitation and representation of
> the divine creation of light, and because from the very outset
> they are ordained to serve this purpose. There can be no ques-
> tion, therefore, of poetical or any other license in the use of
> these images.[165]

Thus ultimately his reading of figure is not justified solely of the basis of literary observations, even according to Barth's interpretation of what he is doing. Rather, his figural reading is justified also on the basis of a theological understanding of the biblical text. The reason that light serves as an image of God's revelation, will and righteousness in the rest of the canon is because the image participates "originally and properly" in the reality which it represents, namely God. Thus Barth can say of light, as he does of the whales in Gen 1:21, that they are "signs set up by God Himself."[166]

If we now return to the table of terms at the beginning of this section, we can see that for Barth, what I have been calling "figure" is not in opposition to the "letter" or simple sense as would be "allegory" or "metaphor," that is, the elements of the second column of the table. For Barth the first column of the table embraces both simple and figural reading, while the second indicates violations of both kinds. Thus, figure and allegory are not interchangeable terms for Barth. Allegory is opposed to plain sense reading, while figure is, as I have been suggesting, "coinherent" or inextricably bound to plain sense reading for Barth. To suggest that figural reading is not within the bounds of plain sense reading would amount to a truncation of biblical interpretation in Barth's terms and a failure to appreciate the polyvalence of the biblical text. This may be part of Barth's ambivalence toward "historical critical" methodology, and part of historical critical disaffection for Barth's exegesis. Historical critical methods prohibit on a methodological level this figural aspect of plain sense reading which Barth sees as essential for a theological or religiously fruitful reading of scripture, indeed for a "biblical" reading of the Bible.

Conclusion

We have seen that for Barth, the primary assumption controlling his reading of the plain sense of scripture in general and Genesis 1–3 in particular is his understanding that the Bible's central function is to witness to Jesus Christ. Thus, the text becomes polyvalent. This is distinct from what we called Augustine's understanding of polysemy, for this involved Augustine's noting distinct levels of meaning in the text. Barth does not want to suggest that the text speaks on different levels, but that the text only speaks "plainly." Within the plain sense, the text is polyvalent, or gathers up and unites themes, motifs and stories from seemingly disparate areas of the canon to shed light on the text at hand. Playing into and supporting this notion of witness to Christ which calls for the corresponding notion of textual polyvalence are Barth's appreciation of genre, narrative structure, secular science and historical criticism. These aspects of his macroexegesis set the parameters for his close reading, or what we have been calling his microexegesis. This includes a concern to elucidate verbal meaning, inquiry into authorship and editing, canonical setting, prooftexting and "reading" the narrative silences. We have seen how for Barth the elements of verbal sense and ruled reading are almost impossible to tease out one from another, as was relatively easy to do for Augustine and Calvin.

Notes

1. Karl Barth, *Church Dogmatics, 3.1*, The Doctrine of Creation, eds. G. W. Bromiley and T. F. Torrance, trans. J. W. Edwards et alii (Edinburgh: T. & T. Clark, 1958), 22. *Church Dogmatics* hereafter abbreviated as *CD*.

2. This term was chosen specifically to be distinguished from the term we used to describe Augustine's reading of different "levels" of meaning in the text. For Barth, there are not different levels of meaning, but within the one level of meaning the text catches up different themes, motifs, and stories, and lets them interpret each other. In other words, Barth sees the text as polyvalent within the plain sense, but not polysemic. Also, it is the *text* itself which is polyvalent: not the reader but the text has the capacity to unite or cause to interact the themes, motifs, and stories. The reader reads "plainly" by recognizing this polyvalence.

3. Barth, *CD 3.1*, 23.

4. Ibid., 23–4.

5. Ibid., 23.

6. Ibid., 24.

7. Ibid.

8. Barth, *CD 3.1*, 294ff. Notice how the coinherence of literal and figurative reading is seen to be one of the results of the narrative reading of the Bible which is one of the marks of pre-critical biblical hermeneutics according to Frei. Cf. Hans W. Frei, *The Eclipse of Biblical Narrative: A Study in Eighteenth and Nineteenth Century Hermeneutics* (New Haven; London: Yale University Press, 1974), 23. See also George Hunsinger, "Beyond Liberalism and Expressivism: Karl Barth's Hermeneutical Realism," *Modern Theology* 3 (1987): 209–224.

9. Here hermeneutics and the Christian life intersect. Reading of scripture cannot be separated from Christian formation under the yoke of obedience to the Spirit.

10. Barth, *CD 3.1*, 24.

11. Karl Barth, *Die Kirchliche Dogmatik, III/1*, Die Lehre von der Schöpfung (Zollilkon-Zürich: Evangelischer Verlag, 1945), 336 ff. Another example of his understanding of the polyvalence of the text is his consideration of the phrase "deep sleep" at Gen 2:21. He says that the "simple meaning" (*bedeutet zunächst schlicht*) of this deep sleep is that "man does not actively participate in the creation of woman and therefore

in the completion of his own creation"; Barth, *CD 3.1*, 294f. But this phrase also has a prefigurative character, says Barth, for it speaks also of "the whole inner basis of creation, God's whole covenant with man." Examples of this sort of reading abound in Barth's exegesis of Gen 1–3. To list them all would be tedious and not very illuminating, but reading them is an adventure!

12. His textual evidence for this is 1 Cor 16:2, Acts 20:7 and Rev 1:10.

13. Barth, *CD 3.1*, 228.

14. Ibid.

15. Calvin and Barth both understand the biblical text, of course, to be inspired as does Augustine, but their formulations of this are different and are not the controlling assumptions in the understanding of the text's capacity to refer. On Barth's understanding of the inspiration of scripture see Klass Runia, *Karl Barth's Doctrine of Holy Scripture* (Grand Rapids: Eerdmans, 1962), 137–68. For Barth's theological reading of Calvin, see Karl Barth, *Die Theologie Calvins. Vorlesung Sommer-Semester 1922*, ed. Hans Scholl (Zürich: Akademische Werke, 1993) and Hans Scholl, ed., *Karl Barth und Johannes Calvin: Karl Barths Göttinger Calvin-Vorlesung von 1922* (Neukirchen-Vluyn: Neukirchener, 1995).

16. Barth, *CD 3.1*, 81. See also his consideration in *CD 4.1*, 508: "Saga in general is the form which, using intuition and imagination, has to take up historical narration at the point where events are no longer susceptible as such of historical proof. And the special instance of biblical saga is that in which intuition and imagination are used but in order to give prophetic witness to what has taken place by virtue of the Word of God in the (historical or pre-historical) sphere where there can be no historical proof."

17. The problem of the historical referentiality of these chapters of Genesis which caused theological upheaval and embarrassment in American theology and church life in the early twentieth century will not be addressed here, but is detailed clearly in Norman Francis Furniss, *The Fundamentalist Controversy* (New Haven: Yale University Press, 1954); Bradley J. Longfield, *The Presbyterian Controversy: Fundamentalists, Modernists and Moderates* (Oxford and New York: Oxford University Press, 1991); Ronald L. Numbers, *The Creationists: The Evolution of Scientific Creationism* (Berkeley: University of California Press, 1993).

18. Barth, *CD 3.1*, ix–x. Note especially how the task of dogmatics at this point becomes "repeating the saga": more will be said on this later. This appears to have influenced Hans Frei's hermeneutical observation that reading the literal sense in the Christian tradition might be more fruitfully understood as repeating the story. Cf. his tentative comments about "verbal repetition as the highest form of understanding" in Hans W. Frei,

"The 'Literal Reading' of Biblical Narrative in the Christian Tradition: Does It Stretch or Will It Break?" in *The Bible and the Narrative Tradition*, ed. Frank McConnell (New York: Oxford University Press, 1986), 64.

19. Barth, *CD 3.1*, 62; *KD III/1*, 66. Throughout this section at this point the word Barth uses for history is "*Geschichte.*"

20. Barth, *CD 3.1*, 59. See also his comments regarding the "secular concept of the 'history of religion,' i.e. the history of the religious spirit which as such can only be one history among many others in the context of history generally," on 59-60.

21. Barth, *CD 3.1*, 63.

22. Ibid., 66.

23. Notice the striking correspondence between the language which Barth uses to describe this reversal and the language which Frei uses to describe what he sees to be the modern hermeneutical error which looks for the meaning of the text in its "ideal reference." Frei, *Eclipse*, 84-85; 99-104. It is interesting to note here that while Barth and Frei are referring to the same "error" in reading, Barth uses the term "*Geschichte*" translated as "history," whereas Frei uses the term "narrative."

24. Barth, *CD 3.1*, 66; *KD III/1*, 71.

25. Barth, *CD 3.1*, 67.

26. "*Unhistorisch*" equals "*praehistorisch*" but neither term equals "*geschichtslose.*" Cf. Barth, *KD III/1*, 87.

27. Barth, *CD 3.1*, 78; *KD III/1*, 84. The translator has chosen the phrase "history in the historicist sense" to render "*historische Geschichte.*" Since there is to be no connotation here of historicist philosophy, we prefer to use the term "academic historiography" to describe what the English version calls "historicism." In quoting the English translation of Barth's text, however, the term "historicism" will be maintained.

28. Barth, *CD 3.1*, 78. Here is where Barth introduces the distinction between the terms "*Historie*" ("history in the historicist sense") and "*Geschichte*" ("history"). "*Historie, d. h. die dem Menschen zugängliche, weil übersehbare, weil ihm wahrnehmbare Geschichte ist objektiv: kreatürliche Geschichte im Zusammenhang mit anderer kreatürlicher Geschichte...*" Barth, *KD III/1*, 84. Note his use of the distinction again in *CD 4.1*, par. 60, "The Pride and Fall of Man," 505.

29. Barth, *CD 3.1*, 80; *KD III/1*, 87.

30. Barth, *CD 3.1*, 78; *KD III/1*, 85: "*nicht nur unhistorisch sondern auch historisch.*"

31. Barth, *CD 3.1*, 79; *KD III/1*, 86: "*...die Bibel die Schöpfung erzählt als Geschichte, die...jedenfalls keinen menschlichen zeugen hatte...Wo kein*

Historiker ist, da kann es...kein Historie geben."

32. Here we see elements of similarity to Gadamerian thought in the insistence on the lesser value of history scientifically conceived. Hans-Georg Gadamer, *Truth and Method*, Second Revised ed., trans. Joel Weinsheimer and Donald G. Marshall (New York: Crossroad, 1991), part 2. Compare with Barth, *CD 3.1*, 78; *KD III/1*, 85: "We cannot overlook the fact that all history is properly and finally important and noteworthy only to the extent that it has this element and is thus not only historical [*historisch*] but 'non-historical' in the historicist sense [*unhistorisch*]. We cannot overlook the fact that all historical writings become soulless and intolerable to the extent that they try to be just historical and nothing more." The difference between Gadamer and Barth is that where the former would want to talk about "*Wirkungsgeschichte*," the latter would talk about history "immediate to God."

33. Here Barth speaks of the accounts of the resurrection of Jesus Christ. Properly speaking, of course, there are none of these in the canonical New Testament. It might have helped Barth to deflect criticism from more conservative quarters on this matter to make his terms a bit more precise by speaking at this point of the *accounts* of the resurrection appearances.

34. Barth, *CD 3.1*, 79; *KD III/1*, 86.

35. Barth, *CD 3.1*, 80.

36. Ibid., 81.

37. Barth, *CD 3.1*, 81; *KD III/1*, 88: "*...das Historische und Unhistorische in der wirklichen Geschichte beieinander und zusammengehören.*"

38. Barth, *CD 3.1*, 82.

39. Cf. his comments on "special biblical hermeneutics," *CD 1.2*, 466, 468, 720, 725.

40. Bultmann's famous article, "New Testament and Mythology: the Problem of Demythologizing the New Testament Proclamation," was published in 1941. Cf. Schubert M. Ogden, ed., *New Testament and Mythology and Other Selected Writings* (Philadelphia: Fortress, 1984). Barth's volume 3.1 of the *Kirchliche Dogmatik* was published in 1945. Barth seems to reject consciously Bultmann's definition of myth as that which expresses the otherworldly in terms of this world. Barth's description of the interpretation of myth is clearly not ignorant of Bultmann's work.

41. Barth, *CD 3.1*, 84.

42. Ibid., 84; *KD III/1*, 91–2: "*Sie wollen in allen ihren Aussagen wörtlich genommen sein: gewiß nicht in einem flachen, sondern in einem tiefen, nicht in einem engen, sondern in einem umfassenden Wortsinn, aber so, daß auch der nächstliegende, direkt erzählende Sinn sein Recht hat und*"

behält--so also, daß auch aus der Erzählung als solcher durchaus nicht
ein Bild für allerlei zeitlose und also unerzählbare Beziehungen und
Verhältnisse wird--so vielmehr, daß auch und zuerst die Erzählung als
solche gelten und ernst genommen sein will, und so, daß auch der tiefere,
umfassendere Wortsinn nicht anderswo als auf der Ebene der ges-
chichtlichen und als erzählbaren und in der Fortsetzung tatsächlich
erzählten Dinge zu suchen ist."

43. Barth, *CD 3.1*, 85.
44. Ibid., 86.
45. Ibid.
46. For the German terms, see Barth, *KD III/1*, 92–95.
47. Barth, *CD 3.1*, 64.
48. Ibid., 64. Notice that Barth is here describing as one error with two sub-categories the "errors" described by Frei in *The Eclipse* as the two distinct possibilities of reading the text as referring either ideally (Barth: "metaphysical") or ostensively (Barth: "physical"). *Eclipse*, 86–104.
49. See the *Confessions*, 11.3 and 12.18, 23, 31.
50. Barth, *CD 3.1*, 65.
51. Ibid.
52. Ibid., 94.
53. Barth, *CD 3.1*, 252. See also the discussion on 277–278: "We have obviously missed the sense of the saga if we think that it is referring to a place of springs or a delta. It speaks of a river which miraculously divides itself rectangularly in the four directions of the compass. Ought not the system as such to warn us against trying to find it on any map?"
54. Barth, *CD 3.1*, 253.
55. Ibid., 100.
56. Ibid.
57. "An accidental omission of these words is almost inexplicable in a passage where every word counts. The translators of the Septuagint thought it necessary to supply them... [a] harmonizing which missed the intention of the verses." Barth, *CD 3.1*, 135.
58. Barth, *CD 3.1*, 144.
59. This observation is, of course, not entirely novel. See for example Robert M. Graves, and Raphael Patai, *Hebrew Myths: The Book of Genesis* (New York: McGraw-Hill, 1965), 21–29.
60. Barth, *CD 3.1*, 156.
61. Ibid., 159.
62. Ibid., 162.
63. Ibid., 171.
64. A correspondence is also drawn between the first saga's granting of

humanity dominion over the creaturely realm in Gen 1:26, 28 and the second saga's expression of this concept of dominion in Adam's naming the creatures. See the discussion above regarding the fourth day and the parallel drawn between the lack of divine naming of the sun, moon and stars there and the divine instruction in the second saga for Adam to name the creatures in Gen 2:19-20, 23.

65. Barth, *CD 3.1*, 178.
66. For a similar but less detailed approach, see Benno Jacob, *Genesis*.
67. Barth, *CD 3.1*, 241.
68. Ibid., 254.
69. Barth, *CD 3.1*, 268. Barth also describes Eden as a prototype for the tabernacle, the man who is assigned the service of tilling the ground as a prototype of the priests and Levites who serve the Temple, and the two trees at the center of the Garden as a prototype of the Holy of Holies. Cf. *CD 3.1*, 254.
70. Ibid., 276-7.
71. Ibid., 281; Barth, *KD III/1*, 321.
72. Barth, *CD 3.1*, 282.
73. Ibid., 289; *KD III/1*, 329: "...*vor dem Übergang der praehistorischen Schöpfungsgeschichte zur historischen Bundesgeschichte.*"
74. He cites as evidence to support his own reading of this "parallel" the Septuagint translation of Gen 2:18 "I will make," ποιησωμεν, and the Vulgate, *faciamus*. "So strongly was the parallel to Gen 1:26 felt even at this early time that it was thought necessary to introduce here too that mysterious plural."
75. Barth, *CD 3.1*, 308.
76. Ibid., 311.
77. Ibid., 312.
78. Barth, *CD 3.1*, 120. It does not appear that Barth is right in saying that "modern science is the first to take offence." We saw how Augustine for one certainly noticed the problem.
79. Ibid., 137, here citing Luther's 1527 *Sermon on Genesis*. Barth himself might argue that we must accept the fact that the *text* says that the heaven is placed between the waters.
80. A related point is made by C. Kaiser with regard to the relation between theology and science in the middle ages: "Aristotelian science was perceived by many to be a challenge to faith in a personal God much as Newtonian physics was later to become in the eighteenth century and evolutionary biology in the late nineteenth... The 1277 Paris condemnation of propositions associated with Aristotelian physics and Averroist philosophy is the most dramatic instance of a conservative Christian

response to Aristotelian natural philosophy..." Kaiser, "Calvin and Natural Philosophy," 79, n. 3. The point to be made here with regard to Barth and the modern period is that one should not assume that premoderns had a necessarily easier time reconciling reigning worldviews with theology and biblical interpretation.

81. Barth, *CD 3.1*, 160.
82. Ibid.
83. Ibid., 173.
84. There is much debate as to the extent to which Barth rejects and/or appropriates the models and methods of historical criticism. See Barth's Forwards to his *Römerbrief*, and his comments on historical criticism and biblical interpretation in *CD 1.2*, 464, 494. See also A. Jülicher's review of the first edition of Barth's Romans commentary. A. Jülicher, "A Modern Interpreter of Paul," in *The Beginnings of Dialectical Theology*, ed. J. Robinson, reprint, 1920 (Richmond: John Knox, 1968), 72-81, originally published in *Die christliche Welt*, 1920. See also Bultmann's review of the second edition of the commentary, in James M. Robinson, *The Beginnings of Dialectic Theology, Vol. 1*, trans. Keith Crim et alii (Richmond: John Knox Press, 1968), 100-20. Cf. E. Jüngel's narrative of this debate in Eberhard Jüngel, *Karl Barth: A Theological Legacy*, trans. Garrett E. Paul (Philadelphia: Westminster, 1986), 70-82. See also Rudolf Smend, "Nachkritische Schriftsauslegung," in *Parrhesia: Karl Barth Zum Achtzigsten Geburtstag* (Zürich: EVZ Verlag, 1966), 215-37, Bruce McCormack, "Historical Criticism and Dogmatic Interest in Karl Barth's Theological Exegesis of the New Testament," in *Biblical Hermeneutics in Historical Perspective: Studies in Honor of Karlfried Froehlich on His Sixtieth Birthday*, eds. Mark S. Burrows and Paul Rorem (Grand Rapids: Eerdmans, 1991), 322-38, and Walter Lindemann, *Karl Barth und die kritische Schriftsauslegung*, (Hamburg-Bergstedt: Herbert Reich Evangelischer Verlag), 1973.
85. Benno Jacob, *The First Book of the Bible: Genesis*, trans. Ernest I. Jacob and Walter Jacob, reprint, 1934 (New York: KTAV, 1974). Cf. *CD 3.1*, 99. Hermann Gunkel, *Genesis* (Göttingen: Vandenhoeck und Ruprecht, 1902). Cf. *CD 3.1*, 63. The interesting thing about Barth's readiness to accept Jacob over Gunkel is that Jacob is less willing to incorporate the conclusions of historical-critical research than is Gunkel. For instance, Jacob is not willing to accept the Documentary Theory (which Barth does accept), and Jacob insists on reading the final form of the biblical text as a whole regardless of its origins (as does Barth). Jacob's approach is more philological-exegetical than historical and he attempts to read the Bible primarily as the religious text which he holds it to be rather than as

a resource for the study of the Ancient Near East. It could be these elements which make Barth often more sympathetic with Jacob's readings than with, for instance, Gunkel's readings. See the Foreword by Harry M. Orlinsky to the translation of Jacob's commentary, as well as the Preface in the same volume.

86. Franz Delitzsch, *Neuer Kommentar Über die Genesis* (Leipzig: Dörffling und Franke, 1887). Cf. *CD 3.1*, 87. Walther Zimmerli, *Erstes Buch Mose, 1-11* (Zürich: Zwingli-Verlag, 1943). Cf. *CD 3.1*, 78. Alfred Jeremias, *Das Alte Testament Im Lichte Des Alten Orients* (Leipzig: J. C. Hinrichs, 1930). Cf. *CD 3.1*, 99.

87. Of course, there are instances in his interpretation of Gen 1-3 where Barth uses historical critical conclusions regarding the text to his theological advantage. For example, in his discussion of Gen 1:3, "And God said," Barth says that "the critical understanding... is quite correct. All ideas of creation as divine emanation or creature as deity are forcefully and completely excluded by Gen 1:3." Barth, *CD 3.1*, 116. See also the discussion at ibid., 162-3 regarding Gen 1:16 where he points out that the ruling of the sun and moon here "is only a reminiscence of the dethroned Babylonian and Egyptian conception of their role." Again, on 243, he points out that the creation of man in the second creation saga is "distinguished from the Babylonian and other pagan traditions by the strong emphasis on his creatureliness... (and) in contrast to the Greek conception of man, the creation of man as it is described here does not signify that a divine or God-like being had found a prison in an inadequate physical organism..."

88. He cites H. Gressman, *Altorientalische Texte Zum Alten Testament* (Leipzig: De Gruyter, 1926), Delitzsch, *Neuer Kommentar über die Genesis* (Leipzig: Dörffling und Francke, 1887) and Gunkel, *Genesis* (Göttingen: Vandenhoeck und Ruprecht, 1902). Cf. *CD 3.1*, 87.

89. Barth, *CD 3.1*, 87.

90. E.g., "There is an indisputable literary connexion between 1:1 and 2:4a...the summary in 2:4a is subjected by 1:1 to a distinctively critical refinement. It is the works of the divine ברא which are the תולדות, the 'generations' of the heaven and of the earth..." Barth, *CD 3.1*, 100.

91. Barth, *CD 3.1*, 79.

92. Ibid., 130.

93. See his discussion, for example, of the understandings of Gen 1:20 in the Septuagint, the Vulgate, Calvin, Luther and the Zurich Bible. Barth, *CD 3.1*, 171-2.

94. "The fact that in the Greek translation it is called 'Paradise' must not mislead us. For while it is true that at a later date, and under Greek

influence, Paradise became a kind of Elysium, in the Persian from which the term derives, and then in the Hebrew, it simply means a walled-in and therefore enclosed and limited place, e.g., a royal park." Barth, *CD 3.1*, 250. "The Septuagint wrongly took this to mean that God put the finishing touches to His work on this day, and since this is obviously an impossible statement in relation to what follows it amends it by turning the seventh into the sixth day." Barth, *CD 3.1*, 220.

95. E.g., he points out that while ויעש אלהים occurs for the first time only in Gen 1:7, it is a paraphrase or functional simile of ויאמר אלהים in Gen 1:6, and indicates no new activity or rupture in the narrative flow. Barth, *CD 3.1*, 136.

96. E.g., in Gen 1:9 יקוו and ותראה are both in the passive, leading Barth to argue that it is not the waters themselves which are active but the Word of God which is the active element here. Barth, *CD 3.1*, 145.

97. Barth points out how the recurrence of the verb בדל in Gen 1:4, Gen 1:6, Gen 1:7, Gen 1:14 and Gen 1:18 functions to underscore the action of separating the created realm from the realm of chaos. Barth, *CD 3.1*, 160.

98. At Gen 1:26, "Let us make...", Barth notes that the verb form indicates a "divine soliloquy, a consultation as though between several divine counsellors, and a divine decision resting upon it." Barth, *CD 3.1*, 182.

99. Again at Gen 1:26, he makes more precise his discussion of the lexical meanings of בצלמנו כדמותונו by noting that their use in conjunction with the prepositions ב and כ requires that the words "image and likeness" be read as referring to the image of Elohim and not to that of man formed in the image of Elohim. He then uses this observation to ground the rejection of the Vulgate translation "*ad imaginem et similitudinem nostram.*" Barth, *CD 3.1*, 197. He argues that the Vulgate actually mistranslates this phrase, yet at a later point he acknowledges that while it is verbally incorrect, it is materially correct. Cf. *CD 3.1*, 203.

100. He notes that while the first saga speaks of the creation of the "heavens and the earth", the second saga speaks of the creation of the "earth and the heavens" in Gen 2:4b. He points out that the reversal of the word order here is significant, for the second saga gives more attention to the earth than the first. Barth, *CD 3.1*, 196.

101. Barth sees the new name for God, Yahweh Elohim, used in the second creation saga as significant insofar as it denotes in his view the God of the covenant. Barth argues that this is a verbal clue to the "visible prefiguration" of the beginning of the covenant. Barth, *CD 3.1*, 234.

102. "That אדם is taken from and formed from the dust of the אדמה testifies in the first instance that he belongs to it. אדמה is the earth as cultivated

land, the field. Adam thus means man of the earth or field or soil, the husbandman. In Latin, too, *homo* derives from *humus...*" Barth, *CD 3.1*, 244.

103. His concern for the verbal level of the text is itself theologically driven; see his comments on Hebrew as the "true language." Barth, *CD 3.1*, 124–5.

104. Barth, *CD 3.1*, 100.

105. Ibid., 104.

106. This is a term which Barth uses often. One could argue for the conceptual link here between what Barth is doing and what George Lindbeck calls "intratextuality." George A. Lindbeck, *The Nature of Doctrine* (Philadelphia: Westminster, 1984), 113 f. Lindbeck credits Barth with influencing his own construction of intratextuality "as an appropriate way of doing theology" (135), and also credits David Kelsey, David Ford, and Hans Frei with influencing his reading of Barth.

107. Barth, *CD 3.1*, 105.

108. However, attempting to uncover an author's meaning will help one to determine the plain sense of the passage: "The meaning, then, of the author of this first account might well be that..." Barth, *CD 3.1*, 112.

109. "It is clear that when the author uses the words ברא, עשׂה, and נתן he is not describing actions which have to be distinguished from אמר, but paraphrasing..." Barth, *CD 3.1*, 111.

110. "This emphasis on the creative Word of God is a distinctive feature of the P account which has acquired a significance for the whole biblical conception of creation." Barth, *CD 3.1*, 112.

111. E.g., "Here, too, the biblical author drew on mythical tradition... if we assume that the biblical author knew of this or a similar view, we have to add at once that, by making the divine utterance as such the sole agent of the whole process, he turns into its opposite the thinly veiled or blatant naturalism of the creation myth." Barth, *CD 3.1*, 112-13. "Although the rule of the stars is irrelevant in this context, and is not therefore mentioned, it may well have been familiar to the author." *CD 3.1*, 163.

112. "The other advantages and qualities of light... have all claimed the attention of various exegetes, but they do not seem to be of any interest to the biblical author." Barth, *CD 3.1*, 122.

113. "It is self-evident that the author was not thinking of allegorical or metaphysical water but of real water as in the myth and indeed the natural science of his day..." Barth, *CD 3.1*, 139.

114. "An accidental omission of these words is almost inexplicable in a passage where every word counts. The translators of the Septuagint thought it necessary to supply them. But this was perhaps an attempt at

harmonizing which missed the intention of the verses..." Barth, *CD 3.1*, 135.

115. This is true of the above example where Barth refers to the "intention of the verses." Cf. also "contrary to the practice of the text, express mention is suddenly made of one of the species..." Barth, *CD 3.1*, 172. Also, "the saga is telling us... the saga is not interested in... The saga sees it in a different light... It is significant that the witness introduced the account of the creation of woman in this way... There can be no doubt that it had for the editor himself the significance and character of the Word of God." Barth, *CD 3.1*, 139, 152, 294, 304.

116. "The saga wishes the creation of man to be understood in the true sense as a concerted act on the part of the speaker and those addressed by Him." Barth, *CD 3.1*, 192.

117. "We cannot escape the conclusion that the saga thought in terms of a genuine plurality in the divine essence, and that the priestly redaction within which it is presented in Gen 1 did not see fit to expunge this element." Barth, *CD 3.1*, 191.

118. Barth, *CD 3.1*, 273.

119. Ibid., 229.

120. Ibid.

121. For example, he points out that the second saga has an attitude "so wholly different from that of the first saga to the elements of water and earth. What in the former is earth's great adversary, held in check by God, is in the latter one of the conditions not only of its habitableness but of its divinely willed and executed future." Barth, *CD 3.1*, 241.

122. Barth, *CD 3.1*, 213.

123. This is one example where Barth's method can be seen to have influenced the development of the canonical criticism of his student, Brevard Childs. For example, see Brevard S. Childs, *The Book of Exodus* (Philadelphia: Westminster, 1972).

124. Barth, *CD 3.1*, 113.

125. Ibid., 114.

126. Italics mine. Barth, *CD 3.1*, 120.

127. Barth, *CD 3.1*, 132. My edition of *CD* has a misprint: it cites Gen 9:22, which reads, "And Ham, the father of Canaan, saw the nakedness of his father, and told his two brothers outside."

128. Ibid., 132.

129. Ibid., 248-9.

130. Ibid., 280.

131. Ibid., 100. "Augustine is quite right..." (101). "Augustine oversimplifies the problem..." (173). "The Church Fathers only obscure

what the passage is really trying to say..." (220). "The Fathers thus betrayed a great obtuseness and narrowed the horizon with serious consequences when in their handling of creation they usually confined themselves to the hexaemeron, although both externally and internally everything points to the fact that the story of creation is to understood as a heptaemeron..."

132. Calvin tends to disagree more often on the basis of doctrinal fruits of the proposed interpretation, with warrants more loosely tied to the letter of the text. Barth himself acknowledges this of Calvin in at least one specific place: "The description of the creation of the woman in vv. 21-22 induced even from Calvin, who has few christological references in his exegesis, the observation... Properly this is the final word of exegesis rather than the first, but there can be no doubt that both the context and the independent features of these verses force us to look in this direction from the very outset." Barth, *CD 3.1*, 325.

133. Barth, *CD 3.1*, 100.

134. Ibid., 101.

135. Ibid., 116.

136. Ibid., 190 ff.

137. Ibid., 192-7.

138. Barth expands their interpretation in an attempt to reach even closer to the letter of the text: "But between this God and the man who thus corresponds to Him there exists—and we have to emphasize this point by way of supplement to Vischer and Bonhoeffer—a unique relationship in organic creation to the extent that among plants and the different animals of land, air, and water, as is continually underlined, there are different groups and species, but that this is not the case among men, so that in relation to other organic creatures man is an *ens sui generis*, and the distinction of sexes found in man too is the only genuine distinction between man and man, in correspondence to the fact that the I-Thou relationship is the only genuine distinction in the one divine being." Barth, *CD 3.1*, 196.

139. Italics mine. Barth, *CD 3.1*, 195-6.

140. Ultimately, Barth acknowledges that exegesis will not answer all the important questions either a text or a given contemporary theological challenge will raise. For an example of the latter acknowledgment, cf. 200: "The Reformation thesis concerning the loss of the *imago Dei* through the fall is understandable and necessary against the background of the Reformation... but there is no basis for this conception of the *imago* in Gen 1." For an example of the former, cf. 202: "Here, too, we can only say that, if the hope of the Old Testament was not meaning-

less, if its covenant-history really had a supremely definite and concrete goal, if Jesus Christ really was Israel's Messiah, the Son of God and therefore the fulfillment of Israel's own existence, the meaning and goal of its whole course, and therefore the answer to the enigma of Gen 1:26 ff., Paul did not represent any innovation in relation to the Old Testament but pointed to its fulfillment. The decision whether this is the case is not an exegetical question. Then and always it is answered only in the form of faith or unbelief, by proclamation or denial."

141. Cf. his comments regarding the authority of the Fathers, *CD 1.2*, Par. 20 "Authority in the Church," especially 603ff.

142. Barth, *CD 3.1*, 122.

143. Indeed, extended discussion of Exodus 33, the story of the Golden Calf, figures more prominently in *CD* than does any discussion of the Fall story of Genesis 3.

144. Cf. *CD 4.1*, Par. 60, "The Pride and Fall of Man"; *CD 4.2*, Par. 65, "The Sloth and Misery of Man"; *CD 4.3*, Par. 70, "The Falsehood and Condemnation of Man." Obviously, Barth touches on sin throughout the dogmatics, but in a more systematic fashion here.

145. This observation, of course, also supports and is supported by Barth's use of the dualism of the elect and rejected in Volume 2 as he points out in *CD 3.1*, 123-4. This theme continues in his later consideration of Gen 1:6-8 where he notes how the firmament holds back the waters of chaos: "With (the firmament's) creation God has actually said No to a world in which man would at once be lost, and Yes to a world in which man can know that he is protected because he is actually protected. This stability of the firmament, of this boundary, of this Yes and No, of the fulfilled divine decision in favour of His cosmos and against the sovereignty, against the present and future reality, of the primal flood and the element of chaos, corresponds to the stability of the divine throne." Barth, *CD 3.1*, 134.

146. Barth, *CD 3.1*, 135. Here he sounds like Augustine. Indeed, one could reasonably state that for Barth there are no biblical passages in which every word does *not* count.

147. Barth, *CD 3.1*, 225.

148. Ibid., 179.

149. Ibid., 186.

150. Ibid., 259-60.

151. Ibid., 263, 265.

152. Barth, *CD 3.1*, 273. The question here is why "the Garden of Eden seems actually to have been planted in order that man might leave it again, and that it might become to him a lost Paradise."

153. Ibid., 312.
154. Ibid., 314.
155. "Objective christological meaning" is Barth's term. See Barth, *CD 3.1*, 273. On 323, Barth uses similar language: "Because they had Him objectively in mind, passages such as Gen 2 and the Song of Songs could only form the fringe and not the center of its witness, its central witness being to the Son, the expected One."
156. Cf. *CD 3.1*, 224, 319; *KD 3.1*, 253, 365.
157. Barth, *CD 3.1*, 125.
158. Barth clearly has read Augustine and knows that he shares Delitzsch's opinion, or vice versa. That Barth chooses to identify the interpretation with Delitzsch over Augustine is clearly a stab at Delitzsch rather than an indication of Barth's own ignorance of Augustine here.
159. Barth, *CD 3.1*, 125.
160. Ibid., 126.
161. Italics mine. The key German terms are: *wörtlich und konkret... eben als das nicht nur das; indem es dieses konkrete Wunder ist, über sich selbst hinausweisendes Zeichen; sichtbar und griefbar die Darstellung der Gnade*. Whether Barth is consistent here is questionable. E.g., if the earth is "visibly and palpably a presentation of the grace..." then can it really be a "sign which points beyond itself" to something else? Barth, *CD 3.1*, 146; Barth, *KD III/1*, 163.
162. Barth, *CD 3.1*, 146-7.
163. Barth, *CD 3.1*, 148.
164. Italics mine. Barth, *CD 3.1*, 152.
165. Ibid., 164.
166. Ibid., 173. "That the (whales) were also created by God... denotes in the context of Old Testament thinking an act of demythologization the importance of which we cannot overlook... The monsters which myth makes so dreadful are indeed great and dangerous signs—like the sea which they inhabit—of the frontiers of humanity and of God's own will. But they are signs which have been set up by God Himself."

Chapter Five:
Ad Litteram: 'Sinewes Even In Thy Milke'

From the preceding analysis of these selected examples of exegesis, it is apparent that the understandings of the category "plain sense" change from theologian to theologian, and even within the work of each theologian. It should likewise be clear that the intent to read the "plain sense" in the examples of exegesis examined here almost never amounts to a search for *the* single meaning of the text. Each of our three theologians therefore has an intuitive respect for what Rowan Williams has called the "eschatological sense." Conversely, it may be in part the work of these three theologians which informs William's understanding of literal sense as "eschatological sense."[1]

We saw that for Augustine the primary controlling principle which enabled and necessitated him to regard the Bible as coherent, and therefore subject to literal reading, was the understanding of the inspired quality of the text. The text was to be read in a straightforward or "literal" sense because the Holy Spirit was at work in its composition rendering it meaningful, and precluding its being read as parables or symbols of another reality entirely separable from the text.[2] We also saw that for Calvin, the controlling principle driving his "literal" exegesis is the understanding that the Bible bears the storied doctrine of God. It is the doctrine of God which is the "glue" for the biblical narratives and it is this which allows and necessitates Calvin to read the text according to its "letter." For Barth, the primary assumption about the Bible which drives his reading of the plain sense is the central understanding of its witness to Jesus Christ. That is, his theological rationale for the canon and for reading it according to its "plain sense" is pinned to his understanding of its capacity to function as witness everywhere and throughout to the Word of God in Jesus.[3]

Augustine's understanding of the literal sense often appears unrecognizable to the modern reader, for he asks questions which would rarely occur to us to ask, and he fills in silences and narrative gaps with extra-narratival material with which modern readers are not generally sympathetic. This extra-narratival material is often drawn from his Neo-Platonic background and his understanding of the Christian life as pilgrimage of the soul's ascent to beatific vision. Yet while Augustine's "literal reading" of the Genesis creation stories therefore supports his version of the Christian Platonist understanding of creation, we cannot conclude that "literal sense" for Augustine is no more that a factor of the common assumptions of his day. Augustine's interpretation is not merely an arbitrary reading of his view into the text, simply an eisegesis of his own cosmology and philosophy, although to be sure some of this is present. Rather, Augustine is constrained by the verbal sense of the text to attempt to offer what he sees as a "literal reading." While he is mainly impelled by the force of his theological presuppositions, his attention to the verbal sense will not allow them to carry his interpretation on their own steam.

Calvin tends to be far more attentive to verbal meaning and narrative context than was Augustine, and when he fills in narrative gaps he does this with material drawn from his own understanding of the Gospel as the story of Israel, the People of God. While Augustine values allegorical reading on theological grounds, Calvin claims to reject it on theological grounds. However, in many ways he is equally if not more bound doctrinally with regard to the reading of the literal sense than was Augustine, yet without acknowledging it as openly as does Augustine. For example, while it is the doctrine of God which logically unifies the narratives of the Bible for Calvin, this is often slipped in under the cover of the "simple" and "plain" meaning of the text. While he focuses on verbal sense, he is often not admitting his own acceptance of the constraints of Ruled reading.

Barth, on the other hand, shows how a unified reading of the text can be justified on the basis of the literary features themselves which he identifies in the text. While Augustine speaks of distinct levels of meaning, and Calvin focuses his discussion on the simple sense without acknowledging for the most part a "non-simple" reading, Barth is willing to admit both a simple meaning and a deeper meaning, even though he refuses to split these into distinct and separate spheres. The verbal and literary elements of the text are understood to bear "simple meaning" and "deeper meaning," both of which are understood to be features of the "literal sense."

While there are, to be sure, these differences among the three, there are also some broad consistencies. One therefore cannot conclude that the reading of the literal sense within this trajectory is a purely arbitrary act to justify the authoritativeness of one's own reading, whether conscious or unconscious. The most obvious issue underlying the reading of the literal sense is, indeed, the authority of scripture. As we have seen, Augustine was converted to Christianity in part by the allegorical readings of the Old Testament in Ambrose's sermons, and yet he is aware that his allegorical interpretation in

De Genesi contra Manichaeos did not succeed at convincing his opponents of the "correctness" of an orthodox reading of Genesis. Creative interpretation can be countered by creative interpretation; in order to argue doctrine, Augustine decided that he had to pin his reading closer to the words of the text itself. Allegorical reading, he came to believe, was useful as an intra-Christian practice, but for discussing doctrine, especially with those outside that faith, one had to base one's arguments on a literal reading.[4] Calvin, for his part, argued doctrine both with "Papists" and Anabaptists on the basis of the literal sense. The doctrine of his opponents was distorted, he claimed, because they did not attend sufficiently to the literal reading of scripture. The authority of his own understanding of doctrine, however, he claims, is based on the authority of a simple, literal reading. For Barth as well, the plain sense reading is what distinguishes his construal of the text from those of his opponents who do not read "what the text really has to say." The authority of scripture to warrant one's theological arguments and claims is therefore a central concern in the plain sense reading, but as we have seen, plain sense readings in this trajectory are not merely arbitrary theologico-eisegesis on which to argue doctrine. While attention to literary features increases significantly as we move from Augustine to Calvin and then to Barth, all clearly are committed to the explication of verbal sense and deem themselves to be attempting not to "twist" scripture but to lay out its "plain meaning." It is clear that these three readers are tying their claims about the text, God, and the world to elements in the text, and not simply stating that what they are offering are literal and therefore authoritative readings, or authoritative and therefore literal readings. They are not simply arguing tautologically, "I am right; therefore mine must be a literal reading."

On the other hand, one cannot claim that this trajectory insists on an over-determinedness of the plain sense. That is, according to the readings given by the theologians examined here, one cannot conclude that the plain sense of scripture is an objective, static "given" to be mined from the text like a diamond from the river bed. More goes into the reading of the literal sense in all three of our figures than a simple reading of verbal sense alone. Clearly, verbal and literary matters are highly significant in this trajectory. Since the stories come in written form, verbal sense must be engaged in order to interpret them. Since the stories are said to have occurred within time and space, their historical referentiality becomes an issue in their interpretation.[5] Since the texts often take narrative form, and because the understanding of Christian story as a whole in this trajectory generally assumes narrative form such as we find in the Rule of Faith, the narrative context will be an important element in plain sense reading. But there clearly are communal rules which are not purely literary which implicitly shape the literal reading. Because these three theologians come to the Bible with an overall understanding of the "plot" of the story, Ruled reading applies a certain counter-pressure against the verbal and literary elements of plain sense reading.

Therefore, if a hypothetical Christian community of readers who understand themselves to be within the trajectory represented by the three theologians examined in this study were looking for guidance on what it means to read scripture according to its plain sense, one might offer them the following sketch. The reading of the plain sense of scripture within this trajectory involves a close attention to the lexical elements and literary contours of the text, which cannot be attained without recourse to historical and philological knowledge, but which must be shaped by the goals and expectations of the Ruled understanding of the text. That is, the "plain sense" reading will result from a conjunction of verbal sense and prior understanding of the subject matter of the text provided by the conception of the Christian faith supplied by the apostolic tradition. For this reason, seemingly non-literal readings will be allowed, and indeed necessitated. And, for this reason, seemingly non-literal readings can indeed fall within the range of "plain sense" reading. For example, Calvin can say that the tree of life is "plainly" a figure of Christ. Barth can say that the story of the separation of the dry land from the sea tells "primarily" of the passage of Israel through the Red Sea. Augustine says that we must acknowledge the prophetic element in the Biblical text because it is "foremost in God's intention." The reading of the plain sense is thus a religious activity and for this reason cannot be reduced to a narrow understanding of attention to verbal and literary matters alone.

Reading scripture according to its "plain sense" in this trajectory therefore logically entails the assumption of the divine authorship of scripture, however this may be construed conceptually.[6]   The notion of the "directedness" and goal-oriented nature of the text to form readers in the knowledge and love of God and neighbor cannot be left aside as one attempts to read the plain sense. Therefore, the concern for author intentionality will overlap with and cannot be separated from the understanding of Divine authorship. While none of our three theologians specify the mode of Divine authorship in the texts we have examined here, it is clear that God is understood to "speak" through the text, not only to an audience from centuries past, but also to their own contemporary trials and difficulties, and presumably they would say to ours as well.

Indeed, one might even press the point further. Since these three theologians seem to have an implicit ideal for plain sense reading, i.e., to negotiate between the two constraints of attention to verbal-literary contours and commitment to a Ruled reading, one might argue that these two constraints are at work inextricably and yet without conflation. Both constraints are necessarily at play in plain sense reading, yet in order to offer a convincingly plain sense reading, the interpreter must not meld the two constraints into one category. Each tends to exert a counter-pressure against the other which keeps interpretation open and flexible.

If this is a fitting description of what they seem to be trying implicitly to do in their reading of the plain sense, we might set our three theologians up against their own implicit ideal. In other words, we have inductively abstracted an understanding of the plain sense of scripture gleaned from its exemplification in their exegesis, and now we will apply the abstracted ideal back to their exegesis as an (albeit artificial) test of their own exegesis *ad litteram*.

If the implicit assumption is that the two constraints on plain sense reading, verbal sense and Ruled reading, are to be without division and without conflation, one might argue that when Augustine falls short of his own ideal of "literal interpretation," he is to be faulted not with overly-creative readings which "twist" the text, but with distinguishing between the "levels" of meaning at times too sharply. This would imply a wedge being placed between verbal sense and Ruled reading such that different readings had to be given to take account of each. On the other hand, Calvin might be charged with violating the ideal whenever he seems to *neglect* the distinction between verbal meaning and Ruled reading. Here, rather than being faulted with overly literal or "Judaizing" readings, Calvin might be said to conflate the two constraints in plain sense reading. When this is the case, he seems to want to rely on the words of the text themselves, that is, verbal meaning, to do all the "work" of warranting his arguments about the text without acknowledging that he is engaging in Ruled reading as well. This is, of course, an outgrowth of the Reformer's insistence on the perspicuity of the text.[7]

Barth seems to have the most success in conforming to the ideal which all three implicitly aim for with varying degrees of success. It is for this reason that the exposition of Barth in chapter four was not organized around the two categories of verbal sense and Ruled reading, for they are harder to "pull apart" in Barth's exegesis than they were in Augustine's or Calvin's. It is in large part this aspect of his understanding of the "plain sense" which most perplexes and chagrins his historical-critical critics. He speaks of both a "simple sense" and a "deeper meaning," two distinct features, and yet refuses to separate them or indicate that the deeper meaning which he offers is logically or hermeneutically independent from the simple sense. Plain sense reading is a factor of reading the Genesis creation narratives as saga, while allegorical reading would simply be a violation of another order resulting from an improper identification of the genre as myth.

With these observations in mind, we might now return to our consideration in the introduction of some of the concepts internal to "plain sense" reading and the contemporary attempts to understand these. Raphael Loewe's sketch of the Talmudic understanding of *peshat* overlaps with our consideration of the plain sense in this trajectory, insofar as he has pointed out how the notion of authority plays into the reading of the plain sense of scripture. Augustine, Calvin and Barth all, either explicitly as with Augustine or implicitly as with Calvin and Barth, accept the authority of the formulation of the Gospel in the Rule of Faith as the hermeneutical outer limit to what is a justifiable plain sense reading and what is beyond the bounds. However, the distinction which Loewe makes between "static" and "dynamic" exegesis points to an important element in our trajectory's plain sense. According to our examination, we cannot conclude that the plain sense falls under the category of static exegesis and "non-plain" sense under the category of dynamic exegesis.[8] Rather, the plain sense as understood in this trajectory can embrace both the concern to "enlarge the significance of a given text" (Loewe's "dynamic exegesis") *and* to concentrate on the text, "eschewing any accretions" of significance (Loewe's "static exegesis").

Kathryn Tanner's point that canonical limitation of texts combined with the use of the hermeneutical key of the central narrative of Jesus Christ promotes exegetical creativity instead of limiting it is also applicable to our trajectory. We have seen the degree to which these constraints have promoted exegetical creativity in all three of our theologians. The degree of creativity appears to be greatest in Augustine and Barth, each for different reasons and with different exegetical payout. Yet we have seen that even Calvin allows creative readings despite his insistence that he is interested in reading the literal sense alone. Extrapolating from Tanner's observation, we see how the two constraints of plain sense reading, as we have outlined them in our present project, function as countervailing forces: the concern to honor verbal sense pulls the reader toward "static exegesis," to use Loewe's terms, while Ruled reading pulls the reader toward (limited) "dynamic" exegesis.

As for Tanner's argument that privileging the plain sense can function to create a community which is self-critical and self-reforming, we have seen this to be particularly the case for Calvin, not surprisingly. Calvin's plain sense readings have attempted to undercut, for example, the Roman practice of veneration of Mary. However, the critical edge to Barth and Augustine's plain sense readings in the material examined in the present study tends to cut less against practice and more against hermeneutics (in Barth's case) and doctrine (in Augustine's case). Barth's plain sense readings have attempted to undercut the monopoly of historical-critical construals, particularly as regards the genre of the Genesis creation stories. Augustine's plain sense readings usually function to undercut *another* community's doctrine, as we saw here was often that of the Manichees. Here the privileging of "plain sense" does not necessarily prevent the promotion of a rigid communal life. This can be the case, but need not be, as we have seen.

Rowan William's suggestion of the identification of plain sense ("literal" in his terms) with diachronic reading is intriguing in light of our trajectory's understanding of plain sense. It is true that each theologian we examined reads the time of the text as "recognizably continuous" with his time. This is not based on their understanding of the Bible or the nature of time so much as it is on their understanding of the sovereignty of God over time. In other words, that the Bible's time can be read as continuous with my time is anchored in claims about God. Also, our three theologians would not necessarily accept Williams' favoring of diachronic over synchronic readings. They engage within the rubric of plain sense reading in both diachronic reading (taking seriously the text's sequence and intentionality) and synchronic reading (viewing the text as a field of linguistic signs referring backwards and forwards with little regard to strict linear sequence). Another point on which they might differ with Williams is that the plain sense is indeed understood in our trajectory as a resource for problem solving, or at least for evaluating how to approach a theological problem. While Williams indicates that it is Fundamentalists who view the literal sense in this respect, and that this is opposed to his eschatological understanding of literal sense, our three theologians each argued and disputed both doctrine and communal practice on the basis of the plain sense. However, this does not prevent them (Augustine and Calvin moreso than Barth) from holding their own interpretations as eschatologically provisional.

We have seen how Hans Frei's implicit pointing to the logical link between (pre-Enlightenment) reading of the plain sense and a notion similar to the Rule of Faith is applicable to our three theologians. Hand in hand with Frei's observation that the modern period ushers in an "eclipse" of biblical narrative goes a very simple observation, apparently too obvious for Frei to mention: the modern period regards as non-sensical and therefore unimportant the notion of a divine being whose power stretches to the breaking point the explanatory capacity of the categories of human experience. This *par force* renders non-sensical as well any notion such as Ruled reading, which gives shape to such claims about the God of Israel come in Jesus of Nazareth. Since the biblical narratives are religiously important to Christians, Christians do not want them to be regarded as non-sensical or unimportant, and so they tend in the modern period to understand them as Frei pointed out, that is, as referring to something such as human consciousness, experience, etc., or anything *but* a first century healer and miracle worker whose followers claim rose from the dead. In other words, when one can no longer credit the claims and assumptions in the "orthodox" understanding of God and Jesus Christ, one has to find substitute claims and assumptions in conjunction with which to read the Bible. The "references" which Frei identifies, ideal and ostensive, are such substitutes, and these substitutes are then set up as filling the criterion of "ultimate importance" once ascribed to the central Christian narrative. The "eclipse" of biblical narrative can thus also be described as the "eclipse" of the implicit reliance of plain sense reading on the Rule of Faith as outer limit with its claims about the life-and-death importance of the central Christian narrative.

In order to avoid the error of modern hermeneutics, which Frei identifies as equating meaning with reference, Frei suggests that we avoid all extrabiblical explanatory theories and narratives, and let the text mean what it says.[9] Frei's advice can be heeded within our trajectory insofar as Ruled reading is an "intra-biblical" and not an extra-textual explanatory device. That is, the prior understanding of what the biblical texts are "about" is taken from scripture and not from a set of external philosophical or scientific commitments and reapplied to scripture. The central narrative around which the rest of scripture is interpreted is the narrative of the life, death and resurrection of Jesus and its "patterning" throughout the Old Testament. Ruled reading thus allows scripture to interpret itself. The Reformer's maxim, *scriptura sui ipsius interpres*, never meant that interpretation was "presuppositionless."[10] The understanding of the broader subject matter of the biblical texts in our trajectory is itself drawn from scripture, and not from the categories of, for example, idealistic philosophy, or modern notions of facticity and historicity.

Of course, the only reason our trajectory deems it worth interpreting the Bible according to its "plain sense" is that this narrative is claimed to be of utmost and universal existential importance. Because these narratives are understood to be matters of life-and-death significance, they are central to "plain sense" reading. In other words, plain sense reading involves a judgment about what counts as important. Therefore, while it might not take a Christian to read "plainly" as does Barth, for example, presumably only a Christian would *want* to read the Bible this way, or at least would be motivated to carry through such a task. In other words, one would presumably have to claim the centrality and universal human importance of the narratives about Jesus in order to be motivated to engage in a reading, for example, of

Gen 2:24 which understands it to speak "plainly" of the mystery of Christ's relationship to the Church.

The plain sense reading is, as has been shown, a communal act and a religious practice. As we observed in the beginning of our discussion of Augustine's exegetical principles, it is often the presuppositions and attitudes the interpreter holds regarding the text which are more significant in shaping interpretation than any specific methods used. Assumptions about the triune God's relationship to the world undergird the reading of the plain sense in our trajectory. This is because reading according to the plain sense depends on the notion that God, sovereign over time and therefore also over the text, uses the biblical text to witness to His will and to shape His people. If there is anything which a Christian community might glean from the preceding analysis, it might be encouragement to engage in the cultivation of religious imagination and the audacity to allow for the possibility of the truth of the claims of the apostolic faith. There can be no categorical "ruling" out of historical critical or literary methods, as Hans Frei has said, as long as the reader does not permit the methods *par force* to determine one's presuppositions about God, text, and world.

Thomas Luxon opens his recent study of Puritan allegory by asking why John Bunyan's work could be so allegorical when allegory was consistently vilified by the Reformation.

> The 'single literal sense,' the 'tongue sense' of Scripture was virtually a mantra of Protestant and Puritan hermeneutics. The so-called plain style was a homiletical credo... So how does it happen that Bunyan, not unapologetically, writes allegory and that his allegories are so widely hailed not just as literary masterpieces, but as artifacts of English Puritan culture?[11]

Luxon answers this by suggesting that Reformed Christianity harbors a deeper commitment to allegory than is usually supposed, because it is wed to what he calls an "allegorical ontology" or a "bi-polar ontology."[12] He therefore sees Protestantism's use of typology as simply a euphemism for allegory which itself is "designed to mask Protestantism's continued commitment to allegorical structures of thought and representations of reality or truth... under the antiallegorical banner of the one true literal sense of God's word."[13] There is to be sure a small degree to which the present study confirms Luxon's claims. We have suggested that the "plain sense" is, after all, not so plain that it focuses alone on verbal sense but rather within our trajectory it also requires Ruled reading. However, our considerations here of understandings of the plain sense of scripture do not push us to claim what Luxon calls Christianity's "allegorical ontology" which he says denies history any claims to reality and constantly "others."[14] Rather, we have tried to demonstrate the point which Luxon seems almost to have found but finally and unfortunately lost upon the way: the interpretation of scripture in the Christian tradition is wed not to an "allegorical ontology" *per se* but to the Church's Rule of faith, with its own particular understanding of the divine reality and will. The "plain sense" of Scripture in our trajectory is not controlled by a "Protestant dodge," or a "catholic dodge" for that matter. Neither is it a theological double-speak for the sake of rhetorical power. Rather, when the plain sense is not so plain, it is thus because of the very God which the Gospel proclaims to be the Giver of Life and Redeemer of the world. This is what John Donne so elegantly expressed in the lines from his Expostulation 19 quoted at the beginning of our study. Within our trajectory, it is the very substance of the gospel and the identity of the God who created and redeemed the world which directs and guides reading the Scriptures according to the plain sense.

Notes

1. Rowan Williams, "The Literal Sense of Scripture," *Modern Theology* 7 (1991): 121-34.
2. For Augustine, the Divine Author was also the subject matter of the text, and therefore not "separable" from the text.
3. This is, of course, not to say that each of the three do not share these elements. Calvin and Barth both understand the text to be inspired; Augustine and Barth both allow the doctrine of God to impact plain sense reading; Augustine and Calvin would not disagree with Barth that the text witnesses to Jesus Christ.
4. For an interesting example of an analogous Jewish response as to the limiting of teaching *halakah* to *peshat* interpretations, see Uriel Simon, "The Religious Significance of the Peshat," *Tradition* 23 (1988): 60. He refers to the Torah command, "And you shall love the stranger (*ger*) for you were strangers (*gerim*) in the land of Egypt" (Dt 10:19), the targumic interpretation in *Onkelos* of which is "You shall love the convert (*ger tsedek*) for you were sojourners (*gerim*) in the land of Egypt." Simon says, "On the educational and communal level it is better to interpret by way of *peshat*, applying the *mitsvah* to all types of *gerim*, converts and resident aliens. A people like ours, that has attained independence only after having known the soul of the *ger*, not only in Egypt but all over the world, may not, heaven forbid, forgo this."
5. Of course, we have seen that for Barth the genre of the text to be explicated bears directly on the text's ability to refer historically. Therefore genre also bears directly on the community's ability to read as though it referred historically. Thus, the Genesis creation stories are "sagas" and are not to be read as though they are history. The historical referentiality for Barth will therefore vary from text to text and genre to genre within the Bible.
6. Nicholas Wolterstorff offers an intriguing reformulation of this notion: "I suggest that the most natural way of understanding this claim [that God speaks in the Bible] is to understand it in terms of divinely appropriated human discourse." Nicholas Wolterstorff, *Divine Discourse: Philosophical Reflections on the Claim That God Speaks* (Cambridge: Cambridge University Press, 1995), 3.
7. The recourse to "perspicuity" might be seen as an apologetic move somewhat like, or maybe the inverse of, that of Rabbi Meir Leib Malbim (1809-79; Eastern Europe), who sought to demonstrate that the *derashot* of the Hazal were anchored in the underlying grammar and etymology of

the Hebrew text. Malbim says in his Introduction to his commentary on Leviticus, "The *derashah* is the simple sense [*peshat hapashut*] which is inevitable and implanted in the depth of the language and the foundation of the Hebrew tongue." Cited in Yeshayahu Maori, "The Approach of Classical Jewish Exegetes to *Peshat* and *Derash* and Its Implications for the Teaching of Bible Today," trans. Moshe J. Bernstein, *Tradition* 21 (1984): 45. Calvin wants to base any "applied" senses of scripture on the words of the text themselves (not, of course, on their etymology as with Malbim) so that readers do not need the Roman ecclesiastical authorities to validate their interpretations.

8. Here we are not making a critique of Loewe's assessment of Talmudic exegesis; we are simply making the distinction between this view of Talmudic understanding of *peshat* and that of our own theological trajectory.

9. See an especially lucid example of this in "Response to 'Narrative Theology: An Evangelical Appraisal,'" reprinted in Hans W. Frei, *Theology and Narrative: Selected Essays*, eds. George Hunsinger and William C. Placher (New York: Oxford University Press, 1993), 208.

10. E.g., see Elsie Anne McKee, "Some Reflections on Relating Calvin's Exegesis and Theology," in *Biblical Hermeneutics in Historical Perspective: Studies in Honor of Karlfried Froehlich*, eds. Mark S. Burrows and Paul Rorem (Grand Rapids: Eerdmans, 1991).

11. Thomas H. Luxon, *Literal Figures: Puritan Allegory and the Reformation Crisis in Representation* (Chicago: University of Chicago Press, 1995), ix–x.

12. It should not be lost on the reader that "bi-polar" is a medical term which is used to refer to a mental pathology. Luxon continues, "My point is that reformed Christianity, for all of its insistence on literalism, remains profoundly committed to an allegorical ontology. It is incessantly about the business of othering. It others the self and the world into God's allegory of himself and his kingdom; it others the past as an allegory of the present and the present as an allegory of the future. And Christianity's names for the other, whether it be the old self, the other of the past, or the other of the present (as viewed from eternity), are the Jew, the Synagogue, the 'carnal' Jerusalem, the whore, the flesh, and the world. In short, Reformation thought allegorizes the Christian much as medieval theology allegorized ancient Israel." Ibid., 26.

13. Ibid., 40.

14. Ibid., 62.

Works Cited

Ackroyd, P. R. and C. F. Evans. *The Cambridge History of the Bible*. Volume 1: From the Beginnings to Jerome. Cambridge: Cambridge University Press, 1970.

Agaësse, P. "L'exégèse 'Ad Litteram'." In *La Genèse Au Sens Littéral en Douze Livres*. Bibliothèque Augustinienne: Oeuvres de Saint Augustin, 32-51. Paris: Desclée de Brouwer, 1972.

Agaësse, P. and A. Solignac, trans. and intro. *La Genèse Au Sens Littéral en Douzes Livres*. Latin Text of Augustine, with French Translation. Bibliothèque Augustinienne: Oeuvres de Saint Augustin. Paris: Desclée de Brouwer, 1972.

Auerbach, Eric. *Mimesis: The Representation of Reality in Western Literature*. Trans. William Trask. Princeton, NJ: Princeton University Press, 1953.

Augustine, Aurelius. *De Genesi Ad Litteram, Libri Duodecim*. Ed. Joseph Zycha. Corpus Scriptorum Ecclesiasticorum Latinorum. Vindobonae, Pragae: F. Tempsky, 1894.

_____. *La Genèse au Sens Littéral en Douze Livres*. Latin text with French translation, eds. P. Agaësse and A. Solignac, Bibliothèque Augustinienne: Oeuvres de Saint Augustin, vols. 48-49, Paris: Desclée de Brouwer, 1972.

_____. *Oeuvres Complètes de Saint Augustin, Evêque d'Hippone*. Vol. 32, Latin text with French translation, eds. Pérrone et alii, Paris: Librairie de Louis Vivès, 1873.

Ayers, Robert H. "The View of Medieval Biblical Exegesis in Calvin's Institutes." *Perspectives in Religious Studies* 7 (1980): 188-93.

Baron, Salo W. "John Calvin and the Jews." In *Essential Papers on Judaism and Christianity in Conflict From Late Antiquity to the Reformation*, ed. Jeremy Cohen, 380-400. New York: New York University Press, 1991.

Barr, James. "Literality." *Faith and Philosophy* 6 (1989): 412-28.

_____. "The Literal, the Allegorical, and Modern Biblical Scholarship." *JSOT* 44 (1989): 3-17.

_____. "Typology and Allegory." In *Old and New in Interpretation*, 103-48. New York: Harper and Row, 1966.

Barth, Karl. *Church Dogmatics.* Ed. G. W. Bromiley and T. F. Torrance, vol. 3.1, The Doctrine of Creation, trans. J. W. Edwards et alii, Edinburgh: T. & T. Clark, 1958.

_____. *Die Kirchliche Dogmatik.* Vol. 3.1, Die Lehre von der Schöpfung, Zollikon-Zürich: Evangelischer Verlag, 1945.

Bates, Gordon. "The Typology of Adam and Christ in John Calvin." *Hartford Quarterly* 5 (1965): 42-57.

Battles, Ford Lewis. "God Was Accommodating Himself to Human Capacity." *Interpretation* 31 (1977): 19-38.

Bauer, Walter. *Orthodoxy and Heresy in Earliest Christianity.* Philadelphia: Fortress, 1971.

Baumgartner, A. J. *Calvin Hébraïsant et Inteprète de l'Ancien Testament.* Paris: Librairie Fischbacher, 1889.

Benin, Stephen D. *The Footprints of God: Divine Accommodation in Jewish and Christian Thought.* Albany: State University of New York, 1993.

Besse, Georges. "Saint Augustin dans les Oeuvres Exégétiques de Jean Calvin: Recherches sur l'Authorité Reconnue à Saint Augustin par Calvin en Matière d'Exégèse." *REAug* 6 (1960): 161-72.

Birdsall, J. N. "The New Testament Text." In *The Cambridge History of the Bible, Volume 1,* eds. P. Ackroyd and C. Evans, 308-376. Cambridge: Cambridge University Press, 1970.

Blocher, Henri. "The 'Analogy of Faith' in the Study of Scripture." *Scottish Bulletin of Evangelica Theology* 5 (1987): 17-38.

Blowers, Paul M. "The 'Regula Fidei' and the Narrative Character of Early Christian Faith." *Pro Ecclesia* 6 (1997): 199-228.

Bonner, Gerald. "Augustine as Biblical Scholar." In *The Cambridge History of the Bible, Volume 1,* eds. P. Ackroyd and C. Evans, 541-62. Cambridge: Cambridge University Press, 1970.

Bouwsma, William J. *John Calvin: A Sixteenth Century Portrait.* Oxford: Oxford University Press, 1988.

Breen, Quirinius. *John Calvin: A Study in French Humanism.* Grand Rapids: Eerdmans, 1931.

Brown, Peter. *Augustine of Hippo.* Berkeley: University of California Press, 1969.

Bultmann, Rudolf. "New Testament and Mythology: The Problem of Demythologizing the New Testament Proclamation." In *New Testament and Mythology,* ed. Schubert Ogden, 1980 (1941).

Burns, J. Patout. "Ambrose Preaching to Augustine: The Shaping of Faith." In *Collectanea Augustiniana: Augustine, "Second Founder of the*

Faith," eds. Joseph C. Schnaubelt and Frederick Van Fleteren, 373-86. New York: Peter Lang, 1990.

Calvin, Jean. *Commentarius in Genesin, Primus Mosis Liber Genesis Vulgo Dictis.* Ioannis Calvini Opera Quae Supersunt Omnia, vol. 23, Corpus Reformatorum, vol. 51, ed. G. Baum, E. Cunitz and E. Reuss, Brunsvigae: Schwetschke et Filiium, 1882.

Childs, Brevard S. *Biblical Theology of the Old and New Testaments: Theological Reflection on the Christian Bible.* 1st ed. Minneapolis, Minn.: Fortress Press, 1993. 745 pp.

_____. "The Sensus Literalis of Scripture: An Ancient and Modern Problem." In *Beiträge Zur Alttestamentlichen Theologie: Festschrift Für Walther Zimmerli,* 80-93, 1977.

Clark, Elizabeth A. "Heresy, Asceticism, Adam and Eve: Interpretations of Genesis 1-3 in the Later Latin Fathers." In *Genesis 1-3 in the History of Exegesis: Intrigue in the Garden,* ed. Gregory Allen Robbins, 99-134. Lewiston/Queens: Edwin Mellen Press, 1988.

Cohen, Chaim. "Elements of *Peshat* in Traditional Jewish Bible Exegesis." *Immanuel* 20-21 (1986-87): 1-36.

Countryman, William. "Tertullian and the Regula Fidei." *The Second Century* 2 (1982): 208-27.

Coxe, A. Cleveland. *The Apostolic Fathers with Justin Martyr and Irenaeus.* The Ante-Nicene Fathers: Translations of the Writings of the Fathers Down to A.D. 325. Grand Rapids: Eerdmans, 1884.

_____. *Fathers of the Third Century.* Eds. Alexander Roberts and James Donaldson. The Ante-Nicene Fathers: Translations of the Fathers Down to A.D. 325. Grand Rapids: Eerdmans, 1885.

_____. *Latin Christianity: Its Founder, Tertullian.* The Ante-Nicene Fathers: Translations of the Writings of the Fathers Down to A.D. 325. Grand Rapids: Eerdmans.

Crossan, John Dominic, ed. *Semeia 4: Paul Ricoeur on Biblical Hermeneutics.* Missoula, Mont.: Scholars Press, 1975.

Crouzel, Henri. "La Distinction de la 'Typologie' et de 'l'Allegorie'." *Bulletin de Littérature Ecclésiastique* 65 (1964): 161-74.

Dawson, David. *Allegorical Readers and Cultural Revision in Ancient Alexandria.* Berkeley: University of California Press, 1992.

de Margerie, Bertrand. *Introduction à l'Histoire de l'Exégèse.* 3 volumes. Paris: Le Cerf, 1980.

Deason, G. B. "The Protestant Reformation and the Rise of Modern Science." *Scottish Journal of Theology* 38 (1985).

Demson, David E. *Hans Frei and Karl Barth: Different Ways of Reading Scripture*. Grand Rapids: Eerdmans, 1997.

Dodd, C. H. *According to the Scriptures: The Substructure of New Testament Theology*. London: Nisbet & Co., 1952.

Dods, Marcus, trans. *The City of God*. In *The Nicene and Post-Nicene Fathers of the Christian Church*. By Aurelius Augustine. Ed. Philip Schaff. Grand Rapids: Eerdmans, 1978.

Farrar, F. W. *History of Interpretation*. London, 1886.

Fishbane, Michael. "The Teacher and the Hermeneutical Task: A Reinterpretation of Medieval Exegesis." *JAAR* 43 (1975): 709-21.

Flesseman-Van Leer, Ellen. *Tradition and Scripture in the Early Church*. Assen: Van Gorcum, 1953.

Ford, David. *Barth and God's Story: Biblical Narrative and the Theological Method of Karl Barth in the Church Dogmatics*. Frankfurt: Peter Lang, 1981.

Frei, Hans W. *The Eclipse of Biblical Narrative: A Study in Eighteenth and Nineteenth Century Hermeneutics*. New Haven; London: Yale University Press, 1974.

————. *The Identity of Jesus Christ: The Hermeneutical Bases of Dogmatic Theology*. Philadelphia: Fortress Press, 1975. 173 pp.

————. "The 'Literal Reading' of Biblical Narrative in the Christian Tradition: Does It Stretch or Will It Break?" In *The Bible and the Narrative Tradition*, ed. Frank McConnell, 36-77. New York: Oxford University Press, 1986.

Friedman, Jerome. *The Most Ancient Testimony: Sixteenth Century Christian-Hebraica in the Age of Renaissance Nostalgia*. Ohio University Press. Athens, OH, 1983.

Froehlich, Karlfried. "'Always to Keep the Literal Sense in Holy Scripture Means to Kill One's Soul': The State of Biblical Hermeneutics at the Beginning of the Fifteenth Century." In *Literary Uses of Typology*, ed. E. Miner, 20-48. Princeton: Princeton University Press, 1977.

Gamble, Richard. "The Sources of Calvin's Genesis Commentary: A Preliminary Report." *Archiv Für Reformationsgeschichte* 84 (1993): 206-21.

————. "Brevitas et Facilitas: Toward an Understanding of Calvin's Hermeneutic." *Westminster Theological Journal* 47 (1985): 1-17.

————. *Calvin and Science*. Articles on Calvin and Calvinism. New York: Garland Publishing, 1992.

Gelles, Benjamin. *Peshat and Derash in the Exegesis of Rashi*. Leiden: Brill, 1981.

Gerrish, Brian A. "The Reformation and the Rise of Modern Science." In *The Impact of the Church Upon Its Culture: Reappraisals of the History of Christianity*, J. C. Brauer. Chicago: University of Chicago Press, 1968.

Grant, Robert M. "The Place of the Old Testament in Early Christianity." *Interpretation* 5 (1951): 186-202.

Gunkel, Hermann. *The Legends of Genesis*. Trans. Will Carruth. New York: Schocken Books, 1964.

Hägglund, Bengt. "Die Bedeutung der 'regula fidei' als Grundlage theologischer Aussagen." *Studia Theologica* 12 (1958): 1-44.

Halivni, David Weiss. *Peshat and Derash: Plain and Applied Meaning in Rabbinic Exegesis*. New York: Oxford University Press, 1991.

Hall, Basil. "Biblical Scholarship: Editions and Commentaries." In *The Cambridge History of the Bible, Vol. 3*, ed. S. L. Greenslade, 38-93. Cambridge: Cambridge University Press, 1963.

Hanson, R. P. C. *Allegory and Event: A Study of the Sources and Significance of Origen's Interpretation of Scripture*. Richmond, VA: John Knox Press, 1959.

Haroutunian, Joseph and Louise Pettibone Smith, eds. *Calvin: Commentaries*. Library of Christian Classics. Philadelphia: Westminster, 1958.

Harrington, Daniel J. "The Reception of Walter Bauer's *Orthodoxy and Heresy in Earliest Christianity* During the Last Decade." *HTR* 73 (1980): 289-98.

Hay, David M., ed. *Both Literal and Allegorical: Studies in Philo of Alexandria's Questions and Answers on Genesis and Exodus*. Brown Judaica Series. Atlanta: Scholars Press, 1991.

Hays, Richard B. *Echoes of Scripture in the Letters of Paul*. New Haven: Yale University Press, 1989.

Hayward, C. T. R. *Saint Jerome's Hebrew Questions on Genesis: Translated with an Introduction and Commentary*. Oxford: Clarendon Press, 1995.

Hazlett, W. Ian P. "Calvin's Latin Preface to His Proposed French Edition of Chrysostom's Homilies: Translation and Commentary." In *Humanism and Reform: The Church in Europe, England and Scotland, 1400-1643*, ed. James Kirk, 129-50. Oxford: Basil Blackwell, 1991.

Hoffman, Daniel L. *The Status of Women and Gnosticism in Irenaeus and Tertullian*. Lewiston: Edwin Mellen Press, 1995.

Hooykaas, R. "Calvin and Copernicus." *Organon* 10 (1974).

Hunsinger, George. "Beyond Liberalism and Expressivism: Karl Barth's Hermeneutical Realism." *Modern Theology* 3 (1987): 209-224.

_____. *How to Read Karl Barth: The Shape of his Theology.* New York: Oxford University Press, 1991.

Jones, G. Lloyd. *The Discovery of Hebrew in Tudor England: A Third Language.* Manchester: Manchester University Press, 1983.

Kaiser, Christopher B. "Calvin's Understanding of Aristotelian Natural Philosophy: Its Extent and Possible Origins." In *Calviniana: Ideas and Influence of Jean Calvin,* ed. Robert V. Schnucker, 77-92. Kirksville, MO: Sixteenth Century Journal Publisher, 1988.

_____. "Calvin, Copernicus and Castelio." *Calvin Theological Journal* 21 (1986).

Kamin, Sarah. "Rashi's Exegetical Categorization With Respect to the Distinction Between *Peshat* and *Derash* According to His Commentary to the Book of Genesis and Selected Passages from His Commentaries to Other Books of the Bible." *Immanuel* 11 (1980): 16-32.

Kayayan, Eric. "Accommodation, Incarnation et Sacrement dans l'Institution de la Religion Chrétienne de Jean Calvin." *Revue d'Histoire et de Philosophie Religieuses* 75 (1995): 273-87.

King, John, trans. *Commentaries on the First Book of Moses Called Genesis by John Calvin.* 1847. Calvin Translation Society. Grand Rapids: Baker Book House, 1979.

Kraus, H. J. "Calvin's Exegetical Principles." *Interpretation* 31 (1977): 8-18.

Lake, Kirsopp. *The Apostolic Fathers, Vol. 1.* Loeb Classical Library. Cambridge: Harvard University Press, 1912.

Lampe, G. W. H. and K. J. Woolcombe. *Essays on Typology.* Studies in Biblical Theology. Naperville, IL: Alec R. Allenson, 1957.

Lane, A. N. S. "Calvin's Use of the Fathers and the Medievals." *Calvin Theological Journal* 16 (1981): 149-205.

_____. "Did Calvin Use Lippoman's 'Catena in Genesim?'." *Calvin Theological Journal* 31 (1996): 404-19.

Lash, Nicholas. "Performing the Scriptures." In *Theology on the Way to Emmaus,* 37-46. London: SCM Press, 1986.

Lewy, Heinrich. *Die Semitischen Fremdwörter Im Griechischen.* Berlin: Gaertners, 1895.

Lindbeck, George A. *The Nature of Doctrine.* Philadelphia: Westminster, 1984.

Lockshin, Mark. "Tradition or Context: Two Exegetes Struggle with *Peshat.*" In *From Ancient Israel to Modern Judaism, Vol. 2,* ed. E. Frerichs J. Neusner, N. Sarna, 173-86. Atlanta: Scholars Press, 1989.

Loewe, Raphael. "The 'Plain' Meaning of Scripture in Early Jewish Exegesis." In *Papers of the Institute of Jewish Studies, London*, ed. J. G. Weiss, 140-85. Jerusalem: Magnes Press, 1964.

Louvel, François. "Appendix 3." In *Les Ecrits Des Pères Apostliques*, 491-2. Paris: Editions du Cerf, 1963.

Luxon, Thomas H. *Literal Figures: Puritan Allegory and the Reformation Crisis in Representation.* Chicago: University of Chicago Press, 1995.

MacKenzie, Ross, trans. *The Epistles of Paul the Apostle to the Romans and Thessalonians.* By John Calvin. Grand Rapids: Eerdmans, 1973.

Malet, André, with Pierre Marcel and Michel Réveillaud, eds. *Le Livre de la Genèse.* By Jean Calvin. La Société Calviniste de France: Commentaires de Jean Calvin sur l'Ancien Testament. Genève: Labor et Fides, 1961.

Maori, Yeshayahu. "The Approach of Classical Jewish Exegetes to *Peshat* and *Derash* and Its Implications for the Teaching of Bible Today." Trans. Moshe J. Bernstein. *Tradition* 21 (1984): 40-53.

Marcel, Pierre. "Calvin and Copernicus." *Philosophia Reformata* 46 (1981): 14-36.

Marshall, Bruce. "Absorbing the World: Christianity and the Universe of Truths." In *Theology and Dialogue: Essays in Conversation with George Lindbeck.* Notre Dame, IN: University of Notre Dame Press, 1990.

McCartney, Dan G. "Literal and Allegorical Interpretation in Origen's Contra Celsum." *Westminster Theological Journal* 48 (1986): 281-301.

McCormack, Bruce. "Historical Criticism and Dogmatic Interest in Karl Barth's Theological Exegesis of the New Testament." In *Biblical Hermeneutics in Historical Perspective: Studies in Honor of Karlfried Froehlich on his Sixtieth Birthday.* eds. Mark Burrows and Paul S. Rorem, 322-38. Grand Rapids: Eerdmans, 1991.

_____. *Karl Barth's Critically Realistic Dialectical Theology: Its Genesis and Development 1909-1936.* New York: Oxford, 1995.

McKane, William. "Calvin as Old Testament Commentator." *Nederduitse Gereformeerde Teologiese Tydskrif* 25 (1984): 250-59.

Millet, O. *Calvin et la Dynamique de la Parole: Etude de Rhétorique Réformée.* Paris: Librairie Honoré Champion, 1992.

Mitros, Joseph F. "The Norm of Faith in the Patristic Age." *Theological Studies* 29 (1965): 444-71.

Muller, Richard. *Dictionary of Latin and Greek Theological Terms.* Grand Rapids: Eerdmans, 1985.

Neuser, Wilhelm Heinrich, ed. *Calvinus Sacrae Scripturae Professor: Calvin as Confessor of Holy Scripture*. Die Referate des Congrès International des Recherches Calviniennes, 1990. Grand Rapids: Eerdmans, 1994.

Noble, Paul R. "The Sensus Literalis: Jowett, Childs, and Barr." *Journal of Theological Studies* 44 (1993): 1-23.

O'Connell, R. J. *The Origin of the Soul in St. Augustine's Later Work*. New York: Fordham University Press, 1987.

O'Toole, Christopher J. *The Philosophy of Creation in the Writings of Saint Augustine*. Washington, DC: Catholic University of America Press, 1944.

Osborn, Eric F. "Reason and the Rule of Faith in the Second Century AD." In *The Making of Orthodoxy: Essays in Honor of Henry Chadwick*, ed. Rowan Williams, 40-61. Cambridge: Cambridge University Press, 1989.

Parker, T. H. L., trans. *The Epistles of the Apostle Paul to the Galatians, Ephesians, Philippians, and Colossians*. By John Calvin. Grand Rapids: Eerdmans, 1965.

_____. *Calvin's Old Testament Commentaries*. Edinburgh: T. & T. Clark, 1986. 239 pp.

_____. *Calvin's Preaching*. Louisville, Ky.: Westminster/J. Knox Press, 1992. 202 pp.

Pater, Calvin Augustine. "Calvin, the Jews and the Judaic Legacy." In *In Honor of John Calvin, 1509-64: Papers from the 1986 International Calvin Symposium, McGill University*, ed. E. J. Furcha. ARC Supplement, 256-96, 1987.

Pelikan, Jaroslav. "Canonica Regula: The Trinitarian Hermeneutics of Augustine." In *Collectanea Augustiniana: Augustine, "Second Founder of the Faith,"* eds. Joseph C. Schnaubelt and Frederick Van Fleteren, 329-43. New York: Peter Lang, 1990.

_____. *The Emergence of the Catholic Tradition*. The Christian Tradition: A History of the Development of Doctrine. Chicago: University of Chicago Press, 1971.

Pelland, Gilles. *Cinq Etudes d'Augustin sur le Début de la Genèse*. Montréal: Bellarmin, 1972.

Pépin, J. "Saint Augustin et le Symbolisme Néoplatonicien de la Vêture." *Augustinus Magister: Congrès International Augustinien* 1 (1954): 292-306.

Preus, James Samuel. *From Shadow to Promise: Old Testament Interpretation from Augustine to the Young Luther.* Cambridge: The Belknap Press, 1969.

Probes, Christine McCall. "Calvin on Astrology." *Westminster Theological Journal* 37 (1974): 24-33.

Pine-Coffin, R. S., trans. *Saint Augustine: Confessions.* Baltimore: Penguin Books, 1961.

Réveillaud, Michel. "L'authorité de la Tradition Chez Calvin." *La Revue Réformée* 9 (1958): 24-45.

Robbins, Frank Egleston. *The Hexaemeral Literature: A Study of the Greek and Latin Commentaries on Genesis.* Chicago: University of Chicago Press, 1912.

Robbins, Gregory Allen, ed. *Genesis 1-3 in the History of Exegesis: Intrigue in the Garden.* Lewiston/Queens: Edwin Mellen Press, 1988.

Robinson, Thomas A. *The Bauer Thesis Examined: The Geography of Heresy in the Early Christian Church.* Lewiston: Edwin Mellen, 1988.

Rogers, Eugene F., Jr. "How the Virtues of the Interpreter Presuppose and Perfect Hermeneutics: The Case of Thomas Aquinas." *Journal of Religion* 76 (1996): 64-81.

Rosen, E. "A Reply to Dr. Ratner." *Journal of the History of Ideas* 22 (1961).

Salmond, S. D. F., trans. *Harmony of the Gospels.* By Aurelius Augustine. Nicene and Post-Nicene Fathers. Grand Rapids: Eerdmans, 1978.

Sanders, James A. "First Testament and Second." *Biblical Theology Bulletin* 17 (1987).

Scalise, Charles. "The 'Sensus Literalis': A Hermeneutical Key to Biblical Exegesis." *Scottish Journal of Theology* 42 (1989): 45-65.

Seitz, Christopher. "Old Testment or Hebrew Bible: Some Theological Considerations." *Pro Ecclesia* 5 (1996): 292-303.

Scholl, Hans, <ed.>. *Karl Barth und Johannes Calvin: Karl Barths Göttinger Calvin-Volesung von 1922.* Neukirchen-Vluyn: Neukirchener, 1995.

Shaw, John, trans. *On Christian Doctrine.* In *Nicene and Post-Nicene Fathers, Vol. 2.* By Aurelius Augustine. Ed. Philip Schaff. Grand Rapids: Eerdmans, 1979.

Simon, Uriel. "The Religious Significance of the Peshat." *Tradition* 23 (1988): 41-63.

Smend, Rudolf. "Nachkritische Schriftsauslegung." In *Parrhesia: Karl Barth Zum Achtzigsten Geburtstag,* 215-37. Zürich: EVZ Verlag, 1966.

Smits, Luchesius. *Saint Augustin dans l'Oeuvre de Jean Calvin.* 2 volumes. Assen: Van Gorcum, 1958.

Sparks, H. F. D. "Jerome as Biblical Scholar." In *Cambridge History of the Bible, Vol. 1*, eds. P. Ackroyd and C. Evans. Cambridge: Cambridge University Press, 1970.

Starnes, Colin. "Augustinian Biblical Exegesis and the Origins of Modern Science." In *Collectanea Augustiniana: Augustine, "Second Founder of the Faith*," eds. Joseph C. Schaubelt and Frederick Van Fleteren, 345-56. New York: Peter Lang, 1990.

Stauffer, Richard. "Les Sermons Inédits de Calvin sur le Livre de la Genèse." *Revue de Théologie et Philosophie* (1965), 26-36.

Stroup, George. "Narrative in Calvin's Hermeneutic." In *John Calvin and the Church: A Prism of Reform*, ed. Timothy George, 158-71. Louisville: Westminster/John Knox Press, 1990.

Tanner, Kathryn E. "Theology and the Plain Sense." In *Scriptural Authority and Narrative Interpretation*, ed. Garrett Green, 59-78. Philadelphia: Fortress, 1987.

Taylor, John Hammond, trans. and annot. *St. Augustine: The Literal Meaning of Genesis*. Ancient Christian Writers: The Works of the Fathers in Translation. New York: Newman Press, 1982.

Teske, Roland, trans. and annot. *Saint Augustine on Genesis: Two Books on Genesis Against the Manichees and On the Literal Interpretation of Genesis: An Unfinished Book*. Fathers of the Church. Washington, D.C.: Catholic University America Press, 1991.

Torrance, T. F. *The Hermeneutics of John Calvin*. Edinburgh: Scottish Academic Press, 1988.

Tracy, David. *Blessed Rage for Order: The New Pluralism in Theology*. New York: Seabury Press, 1975.

Trench, R. C. "Augustine as Interpreter of Scripture." In *Exposition of the Sermon on the Mount Drawn from the Writings of Saint Augustine*, 1-152. London: Macmillan and Co., 1869.

Turner, H. E. W. *The Pattern of Christian Truth: A Study in the Relations Between Orthodoxy and Heresy in the Early Church*. London: A. R. Mowbray, 1954.

van der Meer, F. *Augustine the Bishop: The Life and Work of a Father of the Church*. Trans. Brian Battershaw and G. R. Lamb. New York: Sheed and Ward, 1961.

van Oort, Johannes. "John Calvin and the Church Fathers." In *The Reception of the Church Fathers in the West: From the Carolingians to the Maurists*, ed. Irena Backus, 661-700. Leiden: Brill, 1997.

van Rooy, H. F. "Calvin's Genesis Commentary: Which Bible Text Did He Use?" In *Our Reformational Tradition: A Rich Heritage and Lasting*

Vocation, ed. H. F. van Rooy, 203-16. Potchefstroom: Potchefstroom University, 1984.

Van Winden, J. C. M. "'In the Beginning': Some Observations on the Patristic Interpretation of Genesis 1:1." *Vigiliae Christianae* 17 (1963): 105-21.

Verhoef, Pieter A. "Luther's and Calvin's Exegetical Library." *Calvin Theological Journal* 3 (1968): 5-20.

Vignaux, Paul, ed. *In Principio: Interprétations Des Premiers Versets de la Genèse*. Paris: Etudes Augustiniennes, 1973.

Walchenbach, John Robert. *John Calvin as Biblical Commentator: An Investigation Into Calvin's Use of John Chrysostom as an Exegetical Tutor*. University of Pittsburgh: Unpublished dissertation, 1974.

Watson, Francis. *Text and Truth: Redefining Biblical Theology*. Edinburgh: T & T Clark, 1997.

White, A. D. *A History of the Warfare of Science With Technology in Christendom*, 1896.

White, Robert. "Calvin and Copernicus: The Problem Reconsidered." *Calvin Theological Journal* 15 (1980): 233-43.

Williams, Rowan. "The Literal Sense of Scripture." *Modern Theology* 7 (1991): 121-34.

Wood, Charles. *The Formation of Christian Understanding: An Essay in Theological Hermeneutics*. Philadelphia: Westminster Press, 1981.

Wright, D. F. "Accomodation and Barbarity in John Calvin's Old Testament Commentaries." In *Understanding Poets and Prophets: Essays n Honour of George Wishart Anderson*, ed. Grame Auld, 413-27. Sheffield: Sheffield University Press, 1993.

Yeago, David S. "The New Testament and the Nicene Dogma: A Contribution to the Recovery of Theological Exegesis." *Pro Ecclesia* 3 (1994): 152-64.

Index of Subjects

Index of Names

✠ ISSUES IN SYSTEMATIC THEOLOGY

This series emphasizes issues in contemporary systematic theology but is open to theological issues from the past. Works in this series seek to explore such issues as the relation of reason and revelation, experience and doctrine, the meaning of revelation, method in theology, Trinitarian Theology, the doctrine of God, Christology, sacraments and the Church. Of course other issues such as ecumenical relations or specific doctrinal studies on topics such as predestination or studies evaluating particular influential theologians may be considered.

Authors whose work is critical, constructive, and ecumenical are encouraged to consider this series. One of the aims of this series is to illustrate that Christian systematic theologians from different denominations may seek and find Christian unity through dialogue on those central issues that unite them in their quest for truth.

Paul D. Molnar, the General Editor of the series, is Professor of Systematic Theology at St. John's University. In addition to *Karl Barth and the Theology of the Lord's Supper: A Systematic Investigation* (Lang, 1996), he has published numerous articles in professional journals relating to the theology of Barth, Moltmann, Pannenberg, Rahner, and others dealing with issues in method in theology, Trinitarian Theology, and revelation.

Authors wishing to have works considered for this series should contact the series editor:

Paul D. Molnar, Ph.D.
Division of Humanities
St. John's University
8000 Utopia Parkway
Jamaica, New York 11439